D1153302

COMING
HOME

COMING HOME

by

Chaim Bermant

London   George Allen & Unwin Ltd
Ruskin House   Museum Street

First published 1976

© Chaim Bermant 1976

ISBN 0 04 920047 x

Printed in Great Britain
in 11 point Baskerville type
by Clarke, Doble & Brendon Ltd.
Plymouth

To the Memory of

Reb Azriel Boruch ben Avrohom Meir

'. . . a just man in his generations.'

Acknowledgements

Parts of this book have appeared under different guises in the *Jewish Chronicle*, the *Observer* and *Present Tense*, and I am grateful to their respective editors for permission to use them.

I am also indebted to Mrs Sharon Ross, who again coped with my manuscript with her usual alacrity and intelligence; to Mr John Bright-Holmes, for a degree of guidance and help which no author has a right to expect of his publisher; and finally to Judy, Alisa, Evie, Azriel and Danny, who shared something of the turmoil which largely inspired this book.

Contents

Prologue

I was born in a part of Lithuania which was then Poland and is now Russia. When I was three my family moved to Latvia: when five I was sent to school in Poland: at eight we all moved to Scotland: at twenty I first went to Israel. In Latvia I was known as a Polack, in Poland as a Lett, and in Scotland as a foreigner. In Israel, however, I was known as a Scot. In a sense I had come home.

PART ONE

I

Barovke

Latvia, Lithuania, Poland! They had, till 1918, all been part
of Russia and Jews still moved from one to the other as if there
was no frontier, sometimes with the necessary permits, not infrequently without. My parents were Russian. In 1918, as a
result of the Brest Litovsk Treaty which gave Poland and the
Baltic states independence, they became Lithuanian. Two years
later Poland seized the Lithuanian province of Wilno, and they
became Polish. Jews were used to changes of identity as they
moved back and forth across Europe, but at this time one could
change merely by standing still.

I was born in 1929 in Breslev, a frontier town just
inside Poland, and three years later my father was invited to
become Rabbi of Barovke, a village over the border in Latvia.

My father, like my mother, was always reticent about his age
and early history. He was bearded for as long as I had known
him and always looked old, and I found it difficult to imagine
him as a young man or a boy. His father, a short, stocky, genial
man with smiling eyes and a large white beard who looked like
every child's idea of Santa Claus, and who was something of a
Santa Claus by temperament, was a pedlar who even in his old
age trudged on foot through the great forests with a pack on his
back selling haberdashery to woodsmen and charcoal burners. He
could never make a living, but never seemed to be troubled by
the fact and whenever he visited Barovke the house seemed to
glow with his presence. My father, who was the second of three
sons, inherited much of his amiability but nothing of his carefree
spirits and during those rare periods of his life when he had no
real worries he was – like my mother – consumed by pseudo-

worries. He was by inclination, temperament and training a scholar and had been sent as a young man to Slobodka, perhaps the foremost seat of Talmudic learning in Eastern Europe.

If study, in Jewish tradition, is the highest good it is never good enough in itself. One was expected to marry and if possible to marry young. Father was a pious young man, industrious, good-looking with a graceful presence and in due course a *shidduch* was arranged for him and he married the pretty, vivacious daughter of a Vitebsk corn and flax merchant. As was usual in such matters Father would either have been supported as a scholar all his life or he would have entered his father-in-law's business, but the Russian Revolution came, the business was no more, and Father had to do something for which fate had left him wholly unequipped – make a living.

At some stage during his first or second year of marriage, which is to say in 1918 or 1919, he was press-ganged into the Red Army. I presume he was press-ganged for he was anything but red by temperament and a less soldierly soldier never bore arms.

When my mother talked of old times, as she often did, especially in her later years, she would usually close with the same refrain : *Vos mi hot zich duch gelept, vos mi hot zich duch gelept* – what one has lived through, what one has lived through.

Her family home was on the western marches of the Russian empire. Early in World War I, after Hindenberg's massive victory at Tannenberg, the Germans broke through and occupied most of the western provinces. Jews had no cause to regard Czarist Russia with loyalty or affection, and they greeted the Germans as liberators (as did the Lithuanians and Poles). The Germans later pulled back and there came the depredations of the Russian civil war, first from the Reds then the Whites, and occasional incursions from armed bands who seemed to be in business on their own. And before one could draw breath there followed the Russo-Polish war and the Polish-Lithuanian wars, from which the Poles emerged triumphant and which they celebrated with pogroms in several centres of Jewish population, including Wilno, the former capital of Lithuania. There had been almost ten years of unbroken turmoil in which the engines of war rolled back and forward, back and forward, crushing everyone in the mud, and if one asked Mother what she did in those years she answered in the words of Abbé Sieyès: 'I survived.'

She was a handsome woman, with large, clear grey eyes, and a self-consciously dignified bearing, as if determined not to be borne down by her lowly circumstances, and always kept us and herself in mind of her patrician origins. She was haughty and snobbish, yet lively and had a forceful way of expressing herself both in the things she said and the way she said them. Father by comparison seemed like a dormouse who had been roused from his sleep.

The wars and revolutions, the general chaos ruined a great many families and many Yeshiva students who had been equipped for a life of prayer, contemplation and study, and who had been supported by their parents or in-laws, suddenly had to fend for themselves. My father's position, however, was not quite desperate, for my grandparents managed to scratch together sufficient funds to set him up with a shop in Breslev as a dealer in suiting materials. However, Father had a mildly pagan streak, which I have inherited in enlarged form, and loved the countryside; if business was slack and the weather was fine, he closed the shop and went out for a walk, which made the business even slacker. He also adhered to the Talmudic precept that one must trust men unless one has cause to distrust them, which was all right for sermons but not for business, and he was soon ruined.

By then he was the father of three or four children. He had been ordained as a Rabbi shortly before his marriage, but so had a hundred thousand other Talmudical students. There was a Jewish tradition that one should not make a living from the Torah, but what was perhaps more immediately relevant was the fact that there was no living to be had from it. The towns and villages of Eastern Europe were teeming with Talmudists laden with learning, but without visible or, indeed, invisible means of support. 'He who does not teach his son a trade', said the Talmud, 'teaches him to steal', but the only trade for which Father and his contemporaries had been trained was that of sons-in-law and that, for the time being (the professional son-in-law has since made a comeback), was no longer a profitable calling. He had to find himself a craft and after a couple of years' training he became a *shochet*, which has a certain amount of prestige as a semi-ecclesiastical profession and because it requires a considerable degree of learning. But it is as degrading and unpleasant an occupation as a man could have, for a *shochet*, not to put too fine a point to it, is a butcher, by which I do not mean a purveyor of slaughtered meat, but a slaughterer, literally, a professional cut-throat.

Insofar as slaughter can be humane, *shechita* is humane – to the animal. It is, however, inhumane to the *shochet*, for there comes a moment as he bends down to apply his knife when he has to face the bulging, bewildered, almost pleading eyes of the animal. Father never became hardened to that moment and was eventually broken by it. Other *shochtim* must go through the same experience, for they are required to combine the training and disposition of a scholar with the employment of a butcher. But still it was a craft and offered an income of sorts.

Father would never have been invited to Barovke had he been merely a Rabbi, for Barovke could have done without religious ministration, but it could not do without kosher meat. He thus lived by the knife, but thought of himself only as a Rabbi. There were two synagogues in the village and he ministered to both. He was, as the village policeman put it, the *Patushka*, the little father, of Barovke, and he gloried in the role.

Barovke was a mixed-up place. The area had been colonised by demobilised Russian soldiers after the Napoleonic wars and the peasantry, insofar as they said anything at all, for they were a dour lot, spoke Russian; the Jews spoke Yiddish; the intelligentsia, German. Who then spoke Latvian? Those whose jobs depended on it, post-masters, school-masters, government officials; in short, those who were paid to do so, for anyone in government service was well paid, or at least regularly paid, which is more than can be said of almost everyone else in Latvia. The old, which is to say the Russian, name for our village was Barovke; the new, or Latvian name, was Silene, and in school it was a punishable offence to call it anything else, though one was as likely to call Barovke Silene as one is to call Dublin, Baile Atha Clath.

The Jews never spoke of the place as anything other than Barovke, not out of stubborn loyalty to old Russia, but because it sounded right; it was the sort of name Shalom Aleichem might have made up, like Kastrilovke or Anatevke, for 'Ke' in Yiddish suggests something small and beloved, and the final syllable conveyed something of its humble size and station. It was a clearing in the forest near the Latvian–Polish border, and one suspects that it came into existence in the first place because of the smuggling opportunities afforded by the border. It consisted of a few dozen shops and houses, some neatly grouped round the small cobbled square, the rest scattered in all directions, as if sown by the wind. They were built on high stone foundations to keep the timber above the level of the snows, with steep roofs and sagging windows, like unhappy eyes in an unhappy face. Doors too sagged, as did shutters, and there was a built-in lopsidedness about the whole place. The more prosperous homes were brightly painted in red and yellow with white window frames. Many dwellings were set in small gardens or orchards, surrounded by an affected, tiny, brightly painted wooden fence, with the tops carved like the onion domes of a Russian church. None in Barovke was so poor as not to have a fruit tree to his abode. Chickens scratched around in the streets, in the gardens and courtyards, and at meal-times pecked around under the tables in the homes, sometimes fighting for the available provender with the cats. I do not know if anyone actually kept a cat, but cats insinuated their way into every household. On the other hand there was no Jewish home with a dog. Dogs, large, gruff, shaggy, snarling creatures, were something one associated with *goyim*. One fled at the sight of a dog, and to this day I am still inclined to cross over to the other side of the road at the sight of a poodle.

Barovke itself was – or so I thought – solidly Jewish, but as one grew older one became aware of another, posher, Barovke beyond, with more substantial buildings, some of them of brick rather than timber, built in regular rows, in neat streets with neat gardens. This other Barovke contained the occasional non-Jewish Jew, but it was otherwise as *Judenrein* as Barovke proper was *goyimrein*.

One was curiously unaware of the Latvia beyond Barovke. One knew of Dvinsk, the nearest big town, and one heard occasionally of Riga, the capital, but Latvia itself was little spoken of possibly because it was still a novel entity, and it was never, in spite of its small size, a cohesive whole. The Dvina, which flows into the Gulf of Riga, cuts through the heart of the country. Those to the north generally described themselves as Livonians, those to the south as Courlanders. If anyone actually spoke of himself as a Latvian he was probably a Jew.

The area as a whole was to the Baltic what the Low Countries were to Western Europe and whenever Sweden, Germany, Russia, Lithuania or Poland engaged each other in war, as they frequently did, Livonia and Courland were their battleground, and the provinces were at different periods incorporated into Sweden, Russia and Poland, but until 1944 the dominant influence was always German. Trade was in the hands of the great German merchants settled in the area since the days of the Hanseatic League, and much of the land belonged to the German nobility. Until 1885, though the country was under Russian rule, the official language was German.

The German influence had a lasting effect on Latvian Jewry, and it was among the first to be affected by the *haskalah*, the movement of Jewish enlightenment which spread eastwards from Germany in the course of the nineteenth century. By the end of the century most of the prosperous Jewish families in Riga and other large Latvian towns were thoroughly assimilated and rather more at home in German than in Jewish culture, but enlightenment was rather slow to penetrate the interior and in small villages like Barovke one began to sense its impact only after the First World War. The community as a whole was, on the face of it, at least Orthodox and observant to a man, though Father had to exercise a constant vigilance to keep it that way. The Jewish Sabbath, for example, begins at dusk on Friday evening, and shop-keepers were inclined to keep their premises opened until the last moment, or even beyond, but not if Father was around. As the sun set Father changed into his Sabbath best, and with his coat over his shoulder like a cloak would progress slowly and majestically through Barovke on the way to synagogue, and shops would shut at his approach like flowers on the approach of darkness.

The local doctor, dentist, apothecary and lawyer were all Jewish, but they were not, strictly speaking, part of the com-

munity. They went about their work bare-headed; one did not
see them in synagogue; they worked and travelled on the Sabbath; it was doubtful whether they ate kosher (it was almost
certain they did not), but no one was troubled by the fact, not
even Father. They were university-trained and such people were
not expected to be observant. One was, indeed, mildly reassured
that they remained Jewish at all, and one felt flattered on the
rare occasions that they graced the synagogue with their
presence. They wore black homburgs, instead of the cloth caps
worn by everyone else except Father; they wore ties; their
jackets matched their trousers. They were the local gentry, save
that, with the exception of the lawyer, Abrasha Pinkashovitz,
they assumed no position of leadership in the community. Their
contacts with it were purely professional. They descended, pre-
scribed, took their money and returned to the elevated universe
whence they came. Father, who prepared some of their sons for
the Barmitzvah, would return from their homes full of wonder.
Telephones! Velvet curtains! English furniture! Carpets on the
floor! But they must have held a lowly place in their professions
to have got no further than Barovke. The first car in the
neighbourhood was owned by the husband of the local midwife
who seemed to spend his entire day in, on or about the car.
Perhaps it didn't have an engine, or perhaps he couldn't afford
petrol, for I never saw him drive it. The second was owned by
Abrasha Pinkashovitz. The doctor, a pale-faced man with rimless glasses, who looked as if he was in need of a cure himself,
went about his work on foot.

Father, for a Rabbi of his school, was a progressive and en-
lightened figure, though he would have denied any such label,
but as in most Orthodox Jewish families it was the womenfolk
who exposed one to the modern world. Father had a substantial
library, but with never a volume devoted to anything other than
holy writ. There were the basic books themselves, the commentaries on them, commentaries on the commentaries, and commentaries on . . . whereas my mother and sisters read profane
literature in several languages and I was seven or eight before it
dawned upon me that not everything in print had been dictated
by God to Moses on Mount Sinai. I was aware that people wrote
letters to each other, but it was something of a revelation to dis-

cover that books could be the product of mortals, some of them, like Pushkin, Dostoevsky, Tolstoy, not even Jewish.

'Do you mean,' I asked, 'that you can write a book and people will pay you to read it?'

'Yes,' said Mother, 'if they like it.'

And I got myself a pencil and paper and began: 'Once upon a time there lived an old woman who never died . . .' It was inspired by the sight of an old woman who had lived in Barovke and who was recalled even by the village ancients as being old when they were born. She was bent double with age and was said to be a hundred and seven.

The fact that Latvian Jewry was drawn to German culture made them suspect in Russian eyes and shortly after the outbreak of World War I many Jews – including my father's family who were anything but Germanised – were deported into the interior. There then followed years of turmoil and terror, not unlike those experienced by Mother's family except that my father's parents went penniless into the war and came penniless out of it. In 1915 the Germans occupied Latvia. They pulled out in 1918 and in November of that year an independent Latvian republic was proclaimed, which was almost immediately threatened by a Bolshevik and then a German invasion, and it was not until 1920 that the Latvians were finally masters of their own country. There then followed a period which many Jews spoke of as *'die golderne yorn'*, the golden years. Jews, in common with other minorities, enjoyed and were encouraged to enjoy, cultural autonomy. There was a network of Jewish schools which formed part of the state system and which offered a choice of education in Russian, German and Yiddish. There was a Hebrew teachers' seminar, a Jewish music conservatoire, a Yiddish theatre, a flourishing Jewish press. Then in May 1934 – about a year after we settled in Latvia – there came a Fascist coup under Karlis Ulmanis. Cultural pluralism was abandoned in favour of a policy of rigorous Latvianisation. All the Jewish schools were closed except the religious ones, and they were placed under the control of the Agudah, a right-wing ultra-religious party. The non-Jewish schools had classes on Saturday from which many Jewish children had in the past been excused. Saturday attendance was now made compulsory, and Barovke was particularly affected, for it did not have the alternative of a Jewish state school, and Father protested that Jewish children were being compelled to desecrate their Sabbath.

It is difficult perhaps for the western reader to appreciate the petulant temper of East European authority, and the protest must have involved Father in a prodigious, indeed, reckless display of courage, for apart from his natural timidity, he was in an exposed and vulnerable situation. Though he was born in Latvia he did not happen to be living there when the state was proclaimed and as far as the authorities were concerned he was a Russian, a Polack, possibly even a Red, but at all events a foreigner, and a Jewish foreigner at that. The headmaster of the school, a dapper little dried-up, yellowish being, like a Chinese ivory figurine, with a huge bald head, no eyebrows, and blue lips, was the local representative of the ruling party, the Gauleiter, so to speak, of Barovke, and he made the protest known to his superiors. An obscure Rabbi – and he an alien – in an obscure village was questioning the every authority of the state. Word went forth that Barovke should be rid of its meddlesome priest. And Father, by now comfortably established in a small house with a red roof and green shutters, set among cherry trees, with two daughters at school and a son approaching school age, and a fourth child still in early infancy, was served with an expulsion order. For the first time in his life he had known something like economic security. His position as Rabbi carried prestige but no salary, but as a *shochet* he charged so much per head per animal slaughtered. There were slack weeks in the summer and winter, and frantically busy ones on the approaches to the festivals, but overall he was able to earn an average of about one pound a week, which, though it offered no luxuries, meant that none of us went hungry, ragged or cold. Now, his humble sufficiency threatened, he turned for help to one Mordechai Dubin, the Agudah leader.

The Agudah was founded in 1912 to combat the inroads which Zionism was making into Jewish life and it represented a type of Orthodoxy which was too rigid and extreme even for my father – who was, in any case, a lifelong Zionist – but it was favoured by the Fascists as a pliable and submissive partner. The Kingdom to which it aspired was not of this world. What others

demanded as of right, the Agudah was prepared to seek as a
favour. Mordechai Dubin, head of the party, was a personal
friend of Karlis Ulmanis. Many Jews regarded the cringing
unctious attitude of the Agudah with bitterness and contempt,
but many others believed that they owed their lives to the inter-
cession of Dubin with higher authority and my father was
among them. The expulsion order was rescinded. But his
troubles were not over, for his labour permit, without which he
could not function as a *shochet*, was not renewed, and there all
of Dubin's influence proved unavailing.

We were not left entirely destitute. Father could still pick up
the odd shilling from private tuition. It was illegal for him to ply
his trade and illegal for butchers to employ him, but he was
still brought an occasional chicken to slaughter (which he killed
in the back-yard) and, with the assurance that the policeman
next door would keep a blind eye to his movements, he darted
down to the abattoir with his knives under his jacket, despatched
a few sheep, and sneaked back, and in this way he was able to
earn something like six to seven shillings a week which was just
about enough to survive on in Barovke in 1936.

There is an old Yiddish saying that you shouldn't have to get
used to what you can get used to (it sounds better in Yiddish),
and we got used to it. We subsisted on herrings and black bread
during the week, and somehow managed to eat reasonably well
on the Sabbath and festivals, with white bread on the table and
stuffed pike, and Mother's invariable compote of stewed prunes.
We might have continued like that for years, but if one can get
used to poverty, Father could not get used to his furtive existence. He felt like a hunted criminal and was beginning to crack
under the strain. Finally, he found a job in Glasgow.

Father often had regrets about the nature of his calling, but
in later years he used to say :

'If I had been a prosperous businessman I would never have
left Latvia, if I had been a doctor or a lawyer I would certainly
not have left. Why did I leave? Because I was a broken down
shochet and couldn't make a living. Boruch Sholem (a local mag-
nate) is dead; Dr Heller is dead; Abrasha Pinkashovitz is dead,
and if I wasn't a *shochet* we'd also be dead.'

II

Exile

Throughout those harassing years many, perhaps most East European Jews had two sources of comfort, their God in heaven and/or an uncle in America; in the event, the latter sometimes proved more useful than the former. Mother did not have an uncle in America, but she had one in Britain, which we thought of as an offshore island of America, and was therefore almost as good. Nor was he an ordinary uncle. He was, it was said, not only prosperous – which was the least one could expect of a relative in the west – he was a J.P., a Justice of the Peace, which was translated to us simply as a Judge. Nay, a JUDGE. In every Jewish community there was a *Beth Din*, a Rabbinical court, which dealt mainly with religious matters but to which Jews often resorted for arbitration. Father, as a Rabbi, had served on such a court on innumerable occasions and could thus be considered a judge of sorts. But this distant uncle, Louis Daets by name, functioned on a more exalted plane, and dispensed justice to *goyim* and in our imagination he flourished as a veritable Solomon. We received cuttings about him from the Yiddish press, which were passed along the pews in synagogue, in the English language Jewish press and even – so far had his fame spread – in the English language *goyish* press.

He was a distinguished-looking man with a fine head of hair, piercing, rather stern grey eyes, like my mother's, a formidable nose, an Edwardian moustache and beard, an Edwardian wing collar and cravat, replete with pearl tie-pin, and a gold watch and chain with a pendant medal across a substantial stomach. The most impressive thing about the portrait was the beard. Barovke was full of beards, but they were wild, shaggy outcrops with a will and vigour of their own. This beard was cultivated, tamed, contained, as if every particular hair had been individually laid in place. He looked every inch the judge. Such an uncle was as good as money in the bank, and it was to him that we finally turned when things in Barovke became impossible.

It so happened that there was a vacancy for a *shochet* in Glasgow, and Uncle, who apart from his other duties, was Chairman of the Board of *Shechita* (he was Chairman of the Board of almost everything else), offered Father the job. From then events followed in rapid succession. It was decided that Father would go to Glasgow (borrowing the necessary fare from Uncle) and would send for us as soon as he had saved enough for the tickets, which might take a year. In the meantime, my eldest sister, who had finished elementary school in Barovke, would go to a gymnasium in Dvinsk (or Daugapils, as it was known in Latvian, or Dunabourg in German), I would be sent to Breslev and my other sisters would remain in Barovke with my mother.

There was a great family reunion before Father left, and relatives came by the waggon load from Breslev, Dvinsk and nearby Kreslavka. I don't know where they could all have slept, for our house had only three rooms of which but two were bedrooms – though in Jewish homes in those days, as in Israel now, every room, including the kitchen, could be made to serve as a bedroom. (There was no inn in Barovke and important guests usually stayed with us, usually in my room, sometimes in my bed. There was a small man with a great bushy beard, a charity collector, who often slept in my bed and who farted with such force that I was almost blasted out of bed.) And finally there was a great public dinner at which all of Barovke was present. I don't know what there was to eat or drink, but the speeches were many and endless. I came and went several times, but whenever I returned there was always someone on his feet paying tribute to my father, all genuinely meant and some delivered with tears. I remember in particular an elderly bearded figure called Simshon Ber, not for what he said, but because the tears he shed did not penetrate his beard but rolled down it like water off a duck's back and stained the table-cloth.

My parents lived on the memory of that day for many years,

for the tributes that came their way in Glasgow were few and sparing.

I left for Breslev some time before Father left for Glasgow and he accompanied me on foot as far as the Polish border (there was room beside me on the open cart but he wanted to save the fare). It was a blazing hot day and he kept removing his homburg and wiping his hatband and forehead. The horse was plodding slowly along the dry, rutted track and I kept dropping off to sleep. Father and I never had much to say to each other, especially when we had much to say and were, I think, rendered inarticulate by affection. When we reached the border Father blessed me, but we did not kiss or cry, for we have always been afraid, or reluctant, perhaps even unable, to show emotion in our family, and to that extent we were Englishmen ready made, except that I have sometimes felt – unjustifiably as I discovered – that Englishmen have no emotions to show.

I continued onwards towards Breslev while Father returned towards Barovke, and I watched his erect black-clad figure recede through the haze of the hot afternoon. He did not turn round once.

I was six and about to receive my first bitter taste of exile. I stayed with my mother's family. They had been prosperous corn and flax merchants before the First World War but had lost everything in the Russian Revolution. To my unsubtle mind people who lost everything were left with nothing, but instead I found people of substance who seemed better off in the depths of their penury than my father at the height of his prosperity.

There were two Breslevs, the old and the new, with the latter, which was also known as the Domques, built on high ground overlooking the former. Old Breslev was of timber, the new of stone. New Breslev had electricity, the old had none. Old Breslev was entirely Jewish, the new, entirely Polish, and any non-Jewish Jews who happened to be there kept quiet about their antecedents or were practising Christians. My grandfather's house was one of the largest in old Breslev, a two-storey affair, solidly built, with outhouses and a large, cobbled courtyard. The house seemed to be the general meeting place of everyone in Breslev. A constant whirl of figures, young and old, passed through it, and although

one was always surrounded by people I never had any company
or friends. My main source of delight was the cellar, a large dark
place, which extended under the entire area of the house, the
courtyard and outhouses and which, during the German occupation in World War II was to be the scene of an unspeakable
tragedy.

There are three years which I regard as the black years of my
life. The third was the year I ceased to be an undergraduate
and became a school-master. The second was so painful that I
still cannot bring myself to write about it almost thirty years after
it passed. The first was that year in Poland. I have often wondered
why I was so unhappy in Poland and the most obvious reason
was that I was so happy in Latvia. In Barovke, first of all, I was
at home. We were, in retrospect, poor, but who was not? One
might have had regular meals only on the Sabbath, but one rarely
went hungry the rest of the week and everyone in Barovke ate
reasonably well in season. There were eggs in plenty in the spring
and summer, fruit in plenty in the summer and autumn, and
there was bread and milk at other times of the year, and if one
waned in winter one waxed in the summer.

Then Barovke itself, and its surroundings, were a constant
source of joy. There was a small lake at one end of the village and
a large lake at the other, with a blithe, silvery, chuckling stream
linking the two, and in the hot summer we were hardly out of
the water, wading, swimming, fishing (darting by hand after
the tiddlers who sought refuge under the stones). In the winter,
muffled up like eskimoes, we went skating, sledging, skiing. It
was a free, open life and an important part of the openness and
freedom was the fact that the *goyim* were friendly: in Poland
they were not.

Antisemit (with accent on the last syllable) was an expression
with which the Jewish child in eastern Europe became familiar
early in life. It entered into adult conversation a hundred times a
day and in every possible context, and one took it to be one of the
ills of life, like rheumatism, which was more painful at some time
than others, but which one learned to live with. All *goyim* were
presumed to be *antisemitten* unless they showed definite proof to
the contrary, whereupon they were pronounced *Judenfreint* —
philosemites. Thus, for example, *Patushka*, or 'little father' as the

local Russian Orthodox priest was known, was a *Judenfreint*, as was the village policeman, a mild-mannered little man, with a Hitler moustache and a woebegone expression. *Patushka* sometimes played chess with my father, to whom he had an uncanny resemblance. They were both bearded and (in winter) both wore the same tall fur hats. They also both liked a *schnaps*, though Father was a Sabbath and festival drinker whereas the *Patushka* packed a flask in his canonicals and was inclined to swig at it any time. He also, it was said, kept two concubines which, as Father observed, was perhaps easier than keeping one wife.

The policeman was our next-door neighbour and his wife was my mother's best friend. She was a large, blonde, German lady and, like Mother, was in delicate health which, in Barovke, was accepted as a proof of refinement. Like Mother she was comparatively well read and considered herself a cut above most other people in the district, and like Mother she felt that fate had not given her the station in life to which she felt entitled and looked out at the world with baleful, aggrieved eyes.

My sister's best friend was Anushka, a young peasant, a bright-eyed, red-cheeked, wet-lipped creature, with long, jet-black hair, lusty, care-free, effervescent and even to my young eyes she represented an uninhibited world which would always remain outside my experience. She seemed in motion even when still and made the Jewish girls one knew seem tame, languorous and repressed.

On market days Barovke was flooded with peasants and some of the small boys tried to provoke me by putting their forefingers together in a cross and kissing it, totally without effect, for I thought they were indulging in some sort of religious ritual. In short, given my limited experience, Barovke *goyim* were *Judenfreint*.

In Breslev, however, they all seemed to be *antisemitten* and, again, given my limited experience, they all were. I did not make one friend or acquaintance during that year in Breslev and wandered by myself from one end of the town to the other, up and down the main road and into the sideways. One day I wandered beyond the town and into the countryside when I saw two boys, a little older than me, sitting on a fence and regarding my approach with less than friendly interest. I looked at them, and they looked at me and I turned about with as much dignity

as I could muster and began to walk back, breaking into a trot
when I heard their steps behind me. They were upon me in a
minute, knocked me to the ground and set about me with boot
and fist. When I reached home battered and bleeding my grandmother turned on me. Idiot! Didn't I know it was dangerous to
go beyond Breslev on my own? And of course I didn't. In Barovke
one had been safe to roam at will. I had heard of Jewish persecutors as part of distant or not so distant history, but otherwise
thought of antisemitism as a mere matter of sentiment, that some
people disliked Jews much as others disliked, say, borsch. It had
never occurred to me that one could still be knocked down, kicked
and beaten just for being Jewish.

If the surrounding countryside was dangerous, one was not
entirely safe in town. I was once chased along a backstreet by a
one-legged boy with a crutch. He proved to be faster with his
one leg than I with my two and hooked my feet from under me
with his crutch, and I went flying on my face.

If the *goyim* were hostile, the Jews were not particularly
friendly, and while I suffered among the former as a Jew, I
suffered among the latter as a Latvian. I was a sort of Jews'
Jew.

The Breslev Jewish day-school, as far as I remember, was not
a state school but was financed by the local Jewish community.
Premises were decrepit and cramped. I remember a dainty little
woman teacher who taught us German, but otherwise the only
things about the school to impress themselves upon my memory
were the bullying and harassment and the fact that the male
teachers wore no hats. There is nothing in Jewish canon law –
certainly nothing in any of the authoritative codes – requiring a
man to have his head covered, but the head-covering had through
usage assumed an obligatory nature, and to my mind the idea of
a Jewish teacher in a Jewish school without a hat was as improb-
able as a Jew with a foreskin (I was to meet such Jews too). A well-
capped bearded ancient in a crumpled suit came in every day
to give us religious instruction, but he was apart from the rest of
the staff, a neglected figure and his fusty, musty presence somehow symbolised the place of religious studies in the curriculum.
The school was in the main concerned to introduce young Jews
painlessly into the mainstream of western culture and I was not

quite ready for it. In coming to Breslev, indeed, I was getting the worst of both worlds. Barovke school, would, of course, have offered no Jewish instruction at all, but it was a stately edifice of stone, three storeys high, red-roofed, white-walled, with a spacious playground and playing fields. Rooms were lofty, windows were clean, floors were polished, and there was discipline and order. In Breslev now there was chaos. In later years, in Scotland, when I was of an age and size to look after myself I thought the school discipline excessive, but it is woefully necessary to a small boy thrown among strangers. I was bullied in school, I was bullied out of school. No day passed without its moments of mortification and I went to bed in tears and woke in trepidation. And if my own private world was depressing there was little relief to be found in the outer world. One sensed doomsday in the very air of Breslev and the hatred of the surrounding peasantry could be felt like the weight of a humid day.

Poland, which had become independent in 1918, grew to almost imperial proportions after a series of wars with her neighbours, found herself with minorities including Lithuanians, Ukrainians, Germans and Jews who formed more than a third of her population. Jews alone, who numbered some three million, formed ten per cent of the population.

The Treaty of Versailles had promised minorities their own schools, the freedom to follow their own national traditions and the abolition of all religious discrimination, but most of the promises were breached both in the spirit and the letter. Jews were widely regarded as enemies of Poland. In former German areas they were accused of taking sides with Germany; in Ukrainian areas with the Ukraine; in Breslev, part of the former Lithuanian province of Wilno, they were doubly distrusted as Lithuanians and Jews. Moreover, as it was in a border zone, the surrounding areas were settled with 'trusted' families from central Poland who brought with their fierce nationalism a raging xenophobia. The government in particular seemed set to undermine the whole economic base of the Jewish community.

The drink and tobacco trade which had been largely in Jewish hands was made into a state monopoly which refused to employ Jews. Galician Jews who had been employed in large numbers on the Austrian railways, were thrown out of work when the area became Polish. The growth of agricultural cooperative and state trading corporations was gradually eliminating the Jewish middle man and there was a growing tendency to boycott Jewish goods, with the result that small towns like Breslev, which were only beginning to rebuild lives and fortunes shattered by the war, found, as the 1930s proceeded, a gradual waning of prospects. There had been heavy emigration to America in the previous decade, but new laws virtually closed America to East European immigrants. There had been a flow of migrants to Palestine, but that petered out after the 1929 riots, and people turned in every direction for a new refuge. Some moved to Argentina, some to Brazil, some to China. Many subsisted on remittances from *reiche krovim*, rich relatives abroad. (The mere fact of being abroad was in itself taken as a proof of riches.) If the mood of Breslev was thus gloomy it had something to be gloomy about.

A few months after I went to Poland my father set out for Scotland, and after about a year he had saved up enough money to send us tickets to join him. My exile was about to come to an end. That Passover my mother and sisters came over from Barovke for a family reunion and there were some two dozen of us at the *seder*, the celebration, part banquet, part holy communion, with which the festival opens. The winter snows had melted, but it was a bleak, icy night and I remember slithering on the frost-covered pavements on the way home from synagogue, and something of the bleakness of the outside night invaded the large dining room and clung to our spirits. Grandfather had been dead for some time and my uncle Chaim-Kasre, with his dark-eyed, full-bosomed wife on one side, and Grandma on the other, presided over the gathering. Grandma, a handsome formidable woman with a determined jaw, suddenly seemed old and frail. She had lately lost the sight in one eye and the black patch on her glasses made her look slightly ridiculous. She did not cry, for that would have been unlike her, but what was passing through her mind was passing through ours. The young were young and the world was getting smaller and who knew but we might not meet again, that this might be the last she would see of us and we of her. None of us, of course, could have guessed that not even she would be allowed to fade out of life gradually and peacefully.

In 1940 Poland once again vanished from the map of Europe

as Germany and Russia divided the country between them. In
June 1941 the Germans invaded and occupied the Russian-held
areas. The young fled to the forests or eastwards into Russia. My
uncle Chaim-Kasre, who was one of the leaders of the community, tried to restrain them. 'What are you afraid of, what
can they do to you?' he asked and, as a survivor told me later,
'it seemed a reasonable question. You felt that if you had lived
under the Poles and the Russians you had little to fear from the
Germans.' And for a year or so they suffered the privations usual
in war-time but otherwise lived a more or less normal existence.
Schools and synagogues remained open, festivals were celebrated, people even married and had children. Then in 1942 the
atmosphere changed and it became clear that the Germans were
bent upon a policy of extermination. There was a further flight
to the east, but the old and those encumbered with children took
refuge where they could and some forty people, including my
grandmother, hid themselves in the cellar which had formed
my private universe during my Breslev year. None of them came
out alive.

We received a telegram in 1944 informing us of the death of
grandmother, uncles, aunts, and cousins, but without details of
where, when or how. I learned the details thirty years later at a
gathering in Tel-Aviv.

For many years the tragedy of East European Jewry was
summed up for me by something I witnessed as we passed the
Jewish Cemetery on the way out of Breslev. There was in
Breslev a young widow with three children who remarried and
prepared to set out for a new life in America. However, the oldest
child, a girl of twelve, was mentally backward, and the mother,
fearing that she might jeopardise the chance of the rest of the
family to emigrate, abandoned her. Backward or not, she could
not have been all that insensitive, for as we passed the cemetery
we saw her hugging her father's tomb-stone, her face thrown
back, crying to the cold heavens at the top of her voice. We
travelled on a slow-moving cart, and it was a long time before
the sound of her voice died in our ears.

I rejoined my mother and sister in Barovke to prepare for our
emigration and found their position already transformed. Father
was sending us £10 a month and we were rich, and one obvious

B

sign of it was the succession of *meshulochim*, charity collectors, who can smell money as instinctively as bears smell honey and who almost laid siege to our house. There were people in Barovke who earned more, but their income came in erratic lumps, and even when the going was good they were afraid to spend it in case it should go bad, whereas Father's two fivers in their registered envelope came as assuredly as day followed night. British bank-notes now look much like any other currency and are usually worth less, but there was a grave dignity to those large white flimsy fivers with their glossy black print and their whirly figures; they looked as if they had been painted by hand. Framed they would have looked like a college diploma.

The fact that for the first time since the Russian Revolution Mother was again in funds did little to change her way of life, for though she was from a rich family and Father from a poor one, she was rather better at husbanding cash; but it did mean that Anna, an old, battered, Russian *babushka*, who used to come in as a home-help on the not infrequent occasions when Mother was ill, now came every day. She was a chain-smoker and rolled her own cigarettes from any paper to hand – usually newspaper. She once picked up one of the fivers and began to fill it with tobacco, when Mother snatched it from her grasp.

We became very attached to Anna and went to see her before we left Barovke. She lived in a thatched hovel in the woods which, in an English setting, would have been picturesque, but which to our eyes summed up all that was dreadful in poverty. It was dilapidated and open to the winds and the cold. Inside, apart from a faded icon there was hardly anything but bare boards and bare walls, all seen in half darkness. There was a stove in one corner and a pile of rags in another, which I suppose served as a bed. There was a hunk of wood like a butcher's block which served as a table, but there was no other furniture and no chairs. Such things were often handmade in Barovke, but her husband, a woodsman, had been crippled by a fall of timber and slouched around during his waking hours with a bottle of raw vodka. Anna was the breadwinner, and almost everything she earned he drank, but I never knew so much as a sigh to escape her. She was a typical Russian peasant woman, stoic, hardy, tireless, uncomplaining. She clasped us all to her great bosom before we left – I still remember the smell of stale tobacco – and drenched us with tears.

In the meantime we were hearing wondrous things from Glasgow, its magnificence, its towering buildings, its size, its open spaces, its wealth. People, wrote Father, ate four meals a day whether they were hungry or not, and that at set times – breakfast at eight, lunch at one, tea at five and supper at seven. In Barovke one had a cup of tea and a bun at breakfast and *varmess* – a warm meal – towards evening, but otherwise one snatched a bite whenever one was hungry – provided always there was a bite to snatch. In Glasgow doctors, 'and even professors', attended synagogue religiously every Sabbath, which made us feel it was a holy city. In Glasgow, we learnt, 'great Jewish merchants' kept their shops shut on Shabbat, whereas in Latvia (there were no millionaires in Barovke itself) anyone beyond a certain level of prosperity could, so to speak, arrange his own terms with the Almighty and did not keep, and was not expected to keep, the Sabbath. And most wondrous of all – the *goyim* were friendly. Elsewhere one presumed *goyim* were unfriendly unless they showed proof to the contrary. In Glasgow, wrote Father, it was the other way about, they were *all* friendly – 'even the *beitzimer*'.*

The only non-Jews with whom Father had any contact were our immediate neighbours (whom he would greet with : 'Good morning, nice day,' whatever the state of the weather), and Irish pluckers in the poultry slaughter house, in the Gorbals, so much of the little English that he knew he acquired from an English translation of the Talmud (which he used as a sort of introduction to the English language), and from the Irish pluckers, and some of the expressions he picked up sounded odd in his mouth. Thus, he referred to Mother, whose superior airs would humble a duchess, as 'the missus'. A famous Rabbi once lay dying in a Glasgow hospital and Father was among the privileged

* The expression *beitzimer* – singular, *beitz* – was new to me and when I came to Glasgow I found that it referred to a low-class *goy*, but only discovered the derivation of the word over thirty years later from Professor Arthur Hyman, a Hebrew scholar formerly of London and living in Jerusalem. *Beitz*, or rather *beitzah*, is Hebrew for egg. The Yiddish for eggs is *eyer* which in turn was also the Yiddish for Irishman. In Glasgow – as in Liverpool, which was the only other place where the expression was used – the Irish were said to be the lowest class of *goy*, hence the Yiddish for a low-class *goy* was *beitz*, plural *beitzimer*.

few to be admitted to his bedside. 'How is he?' he was asked as he emerged, and Father shook his head gravely : 'He's a goner,' he said.

If the Scots *goyim* were friendly I am not sure whether the Latvian ones were unfriendly and certainly I met no one in Scotland as kindly and affectionate as old Anna, or the policeman with the woebegone expression, next door. The only actual, card-carrying Latvian antisemite I had heard of was Tolk – splendid name for a villian – a border policeman who had shot and killed a Jew trying to smuggle himself over the frontier, though I dare say he would have shot his own father trying to do the same thing. One certainly did not find in Latvia the atmosphere of brooding hatred one had experienced in Poland. The antisemitism which one did encounter was mainly institutional. Any Jew in Eastern Europe who sought to get anywhere could take it for granted that he would meet handicaps at every stage of his progress from which the non-Jew was free, whereas – according to Father – Britain was entirely opened to the talents. Secondary education was free and, if one worked hard enough and was bright enough, one could even get to university for nothing. All this was written, or at least read out to us by Mother, in a continuous tone of wonder and awe. 'Who knows,' she said to me, 'you might even be a doctor.'

No one not brought up in Eastern Europe can appreciate the awe with which a doctor was regarded by Jew and non-Jew. If someone was so ill as to need a doctor – and he had to be very ill (for minor ailments one approached the apothecary) – the house was prepared for his coming. Beds were hurriedly made, jackets were donned to cover braces, the patient was tidied and cleaned and propped up, and when the great man entered everyone rose. One remained standing in his presence and addressed him in a hushed voice. If the patient died it was taken to be the work of God; if he survived at all, the praise of the doctor was sung about the neighbourhood and if he was cured, he was spoken of in hushed tones as a miracle worker. A doctor couldn't fail. My ambition at this time, however, was to be a Rabbi which, in later years, I almost fulfilled.

III

'Mit a gutten Engils'

Glasgow was not, at first sight at least, the golden city I had imagined. Our first stop was Riga, our second Berlin, our third Ostend, the fourth London. From London we travelled overnight and moved from the darkness of night into the half darkness of a Glasgow day. There was a greyness and drabness to everything, the buildings, the streets, the skies, the people. It was full of disappointments.

The first, and perhaps greatest disappointment, was Father himself. I had looked forward to our reunion as a restoration of the close, cosy, intimate existence we had known before. Glasgow, I had envisaged it, was to be Barovke plus regular meals, but nothing was the same any more and Father himself had changed. He had arrived in Glasgow a *heimisher* Rabbi, and was pulled aside with advice – mainly from colleagues who had settled in Glasgow some years before – that he should adapt his appearance a little to his environment, and thus he removed the side-locks which he used to have tucked in behind his ears, and trimmed his beard till it hardly covered his chin. I was later to feel embarrassed by the fact that he had a beard at all, but his flowing whiskers, with their reddish tinge, had been so much a part of his personality that I hardly recognised him without them.

In Barovke I used to accompany him through the mists and across the moist meadows to synagogue every morning. In Glasgow he could not attend synagogue on weekdays for he had to be up about five to get to the slaughter house at six (he travelled on an early morning workman's ticket), so that my visits to synagogue – which in Barovke had formed the centre of my existence – were confined to evenings and weekends, and as time went on my evening visits also lapsed.

In Barovke before going to bed I used to recite a small prayer which still passes through my mind every time I settle down for sleep though it is more than thirty years since I last said it :

'Blessed art Thou, O Lord our God, King of the Universe, who makest the bonds of sleep fall upon mine eyes, and slumber upon mine eyelids. May it be Thy will, O Lord my God and God of my father, to suffer me to lie down in peace and to let me rise up again in peace. Let not my thoughts trouble me, nor evil dreams, nor evil fancies, but let my rest be perfect before Thee. O lighten mine eyes lest I sleep the sleep of death, for it is Thou who givest light to the apple of the eye. Blessed art Thou, O Lord, who givest the light to the whole world in Thy glory.'

Father said an extended version of the same prayer, which seemed to go on for hours. He would stride slowly up and down the floor as he said it in a low, plaintive chant and I would be wakened by the creaking of the floorboards :

'The Angel who hath redeemed me from evil, bless the young and let the names of my fathers Abraham and Isaac be called amongst them, and let them grow into a multitude in the midst of the earth . . .'

And so on till the final verses :

'Behold the guardian of Israel sleeps not, neither does he slumber.
For Thy salvation I hope O Lord, I hope O Lord for Thy salvation,
O Lord for Thy Salvation I hope.'
'In the name of the Lord, God of Israel, may Michael be at my right hand; Gabriel at my left; before me Uriel; behind me, Raphael, and above me, the divine presence of God.'

The lamps were dimmed and I thought I could see the angels amid the flickering shadows and could almost hear the flutter of their wings.

In Glasgow the floorboards did not creak and I was no longer awake to hear my father at prayer; the soft light of the kerosene lamps had given way to the harsh glare of electricity, and the angels were banished from my life. In a sense I have been searching for them ever since, though there have been moments in Jerusalem, when I thought I had found them again.

In his letters to Barovke Father had dwelt only on his joys; he did not touch on his sorrow. In Barovke, though he had been a slaughterer six days of the week, he was a Rabbi on the seventh, and when he entered synagogue people would rise and he would be ushered in to his place of honour by the East Wall next to the ark. On certain special days like the Sabbaths before Passover and the Day of Atonement and, of course, on the Day of Atonement itself, he would ascend the pulpit, draw his prayer shawl over his head, so that his eyes glowed from its depth, and, after turning in different directions, there was still complete silence; then he would begin in a low deep voice, which seemed to issue from the shadows under his shawl rather than himself, swaying slightly as he spoke, and he would be followed with much nodding of heads and many an approving sigh. The message, which took upwards of an hour to deliver, was always the same – repent – but it was rich with homily and anecdote, and ingenious word play, and the synagogue was packed every time he spoke.

There is a verse from the Talmud read on Shabbat afternoons :

'Moses received the Torah on Sinai, and passed it to Joshua, Joshua to the Elders, the Elders to the Prophets; and the Prophets handed it down to the Men of the Great Synagogue . . .'

Who, it was natural to infer, handed it down to my father who seemed eminently worthy of the responsibility. In Glasgow, however, he was reduced to the ranks of mere mortals and never quite reconciled himself to the fact.

Provincial Jewish life in the 1930s was still in the hands of immigrants who, if only to establish their own bona fides as Englishmen, demanded one quality above all others from their Rabbis, that they speak 'mit a gutten Engils', which was the one quality father lacked. He was a good man, a pious man, a learned man with a fine presence, a good Rabbinical diploma, with recommendations from some of the greatest sages in Eastern Europe (written in a Hebrew which would have been Greek to most people in Glasgow), but of 'Engils' good or bad, he had none. He was, as far as Glasgow was concerned, not Rabbinic material, and thus for six days of the week he was a slaughterer and on the seventh day he was nobody, till towards the end of his life, when the sons of immigrants assumed the mantles of their fathers and became leaders of the community. They spoke a 'gutten Engils' themselves and were thus not concerned about the Englishness of their clergy, and Father became Rabbi of an almost defunct congregation in the Gorbals. By then he had mastered the language sufficiently to attempt a sermon in English, though most people who came to hear him would have preferred him to speak in Yiddish. In Yiddish he had sufficient power of oratory almost to penetrate the language barrier, but when he turned to English all his natural facility for words was lost. He would put together his thoughts with the help of the collected works of English Rabbis whose sermons were a patchwork of platitudes couched in clichés.

To reassure himself that he was still part of the ecclesiastical brotherhood Father wore a top-hat on the Sabbath, for the topper, or a tile-hat as it was known in Scotland (cylinder-hat in Yiddish), was virtually the badge of office of the Rabbi. He also had a seat, if not right by the ark, at least not far from it, next to my great-uncle, but it was not in fact his. As a Rabbi he was never required to rent a pew, and as an ex-Rabbi he could never afford to rent one, certainly not in a place of honour next to Uncle on the one side, and the East Wall on the other. Nor did anyone – though he performed many a small service for the congregation – take it into his head to offer him an *ex gratia* pew. He was in fact a squatter, a squatter who was never disturbed, for the actual tenant of the pew took another seat on the rare occasions he was in synagogue, but Father was always mindful of his situation and he saw himself in the traditional role of the Jew, maintaining his place not as of right but on sufferance. I once asked him why he did not rent one of the cheaper pews at the back and he replied that for himself it did not matter, but he could not overlook the fact that he was also a Rabbi. In truth it was rather the other way about, that he sought the place of honour and wore a top hat to reassure himself that he was still a Rabbi although he was soon to discover that a Rabbi in the Glasgow Jewish community had rather less standing than a bankrupt haberdasher.

Glasgow was a hard-headed and, in some ways, a hard-faced, workaday place where material advancement was as a rule given priority over everything else, and the city itself was in many ways a monument to this creed. With its river and hills it has a natural setting as splendid as Athens or Rome, but for over a century it has been at the mercy of speculative builders, railway developers, industrialists, who were allowed to darken every prospect provided they could make tuppence grow where a penny grew before. But with all that, possibly because so sombre a place on earth commends to the mind the heavens, it was in those days a very religious city, not in the sense that it was particularly pious – that Glasgow has never claimed for itself – but because religion exercised the imagination and the energies of a large part of the population (though not always to the extent of affecting its ways), and with it came a considerable deference to the clergy.

Jewish clergymen in those days used to be clad by Church outfitters from head to foot, including even the dog collar, and they found that people would offer them seats in the tram, bank managers extended them credit on liberal terms, policemen touched their helmets in salutation.

Glasgow Jewry, on the other hand, had scant deference for the cloth. The elders were shop-keepers, warehousemen, dealers and traders of various sorts who had made a bit of money, and gave a bit away, and who in their struggle for a livelihood had forgotten any Jewish knowledge they may have possessed without acquiring any compensating knowledge from outside. You were somebody or nobody according to how much you were worth and, to an extent, how much you gave, and if you were rich enough, you were sometimes even absolved from giving. Father, who had tended to view the community with excessive deference when he first came, came to regard it with excessive distaste towards the end of his life. He once said 'ten good men and true would have been sufficient to save Sodom, were there that many good men in Glasgow? There was Ellis Isaacs, and he's dead;

Abraham Goldberg, and he's dead; Hirshow, and he's dead; Hyman Tankel, and he's dead; Eli Jacobs, and he's dead; Jack Mandel, and he's dead.'

He did not include Uncle who was by then in his eighties and still showing every sign of life.

Uncle was another of the disappointments of Glasgow. Instead of the JUDGE, the exalted personage sitting on high, dispensing justice to the multitudes I found a sad little man with a drooping moustache, a baggy suit, soup-stained lapels and a large, eccentric wife in a large, yellow, moth-eaten fur, which she had never left off her shoulders summer or winter. Every time Aunt came on a visit I would rummage among the tufts to establish the origins of the fur and it seemed to me that it was fashioned out of marmalade cats.

Both Uncle and Aunt spoke a broken English (Aunt knew hardly any English at all) which made me wonder what sort of judge he could have been and I soon discovered that a Justice of Peace did not have quite the exalted role I had imagined. He was from time to time required to take his turn on the local magistrate's bench. He did not understand much English but he knew a drunk when he saw one (he rarely saw anyone else) and tended to mete out ten days to anyone who came before him, so that he became known as the Ten Day Wonder. A growing number of Stipendiary Magistrates displaced more and more of the J.P.s whose role had become increasingly ornamental, but during World War II and the immediate post-war years, Uncle was kept busy by a succession of small boys who had lost their sweet ration coupons and needed the signature of a J.P. on their application for new ones, which gave him a function of sorts. He once said: 'I've got the bad teeth of a whole generation on my conscience.'

Uncle and Aunt were first cousins and had left Russia shortly after their marriage early in the century. They reached Glasgow en route for America, but Uncle found friends there and built up a thriving business as a credit draper, or 'tally man', as they were known in Scotland, selling a pair of shoes here, a pair of trousers there, to the working-class areas of Glasgow, and was repaid at the rate of a penny or tuppence a week. They had two daughters both precociously bright and very beautiful, and after World

War I they set out with their children to visit their families in Poland. There, as Uncle put it, 'something unfortunate happened'. He never explained what the misfortune was, but Mother told us. A typhus epidemic was raging in Eastern Europe. Both children succumbed to it and died after a short illness. Uncle and Aunt had set out a young and happy couple with young children, and returned elderly and derelict.

Once they had lost their children they adopted the community as their family and there was hardly a major Jewish organisation of which Uncle was not President, Chairman or Treasurer, but his main joy was the Queens Park Synagogue, a large red-sandstone building which stood, and still stands, near the river Cart in the south side of Glasgow. It was built largely through his efforts and partly with his money, and he haunted the building at all times of the day and night.

There is in the centre of every Orthodox synagogue a *bimah* or raised platform from which the Cantor leads the congregation in prayer, and in front of the *bimah* there is, like the quarter-deck of a ship, an area known as the Warden's Box, which accommodates the lay-leaders of the congregation in their panoply of striped trousers and top hats. Uncle was more in the box than out of it, partly because he almost owned it, but partly because no one else applied himself to the affairs of the congregation so completely. And he was a different man in the box, more erect, more assured. A new light shone in his eyes, there was an extra vigour to his voice. He looked like an elderly, if diminutive, lion.

The relationship between our families was not of the happiest. First of all, Mother could not forgive them for the fact that we had needed their help in the first place. Secondly, she felt that they were patronising us, which to an extent they were. They had taken it upon themselves to pull us into the twentieth century and Mother suspected early in our sojourn that Uncle in his wing collars and Aunt in her moth-eaten fur were possibly not themselves in the avant-garde of contemporary life. It was Aunt (though I may be doing her an injustice) who suggested that as a prospective Briton I could not go through life as Chaim Icyk Bermant, and therefore when I entered Battlefield School in September 1938, I was registered as Hyman Berman and, understanding what was expected of me, I took the matter further.

There was a Jewish boy upstairs from us with the name of Isaac, who was called Francis. Icyk is the Polish for Isaac and I therefore began signing myself Hyman Francis Berman, and I still have an exercise book with that name on the cover. Nobody of course ever called me Hyman or Francis and I was known variously as Hymie, Hi Hi, or Hei Ho and even Haimish. At home I was called Chaim Icke and finally when I enrolled at Glasgow University I saw no reason for departing from the name on my birth certificate and reverted to Chaim Icyk Bermant. Chaim Icyk, moreover, means life and laughter in Hebrew, and although I have not always lived up to my names one can go through life with worse labels.

My own complaint against Uncle was that he was less than avuncular. The Yiddish (and Hebrew) for relatives is *krovim*, near ones, and in Eastern Europe they were literally just that. Their home was an extension of yours, yours of theirs. One came and went without invitation or bidding, dropped in for meals, raided the larder, and even among non-relatives one lived in a world of open doors, except, of course, last thing at night, when there came a heavy clanking of bolts and bars and the clatter of shutters. One of the first things that struck me about Glasgow was that doors stayed shut no matter how hard one pushed and that one had to pull or push a bell, or knock to be admitted. The bells were great fun and for the first week or so after we moved in I was a source of harassment to the entire neighbourhood and beyond, but I could not get over the fact that doors were locked in broad daylight, even when people were at home, and there was no door more thoroughly locked than Uncle's.

I was an early riser and on my way to school I would pass Uncle's two-storey, red sandstone terraced house in Carmichael Place. The house had a bell pull and a bell push, neither of which worked, and one day I stopped by and knocked on the door. No one answered. The next day, feeling something of a challenge, I knocked louder and longer, but there was still no answer. The third time I knocked with such vigour and at such length that an upstairs window was finally thrown open and a bonneted head appeared, which reminded me of the wolf in Red Riding Hood after he had eaten grandma. It was Aunt. What did I want, she demanded, which struck me as an odd question. I wanted in. 'Get on your way,' she said, and slammed the window down.

Father was passing one evening and knocked on the door which, to his surprise, was immediately thrown open and he was greeted with what seemed to him a mixture of embarrassment and dismay. He stepped in to find a house prepared for a party, cups on top of saucers, napkins in cups, gleaming cutlery, cakes on cake stands, little bowls of sugared almonds – and sensing that he was less than welcome he made an excuse to leave.

'Must you go?' asked Aunt, almost propelling him to the door. Father was amused by the incident, Mother was incensed. What uncle would make a party in Latvia or Poland without inviting his nephew and niece, without, indeed, taking it for granted that they would be there? We were obviously being treated as poor relatives which might have been forgivable if they were rich, but if they were rich they displayed little external sign of their prosperity, and in day-to-day terms our standard of living was immeasurably higher than theirs. For most days of the week they lived on the sort of diet we had known back home, potatoes and herring. Father called on them one bitterly cold night to find them bent over the radio with blankets round their shoulders. In the winter they generally went to bed straight after supper, but they were staying up to hear the news. They had no gas or electric heating in the house, and Aunt could rarely be bothered to make a coal fire. Father thereupon lent them a two-bar electric heater which, Mother recalled with satisfaction, was never returned.

Uncle in fact still made quite a lot of money, certainly by any standards with which we were familiar, but gave it away, to Rabbinical colleges and blind homes in Palestine, orphanages in England, impoverished relatives all around the globe and, above all, to Queens Park Synagogue, and I doubt if they ever spent as much as a tenth of their income on themselves.

Jewish generosity is phenomenal, but so, with exceptions, is the Jewish desire to have generosity acknowledged. There are, or were, synagogues in London's East End where almost every inch of wall space was taken up with the names of benefactors written in letters of gold (as they had to donate a mere twenty shillings for the honour, immortality was cheaply bought). Even

Jerusalem is a city plagued with plaques. In the Hebrew University there is not a building, or a square yard of garden without the engraved names of benefactors. Most of the money given by my uncle and aunt, however, was given quietly. They were embarrassed by personal expressions of gratitude, though they did not mind being thanked by post. They were in fact a deeply compassionate pair – Uncle certainly was; I sometimes had my doubts about Aunt – and, like most members of my family, shuddered at any external display of feeling.

In some respects their life stopped with the death of their children. They had not refurbished their house nor added anything to their wardrobe since the 1920s and one suspects they were not in the height of fashion even then. Everything Aunt wore reached down to her ankles or the floor. On the rare occasions when she could be persuaded to remove her fur she wore strange-looking garments with long-pleated skirts and beaded bodices which would have looked bizarre on anyone else, but she was a large woman and carried herself well and they went with her personality. She was a walking period piece.

Their house too was a period piece. The stonework had gathered grime more quickly and extensively than the other houses in the terrace. The iron gate and railings were rusting, the paintwork on the window-frames was peeling; the garden was overgrown and in the autumn schoolboys used to stop by to pick bramble berries from the hedges. The whole house had a woebegone, desolate appearance and reflected something of the tragedy suffered by its inhabitants. The front room, however, which was only used on state occasions, was a splendid place with scarlet wallpaper, embossed with gold, a white marble fireplace, an oval table with a heavy, velvet, tasselled cover, velvet curtains, red plush heavily upholstered chairs, and show cases ranged round the walls, full of small mementoes, silver trowels from the laying of foundation stones, gold keys and silver keys with which Uncle opened various institutions, silver salvers and silver bowls all with inscriptions to Louis and Leibe Sheine Daets for their efforts on behalf of, and their generosity to this or that cause. And every flat surface was occupied with dust and framed photographs, Uncle and Aunt with the Chief Rabbi, with the Lord Provost, with the Lord Lieutenant of the County, with the Moderator of the Church of Scotland, with the Catholic Archbishop of Glasgow, with – could that have been Queen Mary? And a small photo in a silver frame of a stalwart, handsome woman, with black hair piled high on her head, holding a beautiful infant – Aunt Leibe Sheine with the younger of her two children.

Leibe Sheine had two other sisters living in Glasgow but they were not on speaking terms with one another. One sister, living a stone's throw from her very house, was married to one of Uncle's brothers. Brother and sister had married brother and sister, first cousins doubly linked, and both marriages were marred by misfortune.

During the war, relations between Mother and Aunt improved (the females were the warring party; the males rarely fell out with anyone), and after the first air-raids, while we, the children, were evacuated to the country, Uncle and Aunt moved into Battlefield Gardens, into the small room normally occupied by my two older sisters, and they remained there till we came back. There is a traditional Jewish dish called *cholent* compounded of brisket, fat, potatoes and beans which is normally eaten for Shabbat lunch. Aunt indeed prepared it for Shabbat, but in a vast quantity in a great, huge cauldron of a cast-iron pot (they have lately returned to fashion) on which they lived for the rest of the week. Aunt used to go to bed with it, slung low in her hand like a giant hand-bag.

During the war she collected money for the Red Cross and the Mrs Churchill Aid to Russia fund and until the war finished – apart from the Sabbath and festivals – she would never be seen without a pair of boxes in her hand in aid of one or the other. She importuned every acquaintance and, indeed, every passer-by and could, it was said, get money out of an Aberdonian.

Uncle, certainly by Glasgow standards, was something of a Talmudic scholar and when Father or any other Rabbi began quoting some Hebrew phrases he would always butt in with the end of it, but while he was at home with Yiddish, Hebrew or Aramaic he rarely read anything English, except newspapers. Leibe Sheine did not read at all, and I am not sure if she could read, but she was a shrewd woman with considerable insight into

Jewish character and he always deferred to her judgement, especially in matters affecting his beloved Queens Park Synagogue. It was difficult for ecclesiastical employees, Rabbis, Cantors, Beadles, to get a rise in salary, for as Leibe Sheine observed, what did a Rabbi need fifteen pounds a week for when she herself could manage on five, and as a result there was a fairly frequent turnover of clergy. Queens Park was, in its heyday, one of the principal provincial congregations and there was no shortage of candidates. The usual procedure was to invite the man down for the weekend. He would first address the congregation on the Sabbath morning and when he had finished all eyes would travel upward to the Ladies Gallery where Leibe Sheine sat immediately overlooking the pulpit. She never actually gave the thumbs down sign to indicate her disapproval of a candidate, but the congregation could tell by the way she pressed her under-chin against her beaded bodice that the man was doomed.

The first quality she demanded of a candidate was 'a gutten Engils'. Although she spoke hardly any English herself, she had an instinctive feeling for good English from bad and the good orator from the bad – Queens Park in its time has had some outstanding Rabbis, including Kopul Rosen, who, but for his youth, would have become Chief Rabbi after the war, and who later left the Rabbinate to establish Carmel College, England's first and only Jewish public school. He remained in Glasgow for under a year, partly because he was not entirely happy with Leibe Sheine's dominion. He was, she said, a *kenner* (knowledgeable, which indeed he was) and spoke 'a beautiful Engils' (he was one of the foremost orators in the country), but he did not like being told what to do.

If we were disappointed with Uncle and Aunt, they were more than disappointed with us. They would, I think, have liked to adopt us as their second family, but Mother was too prickly, and we remained too stubbornly alien, or to use an expression which echoed about our ears almost endlessly for our first year in Glasgow, we were incorrigible 'greeners'. Other newcomers had arrived in Glasgow about the same time as we, and had built flourishing businesses, spoke reasonable English, were fashionably dressed, kept open house, could make polite conversation, whereas for a long time we looked and dressed and spoke and behaved as if we had just stepped off the immigrant boat, and on those rare occasions when we were invited anywhere we sat together in an awkward, silent huddle. It was not for want of trying to adapt ourselves to our surroundings. Father had already sacrificed three-quarters of his beard. Mother, who had arrived in a voluminous, ankle-length fur coat and cape, of the type necessary to carry one through a Russian winter, had re-modelled it till it stopped short of the calf. My sisters, who had long plaits running halfway down their backs, had hair cuts, and I, who arrived cropped as a convict, allowed my hair to grow till it was long enough for a parting. Moreover, my mother and sisters went to night-school to learn English, while my father struggled with huge chunks of the English translation of the Talmud. But it was all unavailing. We were different and felt different and were deeply, in fact excessively conscious of the fact that we were 'greeners'.

The other newcomers were refugees from Germany and Austria and we resented the common tendency of people to class us together with them. We were *not* refugees, we pointed out, with perhaps excessive vehemence. We came at our own expense, of our own free will. No one pushed us. On the other hand, as we observed with envy, there was little that was 'green' about the refugees, and certainly anyone brought up in Berlin or Vienna, or even Karlsruhe was unlikely to be overawed by Glasgow Jewish society. Indeed, they were hardly in it before they took the measure of it, and were out of it. They were widely read, cultivated people and where they remained part of the community enriched it immensely, but in the main they kept to themselves.

There were several refugees among my contemporaries at school, among them a little pink-faced chap with rimless glasses whom I called the professor. When he enunciated a word of English, he did so exercising every muscle in his face, so that every syllable stood out in relief. In the lavatory one morning I noticed that he had a long, drooping foreskin to his little member, like an overlong sleeve, more foreskin than member in fact. I did a double-take and it was still there, but to make trebly sure I followed him round until he had to go again, and there was no mistaking that he had an appendage which, given his race, shouldn't have been there. And he made no attempt to hide it and indeed when he had completed his business swung it around with something like defiance. I could no more conceive of a Jew with a foreskin than of an elephant without a trunk and for a long time I wondered if I should denounce him as an impostor.

There was a special class for foreign pupils taken by a tall, distinguished-looking, silver-haired woman, called Agnes Smith (the Scottish boys called her Big Aggie), who had an exotic line in spats which came right up to her finely moulded calves. She taught us in German which I, with my knowledge of Yiddish, was able to follow. Within a month the refugee children were out of the special class and in amongst the others, while I had Big Aggie all to myself till the end of term.

Uncle and Leibe Sheine were not our only guides to British life and civilisation. Neighbours, colleagues, friends, all chipped in with their bits of counsel and though we eagerly took instruction from every quarter we tended to lapse into our alien ways. Father had to visit some important communal figure one evening. When he wasn't back by ten, Mother was a little concerned. When eleven o'clock struck and he was still not home she was almost frantic. By eleven-thirty she was on the point of calling the police (she would have called them if we had had a phone) when he came staggering in, white with exhaustion. 'I only intended to stay a few minutes,' he explained, 'but every time I rose to leave, they kept asking me if I couldn't stay, so what could I do? I stayed.'

Similarly when people stopped to ask Mother how she was, she would tell them, and as she was rarely in anything but indifferent health, she had a lot to tell.

We were lavishly entertained one evening by a distant relative who said that now that we had got to know each other we should see each other more and that we should treat his home as ours. I took him at his word and was round there early the following morning. He met me at the gate and without even enquiring whether I had money for the fare (which I hadn't) propelled me on to the first tram.

Some years later Father said that the first thing to learn about the English was that they don't say what they mean and don't mean what they say and we compiled a private family glossary of English words and phrases together with their true meaning, such as :

'How are you ?' (I'm not interested)

'You must come in and see us.' (Keep your distance)

'Make yourself at home.' (Keep your grubby hands off the furniture)

'Do have another.' (Haven't you had enough?)

'Do stay.' (Are we never going to get rid of you?)

'How nice to see you!' (What, you here again?)

'That was a lovely evening.' (Yawn)

'You've got such lovely children.' (What horrible ruffians)

'You must come again.' (That's the last we've seen of you – I hope)

'You shouldn't have bothered.' (Is that the best you can do?)

Back home in Breslev and Barovke there was a tradition of *vos afen lung, dos afen tzung*, what's on the lung, that's on the tongue. The tactful went so far as keeping their mouth shut, but words were approached with a certain deference and to have used them in such a way as to reverse or obscure their meaning would have been regarded as a form of sacrilege. It took us a long time to come to terms with English civility.

IV

Glasgow, My Glasgow

During my first year in Scotland I was in Glasgow but not quite of it. Outside of school hours I divided much of my time between home and synagogue, and was perhaps more in the latter than the former, possibly because I found comfort in being in what I thought of as God's presence but mainly I suspect because the synagogue, though a modern and stately edifice, provided lingering echoes of the old country and it was, I suppose, a way of escaping Glasgow.

I found the size and scale of Glasgow bewildering. I was warned that it would be big, 'twice the size of Riga', wrote Father. I had been to Riga and it was certainly big, but it was open and leafy and one did not have to move far from the city centre to see fields beyond the end of the road, whereas there was something infinite about Glasgow. One moved beyond one street to find another and beyond that more streets, and beyond that still more, with four-storeyed tenements on every side like dark ramparts. After Barovke with its great open skies, its lakes and rivers, woods and meadows, one felt imprisoned.

Our first address was the Gorbals where Father had lodgings with distant relatives and the Gorbals, somehow, was less intimidating than other parts of the town for it reminded me vaguely of Dvinsk. There were Yiddish posters on the hoardings, Hebrew lettering on the shops, Jewish names, Jewish faces, Jewish butchers, Jewish bakers with Jewish bread, and Jewish grocers with barrels of herring in the doorway. The herrings in particular brought a strong whiff of home. One heard Yiddish in the streets – more so, in fact, than English – and one encountered figures who would not have been out of place in Barovke. It was only when we moved into our flat in Battlefield Gardens that I began to feel my exile, for Battlefield – the area was named after the Battle of Langside which took place on a nearby hill – was, certainly in the late 1930s, posh, even elegant. In the Gorbals one ascended to one's flat up a dark stairway smelling of urine. In Battlefield all was light and cleanliness with a slight touch of Dettol in the air. The close, as the entrance to the flats was called, was lined with cream and green tiles; there was a large window on every landing which looked out on a small back-green (soon to be occupied by a large air-raid shelter). The buildings, four storeys high and faced with grey granite, were flanked by small privet hedges and ornamental cast-iron railings, and they looked out on a small garden ringed with trees. No one had access to the garden, not even the surrounding tenants, for it was fenced in and it was only when the landlord could not any longer afford the upkeep of the gardens, that the railings gradually fell away and it came to resemble a bomb site with a small jungle of tall grass and wild flowers. Our flat, with its large kitchen, hall-way, two bedrooms and lounge (or 'big room' as we called it), was palatial compared to anything we had known previously (and in actual cubic feet of air space – for the rooms were all lofty – compared well with anything I have known since), but it was on the first floor and it was an odd sensation to go out of one's front door and not find grass under one's feet. One was, so to speak, suspended above ground. The garden was there to be seen but not used. There were no trees to which one could tie a hammock or in whose shade one could sit on hot afternoons. There was no ground on which to play or picnic. I kept searching for the country beyond Glasgow like a cat trying to sniff its way back to its abode, and for a while I thought I had found it : I had chanced upon a park.

The parks are the glory of Glasgow. They are numerous, large, varied in character and not too tamed, and I doubt if there is a city of similar size in Europe so richly provided with open spaces (and with such easy access to more), but the first park I approached – it was Queens Park – was enclosed behind tall, pointed, cast-iron railings with huge, ornamental gates and I thought I had perhaps stumbled upon some great private estate. I ventured in with some hesitancy, but no one threw me out and the park became my playground.

The second redeeming feature of Glasgow was the trams. They were large and ungainly, and rounded corners with sparks flying in all directions and a screeching like souls in torment, but seen from a distance, before their loud clatter assailed the ears, they had the majesty of galleons in full sail. Different colours indicated different destinations. The red tram went to Milngavie, the yellow to Anniesland, the green to Renfrew Ferry, the blue to Rutherglen, the white to Oatlands. If there was a black tram I should imagine it went to the cemetery, but I do not remember one. The colour code must have been a boon to the illiterate, but a handicap to the colour-blind. It was my impression that the green, blue and white trams went to the rougher neighbourhoods, and the yellow and red to the more elegant ones. When they introduced the Coronation tram, a slimmer, trimmer, stream-lined version of the old model, they painted it in the beautiful cream, gold and green livery of the city, but it was confined at first to the posh Bellahouston, Pollokshields, University run.

The third redeeming feature, and the one which finally reconciled me to Glasgow, was the library. I was not at first aware that one could actually take books out of the library (and that without paying), it was privilege enough to be able to read them. For a few months till I knew sufficient English, I spent my time poring over pictures, but as I graduated to words I became a Beatrix Potter addict. I was nearly nine then and rather old for such literature (except that one is never too old for Beatrix Potter) but among the animals, the mice, the moles, the toads, the squirrels, the ducks, I rediscovered something of Barovke. Our house had never harboured an animal other than a cat and the cat was less pet than mouse-trap. We also had a hen or two, with whom it was difficult to establish any lasting relationship. But to an extent the whole of Barovke and its surroundings were part of our demesne and it was alive with rabbits, squirrels, moles, mice, toads and other Potterish characters, and on hot afternoons, when the village slept, the ducks almost took over Barovke. They would rise from the small lake, which was hardly more than a duckpond, and march in formation, quacking as they went, along the bridle path to the village, over the cobbled square and downhill towards the large lake. Martial music almost came to my ears as I watched them parade.

In spite of the fact that my father was a Rabbi, there was a strong bucolic streak in my family and, I suspect, in most of the inhabitants of Barovke. The devout Jew intones a special prayer when he beholds some marvel of nature, but he is warned not to marvel unduly, for in admiring the beauty of creation he can lose sight of his Creator. It is not a view with which I have ever had any sympathy and neither, I suspect, did my father. He sometimes had to walk twelve miles through the woods to slaughter cattle and sheep in some tiny hamlet beyond Barovke, and he went as much for the walk as for the few shillings it brought. In Glasgow he was sometimes asked to go over to Belfast to help out when the local *shochet* was on holiday. He went willingly and sometimes stayed over for a few days for a walking holiday in the Antrim hills.

There was a point in Queens Park from which one could see Glasgow laid out like a relief map below, row upon row of tenements, with their thick cluster of chimneys, climbing up one side of a hill, toppling down the other. And directly below, like a shallow canyon, lay Victoria Road, which continued in a straight line to Bridge Street, then over the river into Jamaica Street, and up Renfield Street to a vague haze beyond which rose the Campsie Hills, and on clear summer evenings the hills seemed so near that one felt one could stretch out and touch them, but several years were to pass before I actually set foot on them.

If I was coming to enjoy Glasgow itself, I was finding less pleasure in Jewish Glasgow. I still went to synagogue every evening, but was beginning to find it a chore. There is a memorial prayer called the *kaddish* which Jews say thrice daily for their next of kin for the first eleven months after their death and thereafter on every anniversary. It is a duty which many Jews take more seriously than any other, and when I came to synagogue in the evenings I would find about a dozen middle-aged men sitting in small clusters about the large empty building chatting in low voices on the events of the day, and waiting for the service to begin. Beside them one might find five or six Yiddish-speaking elders, among them usually my uncle, who came out of habit and belief and who remained to study a page of the Talmud. There was no one there even remotely my age. I was regarded as the mascot and loaded with sweets and chocolates, and given cigarette cards, and even an occasional penny, but the bribes were not sufficient to ease the sense of desolation I felt in the large, cold, empty building. However, things cheered up on Friday evening.

'And it was evening and it was morning the first day,' since when the Jewish Sabbath as indeed all Jewish feasts and fasts begin, so to speak, on the night before the day after. It means that on fasts like the Day of Atonement one fasts for a night and a day, but otherwise it is a happy arrangement, and as the day sinks the profane week falls away, and the sacred day looms in through the lingering dusk. In Scotland in winter it begins to get dark between three and four o'clock in the afternoon, and Jewish boys were released from school an hour early to prepare themselves for Shabbat. Some boys promptly hived off to the pictures. (One local cinema, otherwise closed in the afternoon, was suspected of running special matinées for these delinquents.) But the more pious among us (and we were not that numerous) bathed and washed and changed and polished our boots and brushed our hair and rushed, smelling of Brylcreem and carbolic, self-conscious, semi-sacred figures, through the profane bustle of Friday evening shoppers, to synagogue.

There was a small parade of shops between our house and the synagogue and their names run through my mind even now like a silent litany: the Union Bank of Scotland (on the corner of our street and the main road); Castlebank Laundry, in canary-yellow livery, and the catch-phrase, 'Mother, here comes the Castlebank man' (it was a very dirty place Glasgow, or very clean, for it had more laundries per head of population than any other town I know of, except perhaps Perth); Brackenbridge the greengrocer; Curries the baker; Holmes the newsagent and tobacconist; Caskie's the outfitters, a large, double-fronted store with two gentleman brothers, their bald heads and wing-collars in attendance.

In Barovke one could get almost anything one wanted in the main general store, herrings, boot polish, pencils, wrapping paper, sugar, marmalade, rat-poison, silk stockings, kerosene, vodka, frying oil, galoshes . . . It wasn't quite Harrods, but it was as near to Harrods as mattered for the needs of Barovke.

One Friday afternoon, shortly after we had settled into Battlefield Gardens, I was sent out to buy a tin of boot polish (or *chromaline* as it is known in Yiddish). I was by then sophisticated enough to appreciate that one probably could not get it in the Union Bank of Scotland, or the laundry, or the greengrocer, or the baker, or even the newsagent, but at Caskie's I stopped, and as I did not know how to describe my need in English, I explained what I wanted in mime.

'Ah,' said the brothers in unison, 'polish.' I stopped, nonplussed.

'No,' I said, 'Latvian.' Caskie's was later to assume a symbolic significance for me.

About twenty boys would filter into synagogue, trailing something of the winter mist behind them, and the prayers we sang were the prayers I had known in Barovke :

'O come let us exult before the Lord : let us shout for joy to the rock of our salvation. Let us come before His presence with thanksgiving; let us shout for joy unto Him with psalms. For the Lord is a great God and a great king above all gods. In His hands are the depths of the earth, the heights of the mountains too . . .'

I was familiar with every tune, for the fathers of Glasgow were the sons of places like Barovke, but if I was inclined to sink into a reverie imagining myself back among the warm crush of worshippers in Barovke, I was chilled out of it by the bleak emptiness of the Glasgow synagogue, with the handful of worshippers scattered among the sea of pews. Moreover, the companionship offered by my contemporaries was incomplete. I was a religious worshipper, they were dilettanti. I came in a suit and shirt which I wore only on Shabbat and festivals – my Sunday outfit as it would have been called in Glasgow – while they as often as not arrived in their school blazers, workaday figures from a workaday world. To them synagogue was an optional extra, and marginal to their existence; it was central to mine. The nearer I drew to others, the more I remained apart, a Jews' Jew.

I was also becoming old enough to be troubled by events outside my own small, private world. This awareness had already
been growing upon me in Barovke. People gathered in small
knots outside the synagogue after service talking in low voices,
with much shaking of heads and many sighs and consternation
radiated from every side. Times were always troubled, but these
times were more troubled than others, and a new figure had
emerged to join Pharaoh, Amalek, Haman, Torquemada and
other Jewish persecutors, Adolf Hitler. At this time, with his
Chaplin moustache, frenzied orations, wild eyes and preposterous
salute, most Barovke boys found Hitler a vaguely comical figure
and we used to blacken our upper lips with charcoal and go
goose-stepping round Barovke sieg-heiling at the tops of our
voices. To the adults, however, he was no joke, and neither
indeed were we, and when we travelled through Germany, my
mother was petrified lest I should do one of my Hitler imper-
sonations; but I was exhausted and slept most of the way, and
woke up near the Belgian border to find myself in a packed
train on the knee of a German soldier.

In Glasgow people felt less directly threatened, but here too
the talk was all of Czechslovakia, Danzig, Memel and – a con-
fusing expression – 'the Polish corridor'. Father acquired a large
radio shortly after we arrived and sat with his ear to the loud-
speaker twiddling dials and pressing knobs, catching the news in
whatever language it would emerge. He found English rather
hard to follow, but he understood German well, and could
derive some meaning from most Slavic languages, and the
whoops, whistles and whines of the radio with occasional voice
fading in and out of the noise dominated the late hours of the
night.

One evening we all trooped down to Battlefield school to be
fitted with gas-masks. For Father this was a moment of crisis,
for in the event of a gas attack he could be smothered by his
own beard, and one of his colleagues suggested that he remove
it entirely except for a token presence of hair on the point of his
chin, but to have gone into the world virtually beardless in such
a situation would have been tantamount to a public declaration
of no confidence in the Almighty. He kept his beard and, as he
said to me after the war : 'You see, nothing happened.'

(The Lubavitcher Rebbe, the leader of the largest and fore-most Hassidic sect, was asked a question on this point by one of his followers in the Israel army about the time of the Yom Kippur war, and he replied that in the first place there wouldn't be a gas attack, but just in case there was, he should carry scissors in his pocket and in the event of an attack he should whip off his beard and whip on the mask.)

One Shabbat afternoon in late August there was a special celebration in the Queens Park Synagogue, and we received the large, sugar-coated biscuits, the sweet wine and lemonade, which were the usual part of a synagogue treat, plus Lyons ice-creams which were particularly welcome on the hot afternoon. Several of the elders of the congregation had forgone their Shabbat after-noon sleep – no small act of self-denial – to be present, and several of them made speeches of such length that we felt our ice-cream was well earned. Uncle, too, spoke. His voice faltered several times and there were moments when I was afraid he might break down. He lived for the weekly encounters with the children. When the next Sabbath came there wouldn't be a young face in the congregation, nor the sound of a young voice, not even mine. The town would be like Hamelin.

V

See You After Four

We rose early and found the hall full of baggage and the kitchen table full of sandwiches. My parents must have been up half the night. My eldest sister was away from home training to be a nurse and would shortly be joining the Army Nursing Corps. The rest of us were to be evacuated. It was a word which I had heard a lot but with whose implications I was still unfamiliar.

We were taken by taxi to St Enoch Station where we found about every child in Glasgow lined up with gas-mask case slung over his shoulder and a label dangling from him like a mail bag. It was all very orderly, though the excitement in the air gave an extra pungency to the smoke from the engine which enveloped the station. There were some tear-stained mothers but few tear-stained children. Most of us felt as if we were about to embark on a prolonged treat and had, indeed, each been handed a large paper bag which contained among other things, one tin of bully beef, a tin of Carnation milk, a tin of Nestlé's milk, and chocolate caramel wafers. We could not wait to get on the train, and when it finally pulled out, our cheers nearly raised the glass roof of the station.

Our destination was Annan in Dumfriesshire, near the English border. My two sisters were billeted on a small farm on the edge of the town, and a large, freckle-faced boy with wavy hair, called Myer Tobias, and I were found billets in the village of Cummertrees, a few miles away.

It was a large house set among trees behind a high wall. The rooms were large and lofty with tall windows, but light was virtually excluded by curtains within and the trees without, and the place was full of dark corners and gloomy passages. In spite of the size of the house and the number of its rooms, its only inhabitants were a heavily built, semi-paralysed old man with a scarlet face so glossy as to be almost glazed, and a semi-paralysed old spaniel with eyes like running sores. They were looked after by a robust, red-faced woman with snow white hair who, with rolled up sleeves and formidable arms, seemed permanently braced for action. It was a summer's day but there was a fire burning in the hearth. The old man sat on one side of the fire, the old dog snoozed by the other; a slight breeze moaned through the trees outside. We sat near the fire while the woman busied herself with tea. The old man looked at us, and we looked at him.

'Nice day,' I said. The old man grunted. The old dog snorted and twitched in his sleep. I had not felt so desolate since I left Barovke.

A few minutes later the woman pushed in the tea trolley and I was startled out of my depression. I stemmed from a world of tea-drinkers, but tea back home was a matter of a glass of tea with lemon, or English tea, as we called it, with a bun or a biscuit or a slice of bread. But this was a wedding feast of a tea, thin slices of brown bread, slices of white bread, with butter and jam, and various bakemeats, with whose character I was unfamiliar, but which I later got to know as bannocks and crumpets and pancakes and scones and madeira cake and fruit cake and Swiss rolls. We did not get such a tea every day, but we did get it once a week, and the memory of the last treat with the anticipation of the next, carried us over the blank days in between. This was an aspect of British life of which no one had told me and I came to cherish not only the tea, but the whole aura of tea-time.

I was under the impression that one was expected to consume everything placed before one, which I did, and when I staggered upstairs to unpack, I sat down on my bed and fell asleep fully clothed.

When I awoke and stepped out into Cummertrees, I was in Barovke, the great open skies with white fleecy clouds racing across them, the fields, the meadows still moist with dew, chickens scratching in back-gardens. There were no lakes as in

Barovke, and no great deep forests, but there were woods bustling
with squirrels and rabbits and, as I discovered at the end of my
first day's explorations, there was a great, deep, turbulent river –
the Solway, whose treacherous tides were to claim the life of more
than one young evacuee. There was no prospect of fishing by
hand, but one could fish by rod; I made myself a rod with a
stick, line, hook and sinker, and although I never caught anything,
I went down to the shore with the hope of hooking a leviathan.
Here was what I had been looking for during all those intermin-
able walks in Glasgow. I was away from parents, from familiar
ways, but in a sense I had come home. A day or two later there
was an incident which took me back beyond Barovke to
Breslev.

Myer and I travelled to and from school by bus. One day after
school, two or three local boys alighted from the bus and followed
us. When we quickened our pace, they quickened theirs, and
Myer, who was born in Glasgow and made of fairly stern stuff,
stopped, turned round and asked what they wanted. I had no
doubt at all what they wanted and grabbed my satchel tightly
under my arm and ran. Together we might have given a good
account of ourselves, separated we were, to use a Scottish expression, Amalakated. Two boys attacked Myer and bruised him
about the head and body, the third caught up with me and gave
me two black eyes and a swollen lip. But worse than the injuries
were the memories they evoked. The *goyim* were not friendly
after all, at least not in Annan. Added to which, Myer would
not speak to me. I was yellow, he said. I had only lately come to
terms with being a 'greener'. Being yellow was new to me. I
presumed he meant I was a coward, which perhaps I was, though
it seemed to me that to run when one is outnumbered – especially
by boys older than oneself – seemed a perfectly natural, perhaps
even a commendable thing to do. That night I wrote a long, tear-
stained letter to my parents, demanding to be taken home. I was
prepared to face the bombers and bombs; I could not face the
antisemites.

When I got to school the next morning I found that Myer and
I were not the only casualties. Half the school looked as if it had
been involved in battle, which, indeed it had. There had been a
concerted attack by the local boys against the evacuees – or

'Glasgow khillies' as they were known. My injuries were not incurred from the fact that I was Jewish, but that I was a town boy, a Glaswegian. It was the most reassuring revelation of my young life. I gloried in the name of Glaswegian, and have not ceased to glory in it since. I became visibly taller, more erect, more robust. I was attacked again, sometimes by myself, sometimes as part of a crowd, but no matter the odds, I always stood my ground and gave as good as I got, sometimes with compound interest. From a mere readiness to defend myself I moved close to assuming the Glaswegian pugnacity, and I had but to suffer the merest slight, sometimes only imagined, to retort with the standard invitation : 'See you after four.' I often came home with a bleeding nose or a mangled ear, but they were a small price to pay for the joys of battle.

I widened my circle of acquaintances and for the first time numbered *goyim* among my friends, including one small chap with glasses, lately down from an approved school, who kept stealing bicycles and bringing them to me. Several of the boys sometimes came home with me, but were made less than welcome by the housekeeper. She complained that their hobnail boots were ruining the carpets and marking the floor, and that they were disturbing the peace of the old man and his dog, though neither gave any signs of disturbance nor, indeed, that they were aware of the outside world at all, but finally both for their sakes and mine, I was moved to another billet, nearer Annan. My host was Mr K – a young farmer with a large, fresh, pink face with dimpled cheeks, and two older sisters, maiden ladies, the one tall, the other short, who looked as if they might be religious, which, as I soon discovered, they were, and, what was worse, they took pains to make sure that I remained the same.

For all the intensity of my Jewish upbringing, I would quite cheerfully have relinquished my faith after a few weeks in Annan, for at every turn it interfered with my pleasures. What kept me in check was partly the presence of my two sisters in a nearby billet, whose religious feelings were more deeply ingrained than mine, partly the efforts of the Misses K – and partly a holy train, replete with Sacred Scrolls of the Law, Bibles, prayer-books, prayer-shawls, and an entire kosher field kitchen, which followed us south to Annan. With the religious requisites, came another – the

Rev. Michaelson, or Ike as we called him, headmaster of the Queens Park Hebrew classes, together with those members of his staff who were not in the army, and as soon as he pitched his tent, we had a small ghetto right in the heart of Annan, which I, inwardly, and sometimes outwardly, resented. He was a tall, silver-haired man, with a thin, white moustache, who peered out over his glasses with an amused look in his eyes, though none of us could understand how anyone who had to teach in *cheder* (Hebrew class) for a living, had anything to be amused about.

Jews, for all their regard for learning, have tended to pay scant regard to teaching and even less regard to teachers, and the task was generally delegated to some local *schleimazel*, unfortunate, who was not much use at anything else, and even where teachers had considerable knowledge, they had no sort of training. One would learn by rote, and if, for example, the subject was *Genesis*, one would begin : '*Breishis*, in the beginning; *boro*, created; *elohim*, God; *es hashomayim*, the heavens; *v'es ho'oretz*, and the earth.' Father, who spent an hour with me in religious studies every evening, used to teach me in this way, and in the course of a year we might cover the entire *Pentateuch*, though by the time I had completed *Deuteronomy* I had usually forgotten *Genesis*.

There were not many Jewish unfortunates in Britain, or rather, they were not so unfortunate as to have to turn to *cheder* teaching, and in places like Glasgow, the religious instruction of the young was generally undertaken by boys in their last years at school – I became a teacher at fifteen – or in their first years at university; and before university bursaries became universal, *cheder* teaching was a form of outdoor relief for Jewish undergraduates.

We all thought that a man like Ike should have been able to do better for himself, and it was only much later, when I joined his staff, that it occurred to me that the reason why he was a *cheder* teacher was that he enjoyed it. When we assembled for a festive meal on Friday night he would, after shouting himself hoarse to reduce us to order, look round with a touching smile of pride and affection. He spoke in the sort of broken English used by music hall comedians when telling Jewish (usually anti-

Jewish) jokes : 'I say der, I vant a got behaviour from you or I'll give you such a *patch* (slap) no grass vill grow der . . . Bleggage, can't you shot your moit . . . If I don't get quiet in an oder minute dere's going to be trobble.' But although he often lost his temper and sometimes his voice, I only saw him raise his hands against a boy twice. Once when he struck an obstreperous lout – now a fashionable and wealthy abortionist – who promptly struck him back, the other time was when he struck me.

He was separated from his wife but she followed him to Annan. She was a sour little woman with thick glasses and bad teeth, and one day she gave me a silver threepenny bit to deliver a message to him, which I promptly did. This happened twice and each time Ike turned red with anger or embarrassment, I don't know which, and when she importuned me a third time to deliver yet another message I wondered whether I should charge her sixpence. If I had anticipated the effect of the message I would have charged a pound. Ike read it with trembling hands, then losing control of himself, gave me a whack across the face which knocked me to the ground. I crept out on all fours, less injured than confounded, and felt like the messenger who had brought David the news of Saul's death. I forgave Ike, but he never forgave himself and for months afterwards he kept offering me sweets, chocolates, biscuits and plying me with extra rations of kosher wine. In one way or another I did well out of his matrimonial troubles.

He organised a kosher canteen which served lunches every day, and at weekends he arranged an endless chain of activities, beginning with the Friday evening service, followed by a meal. There were services again the following morning, followed by lunch, followed by a study group, discussions, debates, and we remained together till night, when the Sabbath was over and we could recite the *Havdalah*, which separated the sacred day from the profane week :

'Blessed art Thou, O Lord our God, King of the Universe, who makest a distinction between holy and profane, between light and darkness, between Israel and the nations, between the seventh day and the six working days. Blessed art Thou, O Lord, who makest a distinction between holy and profane.'

c

And that said, we left our holy little enclave for the profane world about us, which, as fate would have it, was not all that profane. I must have been the first Jew the K sisters had encountered outside of the Bible and they regarded me with something like awe, as if I was a close relative of Jesus Christ. There were boys who complained that the people with whom they had been billeted, or 'foster parents' as they were sometimes called, had tried by one subtle means or another, to bring them into the Church. In my case, however, the sisters were grimly determined to keep me Jewish. Thus, when I came down to breakfast in the mornings, I was sometimes taken aback by the query, whether I had said my morning prayers. They also washed my clothes and astonished me one evening when they asked why I didn't wear a 'fringed garment'.

The devout Jew is expected to wear an undergarment known as *tzitzit*, which is an abbreviated prayer-shawl, short enough to go under a shirt, with a large hole in the centre for the head, and long woollen tassels in each corner. I disliked the garment even in Barovke, for I had a sensitive skin and the tassels tickled. In Glasgow it was an embarrassment, and when I changed for gym, I tried to whip it over my head without anyone seeing, but in my hurry, it more often than not got stuck and the boys asked me what it was.

'A chest-protector,' I replied, which was not very convincing, for as a boy pointed out, about the only area which it did not protect was the chest. 'It's a ball-tickler,' said another boy, and a ball-tickler it remained for the rest of my schooldays.

When I got to Annan, one of my first acts of emancipation was to dispense with the *tzitzit*. I did so with some trepidation, for if it was not a chest protector, I had, subconsciously at least, regarded it as a shield of sorts, and on my first *tzitzitless* day I felt curiously vulnerable, half expecting the skies to fall or the earth to open or, more mundanely, to be knocked down by a bus. I was nervous of going down by the Solway lest I should be swallowed by quicksands, or fall in the water, but when a week passed without incident, I ceased to worry.

The classical way for a Jewish boy to renounce his faith is to eat a ham-sandwich, bare-headed on Yom Kippur and invite God to strike him dead. I know several boys who went through the ritual. None were struck dead, but they were nearly all violently sick. I had no intention of renouncing Judaism. I would have been loth to forgo the Sabbath services with their familiar melodies, and the Sabbath meals with their familiar table hymns (and, to be honest, with their familiar dishes), and certainly I had no wish to do anything which would have estranged me from my family, but foreskin (or lack of it) apart, I wanted to be one of the lads, a boy among boys, and did not want to be separated from them by religious externals.

I solved my *tzitzit* problem in Annan, by rubbing the garment till it was soiled and depositing it in the laundry box. I did this religiously every week until it became a ritual in its own right though it would have been simpler to wear it.

The sisters began their evening meal with a prayer, which seemed excessive for the fare that followed. They had their main meal at lunch-time and the evening meal, which they called high-tea, consisted of eggs with everything. On Monday it was poached eggs, on Tuesday fried, on Wednesday omelette, on Thursday scrambled. Sometimes by way of change we had a kipper or pilchards, but if we did I could never be quite sure what day it was.

The taller and older of the sisters, a mousey-haired woman with streaks of grey, and little blue veins showing through her cheeks, was hard of hearing. The brother, with his large cheerful face and white eyebrows, might utter something about that pig, or this cow, but otherwise had nothing to say, nor was I particularly talkative, so that conversation at table tended to be somewhat halting.

'And did you have a nice day, Hyman?' the older sister would begin brightly, and my reply was always the same :

'Yes.' And we would munch in silence for a time, then the brother might intrude with :

'Gladys is drying up.'

'Gladys?'

'Drying up.'

'She's drying up, Gladys is,' said the younger sister in a loud voice for the benefit of the older one.

'Is she due then, Arthur?'

'She's long past due.'

'She's what?'

'Long past due, Flora.'

'You needn't shout. I can hear.'

The high-tea was the last meal of the day except for a mug of cocoa at bed-time. It occurred to me later that the reason why they confined themselves to a diet of eggs was to keep my fare kosher.

I was still of an age when I tended to measure the wealth of a family by the amount they ate and the hours they worked. The poor, it was generally known, or so it seemed to me, ate little and worked a lot. The Ks ate less well than we did in Glasgow (wartime shortages were to make themselves felt later), and worked harder than anyone I had ever met, and no matter how early I rose in the morning or how late I went to bed, they were always up and about – even on Sunday, and I sometimes wondered if they ever went to bed at all. And if they weren't busy in the house, they were busy in the cow-shed or the dairy, or the hen-house or the kitchen garden. And yet they showed signs of afflu-ence. In Barovke if someone had a cow he was a man of property. The Ks had over a dozen cows in milk, and several heifers, and they farmed nearly a hundred acres of land. They also had a car, not much of one I admit, with spindly tyres, but it went, and Arthur used it to deliver his two sisters to church on Sunday morning, me to Hebrew class, and the pigs to market.

And finally there was the house, large, two-storeyed, square, of yellow brick, with a pillared portico through which, to my knowledge, no soul ever entered on his own feet. The front rooms of British farm-houses are used for lying in state, and the front door for carrying the coffin in and out. The front room in the K household was like a cross between a small natural history museum and an antique shoppe. There were stuffed birds, and what looked like a stuffed ferret, and a collection of giant butter-flies behind a glass case. There was a large monk's chest between the heavy velvet drapes by the window, and a long table with a tasselled tablecloth which reminded me of Leibe Sheine's front room in Carmichael Place. There were several portraits in black oval frames of stern-looking figures, and on the sideboard there was a faded photo of a family group, a woman with three young children about her, and a fourth in her lap, with a tall man with

a heavy moustache standing over them, one hand on his wife's shoulder, another on his lapel. I recognised one of the children in the group as the elder sister, and I asked her who the baby was :
'Poor Albert,' she replied in a sad voice, and said no more.

One slept in the bedrooms and bathed in the bathroom, otherwise all life in the household was confined to the kitchen, which was as big as any two rooms in our Glasgow house.

The one relaxation which the sisters allowed themselves, apart from church, was knitting, and at about nine in the evening, they would switch on the news, open their knitting bags and sit back with needles clicking, emitting an occasional tut at this or that news item. There was no electricity in the house and they worked by gas-light, which they kept turned down low. Arthur, who would come in to hear the news, usually fell asleep as soon as he sat down. The room, for all its size, was always cosy and warm, and sitting among them last thing at night with my mug of cocoa in hand, munching a digestive biscuit, listening to the news, in the soft, greenish flickering light, I felt strangely at one with them. Glasgow, parents, Jews, synagogue, seemed very far away.

'You weren't born in this country, were you, Hyman?' I was asked one evening.

'No,' I said, and added quickly, 'but I'm not a refugee.'

'Not a what?'

'A refugee, Flora – he said, he's not – '

'I heard what he said. Where were you born then?'

'Poland.'

'You must miss Poland.'

'No, I don't, not a bit.'

'Not a bit?'

'Not a bit, Flora.'

'I heard him. Not a bit did you say?'

'Not a bit.'

'Now, isn't that strange?'

I could not see how any Jew who had lived in Poland possibly could miss it. Latvia, yes, but Poland? Yet a few weeks later, a Jewish boy was billeted on us who missed Germany. His name was Heinrich, or Henry. The elder sister announced his impending arrival as good news, but I'm not sure if I welcomed it, for I had begun to enjoy my role as Jew in residence. Moreover, I had never got on with the German boys nor they with me, and apart from anything else, their lack of Jewishness appalled me, much as my excessive Jewishness must have appalled them; but beyond that I had achieved a certain delicate level of contentment which I had not known since I left Barovke and I sensed he would disrupt it, which he did. He was a pale boy with dark, brooding eyes which gave no hint of the mischief behind them, and an elaborate coiffure, on which he spent hours every morning.

We shared a room, but as a rule he had little to do with me and regarded me as one of the local rustics, which in a sense I was, for I was turning native. The sisters had cut down one of Arthur's old overalls to fit me. I also acquired a pair of rubber boots and was using much of my free time to help out on the farm. I was paid for my efforts and was excited to earn my own money, but I also loved the work. Father used to warn me when I was a reluctant pupil that I would end up as a *baal hagolah* (a carter) or even worse, a *pastech*, a shepherd. Neither struck me as a particularly deplorable fate. Now I had become something of a *pastech* of my own volition and, but for the very early rising, found it idyllic. I was particularly anxious to help with the milking, which meant that I had to be up at 5.30 a.m. It was November now and dark at that time of the morning. The ground under foot was covered in frost and breathed out an iciness, which crept up my trouser legs, but, with the exception of Shabbat, when I was not allowed as much as to touch a milkpail, I would leap out of bed at the first chug of the milking-engine. By the time I was down, one sister was already in the dairy and the other making breakfast. My job was to see that the cows had enough to drink and as there was no piped water to their stalls I ladled it out of a milk churn.

One acquires a passing feeling of virtue when one is out and about at an hour of the morning when most of the world is asleep, the opposite of the sort of feeling one gets staggering home at a late hour of the night when most of the world is abed. One feels part of an elect fraternity, the *lamed vovniks,* to use a Yiddish expression, the chosen few on whom the world rests.

Being early to rise I had to go early to bed and Henry and I were sent upstairs with Wee Willie Winkie night lights after the Nine o'clock news, and half an hour later the sisters put their heads round the door to make sure our candles were out, but Henry got himself a powerful torch and read and fumbled under the blankets. He had arrived in Britain about a year after me, but spoke far better English and was near the top of his class. He regarded Ike as 'a broken-down old Jew', and instead of attending the kosher canteen at lunch-time, bought himself fish and chips at a nearby Italian café. He must have had private means. The sisters never asked him whether he said his morning prayers (which he didn't), or wore *tzitzit* (which he didn't) and I think they went a little in awe of him. I at least seemed to conform in some ways to what they knew of the Jew from their reading, but they were never quite sure what to make of him. The elder sister once happened to mention 'how eminently sensible the Jewish dietary laws' were, adding 'that's why the Jews are so clever'. To which Henry retorted that his father was a professor, that his uncles were doctors and lawyers and that his mother too was a doctor, and that his family had not even heard of the word kosher. Pork was a regular part of their diet.

'It's all superstition,' he concluded.

'What was that?'

'He said it's superstition, Flora.'

I was startled not so much by the heresy, but that it should be issuing from one so young, and there began within me a stirring of doubt, which was not the result of my own logical reappraisal of the laws as I knew them, but I wondered whether a boy so obviously intelligent, and so universally praised for his intelligence, could possibly be wrong. Moreover, I was beginning to find the dietary laws, and more particularly my diet of eggs, irksome. Henry once asked if he could have bacon with his eggs, to which both sisters retorted in a horrified chorus :

'Most certainly not.'

Though I had little to do with Henry, I was not otherwise short of company and was on particularly close terms with Arthur, who was possibly in his late thirties or early forties, but regarded me, as indeed I regarded him, as a contemporary. I was ten and he was, I suppose, not much above my mental age, yet he was extremely dextrous, a master of many skills. He ploughed a furrow straight as a die. He was a good herdsman and dairyman, could fix any of the hundred assorted bits of machinery round the farm, strip and mend his own car, which he seemed to have put together from bits of old tractor. And he was an excellent shot.

I sometimes went shooting with him on Sunday afternoons. Christmas was near, and the ground was hard. Trees were bare. The days were usually grey and misty and cold and our breath rose in steamy spurts as we trudged across the rutted meadows. He was indiscriminate about targets, shot at almost anything which moved and usually scored without taking aim. We once saw Henry on a bicycle on a distant path and he asked me with a wide grin whether to take a shot at him : 'Not to kill him, I mean, just a bit of shot up his back-stairs.'

'Your sisters wouldn't like it,' I said.

'No, they wouldn't, would they?'

I sometimes regretted that I stopped him.

Henry had a tube of Brylcreem like a large tube of toothpaste, and once, unbeknown to him, I borrowed a squeeze. I usually limited my hair care to passing a comb over my head, and when I came downstairs with a gleaming coiffure, he asked me where I got the Brylcreem from.

'Bought it,' I said, 'what do you think?'

'I think you got it from my tube,' at which I should perhaps have invited him to see me 'after four', but lacked the audacity.

'I'm surprised a religious boy like you should steal,' he added, 'don't you know the seventh commandment?'

As a matter of fact he meant the eighth, but I didn't reply.

'He's a cissy,' Arthur said to me later, 'all got up and perfumed like a girl.'

Although I regarded Henry with enmity, and he regarded me with disdain, I felt flattered by any attention he cared to pay me. If he wanted company for a walk in to Annan in the evening or down the road to the post-box (he was afraid of the blackout) I was happy to go with him. Whenever he wanted some small service from me, I felt unable to refuse. He patronised me and I was pleased to be patronised.

One Saturday afternoon he invited me to go to the pictures with him.

'On Shabbat?' I said.

'Why not? There is no law about going to the pictures on Shabbat.'

'There is about using money.'

'I'll pay for you, you can pay me back tomorrow.'

And I went, following close behind him, furtively, not daring to look to the right or the left as I entered the cinema. Henry was, I suspect, amused by my agitation. The main film was 'Fra Diavalo' with Laurel and Hardy, but I remember no part of it, for I sat biting my nails, worrying lest the building was bombed and when the casualty lists were published, all the world would know that I, Hyman Berman, son of Rabbi Berman, had, knowingly and wilfully, desecrated the Sabbath. There was no bomb attack, but news of my transgression must have reached Glasgow that night, for the following afternoon, as I was helping Arthur put up Christmas decorations, Father arrived in a taxi, threw all my possessions into a case and took me home.

When I looked out of the rear-window the two sisters were standing together, bent against the wind, wringing their bony hands.

They were too dumbfounded by the sudden turn of events to be quite sure what had happened and must have been wondering if they had done anything wrong.

'Was that man the husband?' Father said to me later.

'No,' I said, 'they haven't got a husband.'

'Are they widows?'

'No, they're not married.'

'*None of them?*'

'None of them.'

'*Nebbich.*'

In a Jewish family, for one child to remain unmarried is a misfortune, for two is a calamity, but for all three to remain single is regarded as a conspiracy of fortune, for all of Jewish life is built round the family and most of its traditions presume children, continuity. To be without children meant that the world was co-terminal with oneself, an end to immortality, so that in Orthodox Jewish families the single are never allowed to abandon hope of marrying and the married never abandon their efforts on their behalf but here were three people content, even cheerful, with

their celibacy. Arthur had no girlfriend, the sisters no men-
friends, at least none that ever called at the farm. Perhaps the
regeneration constantly evident in farming life gave them a sense
of continuity which others looked for in their children.

VI

The Makings of an Englishman

Apart from the blackout I was barely aware of the war in Annan, and in any case, one did not expect a town of that size to be lit up : bright lights one associated with a metropolis like Glasgow. I had heard an air-raid siren but once, and that on the first afternoon of the war, when German bombers came near the Forth Bridge, but when I returned to Glasgow towards the end of December, the city seemed to be blacked out even during the day. I had returned reluctantly in a mood to detest it, and detest it I did.

I had been looking forward to Christmas. As a devout Jew from an Orthodox family I should have been wholly indifferent to the festival, but I was intensely aware of it even in Barovke, for in Barovke, apart from anything else, we had two Christmases, the first, on 25 December, celebrated by the Lutherans, and the second, on 6 January celebrated by the Russian Orthodox Church. The main celebration, organised by the school, was on the former date and although I was not a pupil, I was allowed to tag along behind my sisters and I enjoyed the spirit of the occasion almost as much as the huge bags of sweets distributed by *Jedushka Maroszh* (Grandfather Frost, otherwise Santa Claus, and wearing the same scarlet and white and with the same long white beard). The Lutheran celebrations continued for several days and did not quite peter out before the Orthodox celebrations began. There were illuminated trees everywhere, fireworks, and I was enchanted by the colour, the noise, the bunting and, perhaps above all, by the Christmas carols and especially 'Silent Night', which to the intense annoyance of my father, my sisters sang together when washing up on Friday nights.

When we came to Glasgow I was eager to see what Christmas would bring and glumly discovered that it brought nothing. There were no preparations in the school, no Christmas trees, no Father Christmases, no streamers, no bunting, no fireworks, no carols and no bags of sweets. The shop displays, with their small fairy lights blinking in the misty evenings, and their boxes of talcum powder and perfumed soaps, and dressing table sets in quilted boxes, and their sprinkling of mock snow did carry some intimation of an approaching festival, but they were arranged so long before Christmas – usually early in November – that by Christmas itself they were almost shop-soiled. Most astounding of all, when the great day came many of the shops were open. The Presbyterians, with their almost Jewish capacity for suppressing the pleasurable in religion, were inclined to play down the significance of Christmas. Many families, however, still regarded it as a major event and my younger sister was invited to a Christmas party by a little girl with whom she had become friendly at school, and I was to see her there. I scrubbed my face, brushed my hair, polished my boots, changed into my best suit in the hope that once I was at the door in my festive gear, I too would be invited in. But when I delivered my sister I was told when to collect her and the door was politely but firmly shut in my face.

My second Scottish Christmas was to have been in Annan and it promised to be a splendid and exciting occasion. The sisters were presumably not Presbyterians, for they were making elaborate preparations. Their holy of holies, the front room, with its stuffed aviary, was to be brought into commission. Dust wrappers were taken off the furniture, and Arthur and I began to arrange streamers round the walls. They were expecting some relatives, including several young children, to come up from England. Henry regarded the prospect of the coming days with a shudder, but I was looking forward to the celebrations almost as a member of the family in my own right, and, indeed, I was being treated as such. I wouldn't be allowed to partake of the turkey, but the sisters had prepared a kosher Christmas pudding and kosher mince pies and crackers and a Christmas tree. 'See and hang up your sock,' Arthur had said to me, and, without giving any secrets away, added : 'It had better be a big sock.' And while I was cheering myself with the thought of it all, Father descended out of the grey and snatched me back to the chilly darkness of Glasgow.

I have been troubled by Christmas since, half wanting to be in it, but always having to keep out of it. I was once invited to a kosher Christmas dinner by a Jewish family. The food was good, or at least plentiful, the wine excellent, the occasion depressing. It was not merely that I felt like an intruder at a private feast, I felt that the whole feast was an intrusion. What were we Hebrews doing at table celebrating the birth of Jesus Christ? My hostess, sensing that I was troubled by something, took me by the hand and showed me that the turkey had been slaughtered by the Glasgow Jewish Board of Shechita, probably by my own father, and, as a matter of fact, kosher butchers did rather well out of Christmas. One could argue that Christmas is, after all, pre-Christian and was originally a pagan festival celebrating the winter solstice. It could further be argued that the Christians themselves have de-Christianised it. I once attended a Christmas dinner given by a non-Jewish friend. There was so much to drink before the meal that I sat through the meal itself in a glazed stupor and remember little about it beyond the fact that apart from the traditional fare, and a sprig of holly on the Christmas pudding, there was nothing to distinguish it from any other gargantuan blow-out, and as excessive eating appeals excessively to many Jews, one can understand how the Christmas dinner has become an annual event in many Jewish homes. There are Jews, indeed, who go beyond the Christmas dinner and have Christmas trees, exchange Christmas presents and Christmas cards, and certainly there is something very beautiful about a laden Christmas tree, but I have always felt that for the Jew to celebrate Christmas in any way, suggests not only a slight association with his own faith, but a slight respect for the faith of his neighbours.

The festive mood which surrounds the approach of Christmas is, of course, infectious and one cannot entirely avoid being caught up in it. I have been a journalist for the past sixteen years and, if I may divulge a professional secret, journalists spend a good deal of their time in pubs, not always drinking – though they have been known to do that too – but because they are the bourses of their trade, where gossip may be exchanged, rumour tallied against rumour and where hearsay sometimes gells into hard fact. Also there cannot be many parts of London which have so many delightful pubs in so compact an area as Fleet Street and its neighbourhood, but as November gives way to December and as Christmas looms ahead, the casual imbiber finds himself caught up in a saturnalia. Drinking sessions become longer, drinks larger and more numerous, voices louder, laughter less controlled, and faces become scarlet and steamed up, like boiled lobsters. If one travels home on the underground of an evening, one has to step carefully between pools of steaming vomit.

Journeys to and from town become impossible in the weeks before Christmas. Traffic doesn't move on the roads, and pedestrians can hardly move on the pavements and the bustle and clamour become unnerving and from about the time I settled in London in 1961, I came to dread the approach of the festival and I always tried to get an assignment which would keep me out of the country till the new year. (Yet I must add that when my wife and I were in Israel over Christmas 1962 we did not wish to miss the carols and attended a carol service in the Jerusalem Y.M.C.A.)

It is rather different in the smaller towns and the countryside where religion has lingered rather longer than in the big cities. I lived in Kent, near Tunbridge Wells for a time (I have lived everywhere) in the mid-1950s, and there one could feel the approach of Christmas almost in the softening of the air. People did seem to become kindlier and more helpful and the atmosphere of goodwill was almost palpable. It was the same in Annan and I was looking forward to Christmas with the eagerness with which I normally approached such Jewish festivals as Purim or Passover, and to be whisked to Christmasless, pagan Glasgow was therefore no small trauma. It was a town almost bereft of children. There were few in the street, few in the school and none in the synagogue, Sabbath or weekdays. My eldest sister was working and living in the hospital. The other two were still in Annan (they were less likely to backslide, and in any case were only girls).

Uncle Louis and Aunt Leibe Sheine had moved in with us and slept in the room formerly occupied by my sisters. Mother cooked for her family and Leibe Sheine for hers and they did not get too much in each other's way. Aunt pickled a large jar of herring once a month and prepared a huge cauldron of *cholent* once a week. She and Uncle had herring for lunch and *cholent* for supper, and the smell of herring and *cholent* mixed with that of fried fish (mother's speciality) dominated the house, except on wash days when they were temporarily banished by a heavy cloud of boiled soap.

This was the period of the 'phoney war'. There was no fighting and hardly any bombing and evacuees were beginning to filter back to town, but no acquaintance of mine was among them. Ike was still away and the Hebrew Classes had not been resumed and Father would interrupt his endless, multilingual search for news bulletins to give me an hour or two of private tuition every day. Uncle would also pull me aside on more occasions than I thought necessary to test my Jewish knowledge and was sufficiently impressed to suggest that one day I might be a Rabbi. My parents, however, had higher hopes for me by then, and the word 'doctor' was whispered around the house. I felt that loneliness which the only child must feel, except that even only children could expect to find company in the street. I found none. Instead I found company in comics.

When George Orwell wrote his celebrated essay on boys' weeklies he confined himself largely to the *Magnet* and *Gem*, published by the Amalgamated Press, London, but in Glasgow certainly, and I suspect in other industrial towns, the scene was dominated by a series of comics published by D. C. Thomson of Dundee, the *Beano*, *Dandy* and *Magic*, which consisted of comic strips interlaced with an occasional story, and the *Hotspur*, *Adventure*, *Rover*, *Wizard* and *Skipper*, which were composed entirely of stories. I began reading the comics sporadically at the end of 1938, and regularly after my return from Annan, and it occurred to me later that although all the comics originated from a Scottish publishing house, none of them imparted any-think like a Scottish flavour. I recall only two stories set in Scotland. One was the 'Men of Moidart', and the other was 'The Bad Wolf of Badenoch'. Both dealt with the '45 and its aftermath and one was left with the impression that Scottish history began and ended with Bonnie Prince Charlie. The subject matter of the comic strips was mainly one of the tables turned and trickers tricked.

In the *Beano* the *pièce de résistance* for me was Lord Snooty and his pals. Snooty, as his name implied, was a toff and dressed the part in Eton suit and top-hat. His origins were never quite defined, for he had no parents and lived with an aunt in a castle with a butler and flunkeys. The aunt was a tall, stately woman in a long dress, with several strands of pearls, pince-nez, and coiffure which suggested the late Queen Mary. His pals, however, were scruffy, working-class kids of all shapes and sizes, from near teenagers down to a pair of twins hardly out of their swaddling clothes, called Snitchy and Snatchy. They were, for all the roughness of their appearance, good boys, who, if they did anything boys shouldn't, such as smash a window, always did so by accident, and indeed many of the incidents in the strip were built round such accidents. Their enemies tended to be other working-class kids, rough, without the benefit of Snooty and intent on mischief. The strip fulfilled every schoolboy's fantasy of finding himself among wealthy people in a noble setting.

The principal hero of the *Dandy* was a cowboy, Desperate Dan, a sort of rude, unpolished forerunner of Superman. He did not wear a cloak and did not fly through the air, but he did almost everything else and was indestructible. His punch was far more lethal than his guns and one punch would send his adversaries flying into space, after which he would refresh himself with one of his Auntie Aggy's giant cow pies.

During the war the comics turned patriotic and the various characters found themselves contending with German spies. New characters were introduced such as Addie and Hermy, both suffering from German measles (indicated by tiny swastikas all over their faces), the one moustached, the other plump, and both so ridiculous as to be almost amiable. The danger of laughing at one's enemies is that one can begin to like them, but by then I was graduating to *Hotspur*, *Adventure* and others, which although differing in covers all carried much the same fare – the Wild West, sport (mainly football), detectives (who always had a young assistant and a fast car), school stories, and historical dramas, usually variations on the Robin Hood theme. Once the war began they gave way to daredevil fliers, naval heroes, soldiers, spy stories and scientists working on secret weapons; but one story persisted right through the war years and possibly even beyond – the Red Circle stories about a pseudo-Eton, in the *Hotspur*.

The *Magnet* as described by Orwell must have been defunct by then, for Greyfriars, with its principal anti-hero, Billy Bunter, was appearing in a coloured comic called the *Knock Out* (which has since been knocked out). Red Circle was a sort of Greyfriars, but not nearly so well written and without any character as vivid and well-formed as Bunter. Its most memorable figure was a bullying housemaster called Mr Alfred Smugg (or 'Smuggie'). 'All literature of this kind is partly plagiarism', wrote Orwell of Greyfriars and if, as he suggested, Greyfriars was a cheap imitation of *Tom Brown's School Days*, the Red Circle stories were an even cheaper imitation of Greyfriars. And here too the 'snob appeal,' to use Orwell's expression, was completely shameless. It is very unlikely that any of the boys at the Scottish schools I attended had any hope of going to public school, but the idea of emulating one's betters is deeply ingrained in the Scottish schoolboy, and one's betters at this time certainly went to public school. The Scottish ruling classes, with few exceptions, went south for their schooling, to Eton, Harrow, Rugby. One can thus readily understand why the Red Circle stories appealed to my classmates, but why did they appeal to me?

There were, I think, two reasons. The first was that the comics as a whole provided my sole entry into the non-Jewish universe. I was eight when I came to Scotland and was now nearly eleven, yet, except for exigencies arising out of the war, I had never been admitted to a non-Jewish home. I made friends in the neighbourhood almost as soon as we moved into Battlefield Gardens, even before I could speak English, though it did not take me long to make myself understood, for small children pick up a language as naturally and as casually as they pick up chicken-pox. We played in the central plot of garden, in the street and on the back-greens. We went to the pictures and football matches together, and played football in the recreation ground over the road from Queens Park. And on sunny days, we took sandwiches and bottles of Barrs Iron Brew and had day-long picnics in the park itself, yet they never invited me back to their homes and I never invited them back to mine. It never occurred to me that they should, for if *goyim* were friendly I did not expect them to be that friendly.

There were twelve households in the four-storey block of flats where we lived, of which two were Jewish; ours on the first floor being one and the family Markson on the top floor the other. We and the Marksons were in and out of each other's homes, but in the twenty years I lived in Glasgow there were only two occasions when I set foot in any of the others. The first was during an air-raid when Father was away from home and Mother in a desperate moment of insecurity, took us to a downstairs neighbour, to sit the raid out (nobody in the block ever used the air-raid shelter). The other was, many years later, when a man living above us fell down the stairs and I helped him back up to his flat and his bed. But otherwise I never stepped across a single threshold. Yet this was not due to any hostility or ill-feeling. On the contrary we were on the best and most neighbourly terms, but the neighbourliness stopped short at the front door.

I suppose my parents may initially have thought that this was due to antisemitism, but it soon became clear that Scottish middle-class homes were castles with the portcullis down and the drawbridge up, for even exchanges between non-Jewish neighbours took place in the street, or on the landings, or by the open door, but rarely beyond. Working-class homes, I discovered, were quite different.

In Barovke and Breslev we had lived in open homes with open doors. In time we adapted ourselves to the Scottish closed door, though if I never brought anyone home during our first years in Glasgow it was because I came to realise our home was something less than a palace. There were six of us in the family and a lodger to share three rooms and kitchen, and there were beds everywhere. And more irksome than the beds was the laundry.

When we first came to Glasgow Father was earning £4 15s a week, part of which he sent to relatives in Latvia (we were now *die reiche kreivim*). Mother could not afford to send laundry out (she may for all I know have taken laundry in) and washed everything by hand, including the bed-linen, in the bath (sometimes together with the smaller children). It must have been a back-breaking job for she had to do it crouching, or on her knees. She had never been so industrious in Barovke where our circumstances were infinitely worse, but in Barovke she was the wife of a public figure and had appearances to keep up, whereas in Glasgow she enjoyed comparative – indeed, complete – anonymity. The difficulty, as far as I was concerned, however, was not the washing, but the drying. In Barovke one hung everything out in the open, whatever the time of the year, and one woke on winter mornings to a petrified corps de ballet of woollen combinations. In Glasgow there was only the small back-green, which was meant to accommodate the laundry of a dozen households and on dry days there would be a rush of housewives with dripping laundry, anxious to stake a place on the line. But it usually rained, if not in the morning, then by the end of the day, and Mother finally forsook the line and dried the laundry on twin poles suspended from the kitchen ceiling, and it hung there day and night like a bleeding Sword of Damocles. Mother put out newspapers to catch the drips, which made things even worse, as we lived in a ceaseless suspension of carbolic and moisture and the slow rat-tat of water on paper. On Thursday night Mother fried her fish and as the oil vapour rose upwards it met the water vapour coming downwards to form an almost impenetrable fog.

The laundry was only removed from the pole on Friday afternoons in honour of the Sabbath, and if there be any who are disgruntled with life, let them suspend dripping laundry from their ceiling for six days of the week and remove it on the seventh. They will then discover the true nature of happiness.

I could see laundry poles through the kitchen windows of other homes, but I somehow thought that they were less cluttered, more elegant and certainly more orderly than ours but I don't know what could have made me think so except my reading of the comics. I did not, of course, think that everyone lived like Lord Snooty, but even the *Knock Out*'s Deed A Day Danny, who was working class (his father wore a muffler and smoked a clay pipe), came home at the end of the day to an orderly house with a set tea, whereas with the exception of the Sabbath and festivals, we rarely sat down at table together as a family.

All this, however, does not explain why I was particularly attracted to public school stories, and why my vocabulary was full of public school phrases with whose meaning I was only vaguely familiar – prep, fag, prefect, close, quad, remove, poor-show, well-played. Was it that I was so embarrassed by our domestic circumstances that I wanted to leave home? Or was it, perhaps, that I was already finding the closeness and intensity of Jewish life overpowering, that I longed to be away from parental eyes and parental concern?

Early in 1941, when I was eleven, I found myself in a public school of sorts, or at least a boarding school. The Glasgow Jewish education authorities had found that the provisions they were able to make for Jewish education in Annan were inadequate and in 1940 they acquired Ernespie House, an old mansion (now an hotel), near Castle Douglas in Dumfriesshire. The idea was that we would receive our secular education in Castle Douglas, and our Jewish education in Ernespie House, where they could also see that we ate kosher and conformed to other Jewish obser-vances. The headmaster was a Jewish teacher from Glasgow, Mr Caplan, a shortish man with broad shoulders, smooth, black hair carefully plastered down and parted in the middle, a neat pencil moustache and large glasses from which shone forth an eternal light of self-satisfaction. His wife, a sweet-faced woman with a sour temper, was the matron. She would, I think, have liked to be a doctor and went about in white, delighted in the quasi-medical aspects of her duties, inserting a thermometer here, giving a smile there and exuding an air of ether and lavender. Old Ike came down to look after Jewish studies. As Caplan tried to run the place on public school lines with prefects and housemasters he reminded one a little of Mr Alfred Smugg, and it was easy to imagine oneself if not in Eton, or even Greyfriars, then at least in the Red Circle school.

The building itself helped, for although it could not have been more than fifty years old, it had battlements and turrets and dark cellars which were out of bounds to the boys, which, given the schoolboy's imagination, could easily have functioned as dungeons. There were also extensive grounds, including a good cricket pitch, and a couple of water-towers mocked up to look like ancient keeps. We had pillow-fights with adjoining dorms, cricket matches with a number of third-rate boarding schools in the vicinity, and I imbibed something of the public school ethos.

I was once savaged by a boy much older and bigger than me and ran in helpless fury to show my wounds to Caplan, who summoned the boy and gave him six of the best, but I could see that Caplan was not too pleased with me for bringing the matter to his attention nor did the incident enhance my standing with the rest of the school. I was not quite placed in Coventry, but I was given to understand that one did not tell tales, in other words, that the weak must not invoke authority against the strong. It was, I thought, a crazy precept, presumably established by the strong, but I accepted it.

I also discovered that one could not tell a lie to get out of a scrape, though lies seemed perfectly acceptable on other occasions. I had got my first hint of this at Battlefield School. I fired an ink pellet at another boy which overshot its target and landed plop on the open register on the teacher's desk. She jumped up in a fury and asked the culprit to own up. No one did. She then asked each child in turn. Did you do it? No, miss. Did you? No, miss. You? No, miss. Until she came to me. 'Did you do it?' At which I invoked my supposed ignorance of the language (much as the hard of hearing sometimes bring deafness to their aid). 'I do not understand, miss.' And she went back to her desk and picked up the pellet between thumb and forefinger. 'Did you fire this?' 'No, miss.' And so on till she had been right round the class.

'Come on,' she insisted, 'someone in the class must have done it. I'm prepared to forgive mischief, but I shall *not* tolerate lying.' And a little blonde girl with a great floppy bow put up her hand : 'Please miss, it was the foreign boy.'

The teacher thought the matter too grave to deal with herself, and took me to the headmaster. There my supposed ignorance proved unavailing and I was whacked over my open palm with a leather hawser. 'Not for the ink pellet you understand, but for telling a lie. What for?'

'Telling a lie, sir.'

If necessary lies were forbidden, dilettante lying was perfectly in order and I became a dilettante liar of the first order. Russia was by now in the war and Dvinsk, Wilno, Vitebsk, all of them place names of my early boyhood, were among the first towns to be overrun by the advancing Germans. Mr Caplan would give a commentary on the day's news to the older boys after supper and I would chip in with a commentary of my own, for was I not a native of those very places and claimed to be as familiar with the terrain as if they were my own back yard? I also still knew the occasional Russian word and expression and used them in such a way as to suggest that Russian was my native tongue and I was regarded with something like awe among my contemporaries and even by some of the older boys. I also let it be known that my father had been an officer in the Red Army, nay, the Red Cavalry, though when Father came down on a visit he did not, with his reddish beard, now streaked with grey, his black homburg and brown paper parcel of fried fish he had brought from Mother, look like an ex-cavalry officer (neither for that matter did Isaac Babel, who *was* a Red cavalry officer), but I added convincing detail to my account and no one disbelieved me.

I also exercised my imagination in other directions. After lights-out, we would pull back the curtains in the dormitories, let the moonlight stream in and tell ghost stories. I was new to the game, but quickly entered into its spirit and told the best stories in the school. I would set them in Eastern Europe, tell them in the first person, as if I had experienced them myself, and told them so vividly and with so much incidental detail, that I half came to believe them myself and long after I had finished, when the rest of the dorm was asleep, I thought I could hear the stirring of dark spirits and almost cried out with terror. Caplan once entered the dorm in the course of a recital, but instead of cutting me short, sat down in the darkness to listen.

'Very good,' he said when I had finished. 'Why don't you write them down? Who knows, you might even make some money.' Thus, unwittingly, he set me on a course which, as my parents put it, was the cause of my downfall.

We were wakened by air-raid sirens a number of times but were never required to troop down to the shelters, even when bombs fell on nearby Dalbeatie. Castle Douglas itself seemed a town full of women, mostly with kerchiefed heads. Sunday was our one free day. Matron would examine each of us carefully to make sure that our appearance would not disgrace Ernespie House and we would wander into town in desultory little groups.

The place was largely deserted. All the shops were shut except for two small Italian cafés, both owned by the family Borelli. Sweets were not yet rationed, but they were generally unobtainable and we would sit huddled up in our coats eating ice-cream. Occasionally a visiting parent might take us to tea in one of the hotels, the King's Arms, the Douglas Arms, the Royal, all near one another in the main street. The only other place open was the railway station where, during the first months of our stay, one could still get twopenny bars of Nestlé's chocolate from the slot machines, but now all the machines were empty and rusting and the only one still in working order was a contraption with which, for a penny, one could engrave twenty-four letters on a two-inch strip of aluminium. There wasn't a boy in the school who didn't have three or four of those strips, with his name, address and perhaps a slogan, like 'Britain can take it'.

I followed the news avidly, even where the centre of interest shifted from the Russian front. In Europe one disaster followed another, but there were occasional glad tidings from the Middle East, and I followed the retreating Italians on a wall-map by my bed – Sidi Barrani, Mersa Matruh, Bardia, Tobruk, Benghazi. There was a pro-Axis rising in Iraq, which was bad news, followed promptly by its suppression, which was good news. Then one night, Rudolf Hess, the Deputy Fuehrer, landed out of the skies. He wanted, he said, to talk to the Duke of Hamilton, whose seat was no great distance from Castle Douglas. No one was quite sure what to make of his sudden arrival, but everyone was disposed to treat his arrest as good news. There was need of it. If I was troubled by the earlier events of the war through the effect they had on those about me, by the time the débâcle in Greece came I was old enough, and understood enough, to worry in my own right. For the first time my peace of mind was affected not by what was happening to me, or my family, but by wholly external events. I began to read the papers regularly (I had been following the main B.B.C. bulletins from about the day we acquired a radio) and graduated from the *Glasgow Bulletin* and the *Daily Express* to the *Glasgow Herald* and *Manchester Guardian*.

The surrounding countryside, for the time being, ceased to

preoccupy me. Part of my obsession with the scene in Annan had arisen out of my obsession with Barovke. After a few months in Castle Douglas I was too intent on the present to be obsessed about the past, and I was largely – though never entirely – cured of Barovke and the habit of measuring everything I was experiencing in Britain against everything I had known in *der heim*. I was building up new obsessions to replace the old and drawing reassurance and pride from the Empire, from those huge areas of pink on the map, and I envisaged their spread like a new and healing tissue over the diseased face of the globe. There was, for example, the great yellow patch of the Belgian Congo which seemed too large an area for so small and frail a country as Belgium and I felt it would be better under British control. France, I felt, had behaved shamefully in the war and was no longer worthy of an empire and I took it that the great green-coloured mass of the Sahara would pass to Britain as would, of course, the tan-coloured areas of Eritrea and Somaliland which had belonged to Italy; gradually the whole of Africa glowed pink before my eyes.

There is the well-known story of Greenberg, lately from Poland, who changed his name to Greenhill, took out naturalisation papers and after completing the necessary preliminaries, went down to the Home Office to finalise them. He returned, his eyes red, his face stained with tears. His wife had never seen him in such a state, and she tried to reassure him.

'So they didn't naturalise you? All right, they didn't. You've been a foreigner all your life, so all right, you'll be a foreigner another few years. When my – '

Her husband cut her short. 'Naturalisation? Of course I'm naturalised.'

'Then why the tears?'

And as he unfurled the evening paper he broke down again : 'They've given India away.'

We used to have a sing-song on Sunday evenings in Ernespie House, and the favourite, or at least my favourite, was : 'There'll always be an England, and England will be free – if England means as much to you as England means to me' – all sung with strident, full-throated vigour – and, of course, 'Rule, Britannia'.

The B.B.C. used to play the national anthems of Britain and

her allies before the Nine o'clock news on Sunday night. The more setbacks we suffered, the more allies we seemed to accumulate, and the whole recital must have taken about fifteen minutes. First there was the Polish anthem, then the French, followed by the Belgian, Dutch, Norwegian, Yugoslavian, Greek, Russian and finally, after a drum roll, 'God Save the King', for which we all stood.

When Hitler invaded Russia, Caplan assured us, with dubious accuracy, that 'no one ever defeated Russia – not even Napoleon', and that he had no doubt about the successful outcome of the war. The same view seems to have been taken in Glasgow. Clydeside had been bombed a number of times early in 1941, but the damage did not approach the devastation inflicted on London, or even Merseyside. The skies had been comparatively quiet since and many evacuees had returned to town.

Queens Park, the local grammar school, was reopened in September 1942. I had sat the necessary qualifying exam before that in Castle Douglas and got a place. I returned to Glasgow at the end of August, and was taken to Paisley's, one of the posher gentlemen's outfitters in town – the sort of place where no regular customer paid cash – and there equipped with a green and gold school tie and school scarf and socks with green and gold rings at the top and little green tabs for the garters. My parents must have found it all ruinously expensive, but they got more than their money's worth in *naches*. Clad in my new livery, I was paraded round the family, and Leibe Sheine blinked when she saw me : 'Look at him, an Engils gentleman.'

When term began I made the acquaintance of a pale-faced youngster who had escaped from Belgium the year before and spoke English with an atrocious French accent.

'There's a greener in my class,' I said when I got home.

VII

Queens Park

Queens Park was one of the many board schools opened immediately after the 1870 Education Act and consisted of two tall grey, mock-Gothic buildings erected at the end of the last century, and two rather more handsome structures in red sandstone built between the wars. It had a small garden at one end with a lawn, trees and one might gaze out of the windows on some bleak March day and be cheered by the sight of a daffodil, but as the school expanded, the garden was put under asphalt and a fifth building was erected. The entire school is now to be demolished to make way for a roundabout.

There was, and I should imagine there still is, a strict hierarchy of schools in Glasgow. At the top were the fee-paying schools, Glasgow High, Glasgow Academy, Kelvinside Academy, Hutcheson's, Alan Glen's. They were all in the West End or the centre of town, had more elaborate uniforms (the trousers had to match the jacket), and their pupils tended to speak with a blander, less Glaswegian accent. I had sat an exam for a free place in Alan Glen's, possibly the best of the schools, but failed to get one. I was later astounded to discover how low the fees in the top schools were. Their classes were smaller, their facilities better, their standard of tuition higher, and the fees did not even attempt to cover the cost of the extra benefits. Glasgow, which prides itself on being 'red' and socialistic, in fact subsidised the education of the well-to-do.

The second grade of schools consisted of Shawlands Academy, Albert Road Academy and Queens Park. There was also a third grade of schools of which one was only dimly aware, for they had no liveries, or if they did, the boys did not wear them.

Queens Park was vast, co-educational, with over a thousand pupils, and would today be called a comprehensive school. There were two top streams whose pupils took classics and modern languages, a classics stream, in which I floundered, and five subordinate streams. Towards the end of the war, yet another stream was added, known as the Ag class, for non-academic pupils who hoped to become farmers. They did not, to be sure, look academic, but neither did they look like farmers and came from working-class areas of Glasgow like Springtown and Possilpark, and would not have known a turnip from a toadstool. They were bigger than other boys of their years, had the beginnings of a moustache spreading along their upper lip, dressed in mufti instead of blazers, without as much as a school tie, and had flowing, greasy coiffures. They spoke in accents which I found barely intelligible, but their main distinction was their money. When I turned thirteen Father gave me a shilling a week pocket money. Very few of the boys of my age had more – though several came from wealthy homes – some had less, but the Ag boys went around with jangling pockets of silver. Some of them earned money by delivering papers or taking jobs at weekends, but several of them received generous hand-outs from their parents. I became friendly with a number of the boys, and they introduced me to a side of Glasgow of which I had only been dimly aware. Some would call it the real Glasgow. It is certainly the Glasgow which has been most written about – and that with little accuracy – and I am not sure if the genteel Glasgow of Queens Park is not more representative of the city. They lived in fairly decent homes, and if there was overcrowding it was with furniture, bric-à-brac, bicycles and war souvenirs, including in one case, a trench mortar. Work in the factories and shipyards was plentiful, wages were high, both parents normally went out to work and their children were left to do as they liked and go where they liked. The Ag boys generally went to the pictures three or four times a week.

Queens Park was at one time a fee-paying school. Before the war one had to pay for school books, and one master who, by the look of him, had been with the school since it was founded, lamented the fact that everything was free. 'We had some of the finest lads in Glasgow in this school, but now –' he looked around us with a sad, disdainful twirl of his head and left the sentence unfinished. The older boys, for their part, missed the school as it had been before the war. It had been cheerful and alive, they said, but now it was 'full of old crocks and old dames'. Not all the dames were old. Some, indeed, were disturbingly young and attractive. There was in particular, a young art teacher, who, possibly because she taught art, radiated a certain vague libidinousness, but most of the masters were fairly ancient. Some had delayed their retirement, others had come out of retirement and most of the others looked as if they had been casualties of fate or war. I once had to deliver a message to the staff-room and thought I had strayed into a sanctuary for old men, for I found six sprawling figures, sunk in their armchairs, their glasses over their heads, fast asleep and snoring in unison. They could not all have been as decrepit as they looked, for one of them had to leave in a hurry after molesting a fourteen-year-old girl. She was a particularly well developed wench and he – a music master – said that he was giving her breathing exercises. It could not have been his first offence for he was known around the school as 'Lungs'.

The fact that the school was manned by what was virtually a reserve team did not affect my early progress. I arrived determined to succeed. There was in the assembly hall of the main building, beside the roll of honour of pupils fallen in the First World War, a series of boards carrying the names of the 'dux' medallists, the boys who came top of the different subjects in the different years, and in one *annis mirabilis* one boy came top in no less than eight subjects. His name was Harold Levy, a lean, studious figure, with a tall forehead, and a constant cigarette in his mouth, who, in spite of his tobacco intake, is still happily Inspector of the Central Board of Jewish Religious Education. He had been at Queens Park in the twenties and people would point him out as an example of a brilliant boy who came to a less than brilliant end for he was, as they would add, '*nebbich*, a teacher'.

On my first day at school I fixed my eyes on that prize list and made up my mind that I too would do a Harold Levy. Things, alas, did not quite work out that way, and I came down under a cloud, not the sort of cloud usually written about, but

cloud enough to darken the days of my family. My initial determination, however, gave me sufficient momentum to carry me
through my first three years with flying colours. These, as far
as my parents were concerned, were my golden years and I was
a constant source of *naches*. *Naches* is a particular sort of joy
which a parent looks to from his children; it is not something
which a child expects of his parents, and simply put, it is the
fulfilment of fond hopes. It was not merely that I was working
hard and doing well at school, and coming away with odd prizes
to prove it, but I was also doing well in *Yeshiva*.

Glasgow *Yeshiva* could not compare with the centre of higher
Jewish studies which my father attended in Lithuania. It had
about a dozen boys in their late teens or early twenties who were
full-time students, and about a further two dozen who, like
myself, were in their early teens and would come to study on
weekday evenings and Sunday mornings. I would rush home
from school, gulp down a cup of tea, then rush off to *Yeshiva* to
snatch a page of Talmud. The Principal of the *Yeshiva*, a plump,
elderly bachelor, thought in those early years that I had the
makings of an *ilui*, a prodigy. It was not a forecast which he was to
repeat in later years. There were, he used to tell me, different
degrees of hell for different types of sinners. There are those
who are incapable of doing good, and who in their afterlife
therefore, do not have it so bad, but there are those who are
capable of doing good, but wilfully refuse to do so; they are the
cardinal sinners and suffer the ultimate penalties.

If one approaches the Talmud with the right frame of mind
and a sufficient degree of faith, which is to say, if one believes
that the Talmud incorporates the Oral Law, and that the Oral
Law was dictated with the written Law by God to Moses on
Sinai, and that the Oral Law was received intact by the Rabbis,
one turns the pages with a sense of awe. Where Rabbis seem to
contradict one another it is the business of the Talmudist to
reconcile their contradictions, for no Rabbi, certainly none whose
utterance has found its way to the Talmud, can be wrong. When
this or that passage makes no sense or insofar as it does make
sense, seems plainly absurd, one has to stretch a word here and
reinterpret a phrase there to give it meaning. Apart from the
intricate legal arguments, the Talmud also contains long pas-

sages of *aggadatah*, narrative, from which the devout draw endless lessons and which even to the non-devout offers a fascinating insight into the lives, habits and ideas of the Jewish people round about the time of Christ. But possibly more important than any part of the Talmud is the mood which surrounds the whole. One studies the Talmud with a certain chant and a slight swaying motion and as one gets into it, one so to speak sways oneself into the past, into the world of the great East European *Yeshivoth* : Slobokda, Ponovesch, Mir and further back to the great Jewish academies of Babylonia. One is engulfed by it, and to the devout it is a continuous source not only of enlightenment, but comfort.

My father who rarely knew a day free of frustrations and grief found constant relief in the Talmud. His mood would soften even as he reached up for one of the vast volumes of his Wilno edition, and bent over the pages, and humming softly, he would soon be at peace with himself and the world. For my part I was a little afraid of the Talmud for I was aware of its pull on me. I found the present full of exciting and wondrous things, the future even more so, and I did not want to be pulled back into the past (had I been a *Yeshiva* student today I might have felt differently, for the future has never looked more dismal, nor the past more attractive). If the Principal had described me as an *ilui* at thirteen, he was denouncing me as a *letz*, a scoffer, at fifteen, and given the name I quickly lived up to it; but at first I showed nothing more than a hesitant scepticism. The limited logic I had at my command suggested that if one Rabbi said black was black, and another said black was white, then one or another or both of them were wrong, and if a third Rabbi insisted that they were both right, then he too must be wrong, but my fall from grace was mainly due to the fact that I was becoming not only a sceptical student, but a reluctant one. I felt that my weekday evenings and Sunday mornings could be better used.

I was, throughout my boyhood years, a chronic joiner and in my time I passed through various organisations, including the Scouts, the Jewish Lads' Brigade, the Synagogue Youth Guild, and (of which more later) the Habonim and Bnei Akivah. I joined the Scouts even before the war and enjoyed the hikes and rambles, the songs round the camp-fires, the chumminess. They offered something of the world I was to discover in my reading of school stories, but the only part of the scout uniform I could afford was the lanyard and later the kerchief, but the hat, the shirt, the staff and the kilt (which was part of the scout uniform in Scotland) remained beyond my means. I suppose if I could have come along in plain mufti it might not have seemed so bad, but with the lanyard and kerchief over my grubby shirt, I felt apart from the uniformed pack and finally left.

There was no such embarrassment with the Jewish Lads' Brigade, for there the uniform was provided free. The J.L.B. was founded at the end of the last century by Colonel A. E. W. Goldsmid, an ex-Indian Army officer who was anxious to infuse something of the army's martial spirit into the young, working-class, immigrant Jew, to make a man of him, and, to use a phrase common at the time, 'straighten the ghetto bend'; but by the time I became aware of the J.L.B., it had become part of the army cadet force, with khaki uniforms and shoulder tabs, put-tees, boots and, as a boy sitting next to me in synagogue whispered incredulously, 'real guns with live ammunition'. I was fourteen at the time, the war was still on, I had not yet outgrown my fiercely patriotic phase, and the thought of handling a lethal weapon, and possibly even of shooting at Germans (though I was not sure how such a possibility might arise) was exciting. The school cadet force also offered the chance of handling a gun, but it met on Friday nights and Shabbat mornings. The J.L.B. met on Sundays, and I returned after my second meeting in full uniform, swinging my arms at the side, like a guardsman on parade, and saluted my father with such a clatter of boots that I unhinged the chandelier on the floor below. If I felt every inch the soldier, I did not perhaps look it, for I had grown rapidly upwards but not outwards, and it was difficult to find a uniform to fit. My tunic dangled loosely about me like a mater-nity smock.

The glory of the Jewish Lads' Brigade (Glasgow battalion) was, and still is, its band, the pipes and drums, whose members were splendidly attired in the kilt, spats and sporran, the ceremonial dress of the Cameronians, and after about a month I volunteered to be a piper. I was told to wait a further month and was brought

before the C.O., a very unmilitary looking old man with a red
face, white hair, white moustache and bushy white eyebrows. He
looked me up and down with not too much approval, and asked
if I was of good wind. I wasn't absolutely sure what sort of wind
he meant, but I said I was. He then asked me to roll up a
trouser leg which, a little nonplussed, I did, and he shook his
head.

'No, they'll not do. They're not kilt legs, too spindly.'

I would, I suppose, have left the J.L.B. in any case. I was
very much my mother's son, more than a bit of a snob, and felt
that the boys were rough and uncouth. The huge, shaggy, Ag
boys I knew at school were no less rough, but then they were
goyim. And it wasn't that I was all that genteel myself, but I
expected gentility of my fellow Jews. The one J.L.B. weekend
camp which I attended was a finishing education. Traditional
Jewish fare induces a great deal of wind, which is perhaps why
the Talmud (which has something to say on everything) counsels
that wind must out (though not in the middle of prayer), but I
was sufficiently restrained to emit nothing more than a whisper
(which is perhaps why I incurred an ulcer in my early twenties).
The others suffered from no such restraints and erupted in a
barrage which sent the tent flaps flapping, and which they accompanied with loud whoops, giggles and guffaws. They smoked
heavily and had nicotined fingers and nicotined breath. They
used foul language and told foul jokes. I heard my first homosexual joke :

This pansy went into a men's outfitters and asked for a coat.

'Certainly,' said the man, 'would you like a belt at the back?'

'I'd love one, darling,' said the pansy, 'but I've got to catch
a train.'

The point of the story was lost on me. I didn't know what a
pansy was, indeed, I didn't even know what a homosexual was –
and I doubt if I was the poorer for my ignorance – until I read
Hesketh Pearson's life of Oscar Wilde a year or two later.

None of the boys in the tent was older than sixteen, but they
all had, or claimed to have had, sexual experience, and as they
compared details as to how they went about it, and with whom,
I felt myself turning grey with corruption, though it may have
been green with envy. I felt like an innocent fallen among

delinquents. I was very much happier in the Bnei Akivah, which has many affinities both with the Church Lads' Brigade and the Band of Hope, and where I was more like a delinquent fallen among innocents.

In the late 1920s and early 1930s a number of Jewish youth groups were founded in Germany and Eastern Europe, deriving their inspiration both from the British Boy Scouts and the German *Wandervogel* movement, with the idea of drawing and harnessing the idealism and energies of young people to the Zionist cause. The first such movement to be founded in Britain was the Habonim (the name means simply 'builders') which is still flourishing. I was a member briefly in 1939, but then came the war, and afterwards I joined the Bnei Akivah, which might be described as the Habonim with hats on. It was named after one of the greatest and most heroic of Jewish sages, Rabbi Akivah, who lived about the time of Christ and died a martyr for his faith at the hands of the Romans.

I had joined Bnei Akivah by accident. Although I had numerous friends, almost everybody I knew in Glasgow either went to a football match on Saturday afternoon, if their team played at home, or to the pictures, if the team played away; and I was left on my own. Home was not a comfortable place at such a time, especially in the winter, for the Orthodox Jew does not light a fire (or even switch on a light) on Shabbat, and the only habitable room during the cold weather was the kitchen, where the gas stove burned throughout the day. After lunch the dishes were piled into the sink, my parents went to bed, my sisters to their friends, and I was left on my own. There is nothing more depressing to the overfed than the debris of the last meal, and I fled to the park, and from there went to the library reading room, where I consumed almost everything in sight – the *Adelphi* (Editor Sir B. Ifor Evans – why did his name stick in my memory and nothing else?), *Britannia and Eve, Confectionery and Tobacco News, Punch, New Statesman and Nation, Tribune, The Spectator, Truth,* and, whenever I could get hold of it, *The Tatler* (which wasn't very often, for one very old, very slow and very scruffy reader sat over it all day). I was bent over *The Tatler* one Shabbat afternoon, when I was tapped on the shoulder by a chinless, shoulderless young Rabbi, who asked me

D

if I should like to come along to the Bnei Akivah. I had never heard of it before but given his sponsorship I presumed I couldn't come to much harm. Besides I am disposed to try almost everything once. I went along to a shabby ill-furnished house in Pollokshields and there found the other dozen or so Glasgow youngsters of my age who did not go to football matches on Shabbat, and two or three good-looking girls. The following week I brought along two or three friends (the football season was almost over); they brought along their friends, and by mid-summer there were about fifty youngsters in the group, but what established us as a lasting organisation was our first summer camp.

I had been to camp before, but only for a weekend at a time. Now we were to be away for three whole glorious weeks. We did not, till we were in camp, realise our intense longing to be away from home – at least for a brief spell. We loved our parents and our parents loved us, with a sort of angry, searing affection, like the torrid Israeli sun which I was to experience in later years, and we longed to be out in the cold. To love is to fear and with their affection came anxieties about our health, about our private life, our studies. Whenever I sat down at table I was conscious of the scrutiny of two pairs of anxious eyes watching to see if I was off-colour, or too highly coloured, or if I was eating too little, or if enough, whether it was enough of the right things. To an extent I was the source of greater anxiety than the other boys because I was a *ben-yochid* – not, heaven forbid, an only child, for that would have been intolerable, but an only son, which was enough of an only to get on with, and I was aware from an early age of the burden of hope which rested on me. My sisters were, after all, just daughters, and as such were at the mercy of fate. Good Jewish daughters of good family remained in their father's house until such a time as their redeemer arrived and they set up house on their own, whereas I, as the son, was expected to effect my own redemption and, indeed, that of the whole family, to redress some of the humiliation, frustration and setbacks they had suffered over the years.

They wanted me to go to university, which I also wanted, and be a doctor, to which I did not object. My father would sometimes point out an elderly businessman with a little white moustache who would swagger into synagogue as if the place was his: '*Kuk af*

im,' he would say, '*er is a gornisht but zein sun is a professor*' –
look at him, he is a nobody, but his son's a professor. My father
had by now all but given up hope of a Rabbinical post, but felt
that if I could become a doctor he might recover something of
his fallen grace. A doctor meant *yichus*, social status, prestige. It
also meant solvency, even riches, for a doctor could always marry
money, unless, of course, he married a *shikse*, a gentile, which a
great many Glasgow Jewish doctors did. I recently went through
a list of twelve friends and acquaintances who qualified in medicine in the late 1940s and early 1950s, eight married *shikses*, and
a ninth married a Jewish girl because his mother threatened to
kill herself if he didn't (his wife later left him). I suspect that one
reason why so many Jewish boys marry out of their faith is that
it is the ultimate assertion of a desire to live their own lives, which
is something to which every member of a Jewish family must to
a lesser or greater degree become resigned.

The summer camps were our first experiments in freedom,
away from parental eyes and parental anxieties, which does not
mean that we were free to riot. Our *madrichim*, leaders, were all
earnest young men with a ready, I sometimes felt excessive, sense
of responsibility. Two of them had arrived from Germany shortly
before the war and were *Yeshiva* students; a third, Henry Tankel,
a local boy, was a medical student. The place of Tankel (now a
distinguished surgeon) in the set-up was important for he was in
many ways a model to our generation, as his late father, Hyman
Tankel, had been to that of my parents. Hyman Tankel was, in
my father's words, a *gevir und a mensch*, rich man and a gentleman, which most moneyed people of his acquaintance were not.
Henry was in many ways a chip off the old block. He could have
gone into his father's business, but chose medicine, instead; however not content with that, he won an open scholarship to university and could study for nothing. I had somehow grown up to
believe that brains were a compensation for lack of money, so
that to have both struck me as a sort of extravagance. He was
also deeply religious and in synagogue would spend all his time
at prayer, and the fact that he was one of our Bnei Akivah leaders
made it kosher for our parents. They would hardly have allowed
us to leave home and attend camp otherwise.

By now the end of the war was in sight. Details of what came

to be known as the holocaust were leaking out of Europe. They
at first seemed too horrific to be true for even Germans seemed
incapable of such enormities; but detail confirmed detail and
gradually and painfully we became aware that the great centres
of Jewish life in Eastern Europe were being exterminated. I kept
seeing the faces of my grandfather in Kreslevka, my grandmother
in Breslev, my uncles and aunts and young cousins, and sensing
something of their torments. At the same time ragged handfuls
of refugees, who had somehow been able to make their way out
of Europe to Palestine, were being turned back by the British
authorities. It was a time of great strain for the Jew, especially
a Jew as new to patriotism as I was. But I felt no conflict of
loyalties. The Jews were right and the British tragically wrong
and I could not see how any humane person could have thought
otherwise; but I was troubled by the feeling that perhaps antisemitism was not, after all, a phenomenon peculiar to Eastern
Europe.

Like every Orthodox Jew, I was born and brought up a
Zionist. Zionism formed part of the language of daily prayer, and
Jewish liturgy is full of evocations of Zion :

'Walk about Zion, and go round about her . . .
'Do good, in thy good pleasure with Zion, build thou the walls
of Jerusalem . . .
'For God will save Zion, and will build the cities of Judah, that
they may dwell there and have it in possession . . .
'And of Zion it shall be said, this and that man was born in her;
and the highest Himself shall establish her . . .
'Thou shalt arise and have mercy upon Zion; for the time to
favour her, yea the set time, is nigh . . .
'For the Lord hath chosen Zion; He hath desired it for His
habitation . . .
'By the waters of Babylon, there we sat down, yea we wept, when
we remembered Zion . . .'

Yom Kippur, the most sacred day in the Jewish year, and the
seder, the festive meal which opens the festival of Passover, both
close with the prayer : 'Next year in Jerusalem'.
When a Jew visits a house of mourning he comforts the

bereaved with the words : 'May the Lord comfort you among the mourners of Zion and Jerusalem.'

Our kitchen mantelpiece, whether in Barovke, Breslev or Glasgow, carried a battery of charity boxes, mainly for orphanages and institutions of learning in Jerusalem. Among them stood a larger, more stalwart box, blue and white in colour, with a map of Palestine on the front, for the Jewish National Fund, and it had first call on any spare pennies we had; but it was only after I had been a year or two in the Bnei Akivah that the thought dawned on me that one's Zionism need not be limited to alms-giving and prayer, and that one could go out to Palestine and join the pioneers who were building the new Jerusalem. The matter assumed a particular urgency with me when Labour won the 1945 election and Ernest Bevin became Foreign Secretary, for his anti-Zionist policy left me with a double sense of betrayal. Britain, by its virtual ban on Jewish immigration, had renegued on the Balfour Declaration which had 'viewed with favour the establishment in Palestine of a national home for the Jewish people', and Bevin, by continuing the ban, had renegued on the Labour Party's pro-Zionist past. The speech by Clement Attlee, made at the 1944 conference of the Labour Party, still rang in our ears, for it was the most outspokenly pro-Zionist speech made by any major political figure that I had read :

'There is surely neither hope nor meaning in a "Jewish National Home" unless we are prepared to let Jews, if they wish, enter this tiny land in such numbers as to become a majority. There was a strong case for this before the war. There is an inevitable case now, after the unspeakable atrocities of the cold and calculated German Nazi plan to kill all the Jews in Europe. Here, too, in Palestine surely is a case, on human grounds, and to promote a stable settlement, for transfer of population. Let the Arab be encouraged to move out as the Jews move in.'

He in fact went further than any Zionist I knew, but now less than a year later his Foreign Secretary was telling the remnants of European Jewry clamouring to get to their own homeland not 'to jump the queue'. When the Chamberlain government published the 1939 White Paper virtually closing Palestine to the

Jews, it could at least be said that it was a necessary measure in the wider context of the approaching war, but the war was now over, Britain was victorious. The Arabs, in so far as they had shown their strength at all, had tended to side with the Axis, but the White Paper was still being grimly enforced. It seemed to us then – and I am not of an entirely different mind now – that something of the antisemitic virus spread by Hitler had found root in the British Isles, and especially in the mind of the British Foreign Secretary who did not know Jewish history, was unaware of the extent of Jewish suffering, and certainly had no sympathy for it and who, if not a common working-class anti-semite, was a crass, insensitive bully.

Since coming to Scotland I had hardly, on a personal level, experienced any antisemitism at all. In Breslev one felt it in the very air. In Barovke one could chance upon it. In Glasgow one had to look for it, and I suppose if one looked hard enough one could find it. There was in Queens Park School a special room for persistent late-comers, and I used to call it the *'minyan'* (the synagogue) because so many of us were Jewish. The assistant-head in upbraiding us one morning happened to remark that 'you people' – meaning us Jews – 'are particularly bad about this sort of thing'. A boy in my class, Myer Diamond, was upset by the remark and reported it to the headmaster.

'But look,' I said, 'most of the late-comers are Jewish.'

'That has nothing to do with it,' said Diamond. 'Most of the prize-winners are also Jewish, but you never hear anything about that. The man's an antisemite.'

If that was antisemitism, I could live with it, but once external events made themselves felt, my outlook changed, and I came to wonder whether all *goyim*, once the surface civilities were scratched away, were not antisemites.

I began to weary of the questions I was asking myself and the doubts and uncertainties with which I was beset. I wanted to be in my own home, Palestine, as an immediate solution to what was coming to be an urgent personal problem, and one afternoon I presented myself to the Secretary of the Glasgow Zionist Organ-isation and said I wanted to emigrate.

The Zionist Organisation at that time had an office off St Enoch Square, which is about the busiest thoroughfare in

Glasgow, and as I alighted from the bus, my mind buzzing with plans for my new life ahead, I did not watch where I was going and nearly went under a lorry. There was a loud screeching of brakes. The lorry swerved violently and mounted the pavement. I was totally unaware of the commotion I had caused until a scarlet-faced lorry driver, yelling obscenities, jumped from his cab and began running after me. I quickly jumped on a bus and remained on it till he was out of sight. By the time I got back to the Zionist office, I was white-faced and shaken and something of my built-up emotion and stern determination to get out to Palestine had dissolved. The Secretary, a Mr Barnett, a good-looking young man, with black hair and a blue chin, looked up from his papers.

'Yes?'

'I – I want to go to Palestine.' I felt as if I was addressing a travel agent rather than offering myself for a life of glory or death.

'How old are you?'

'Sixteen.'

'Do your parents know you're here?'

'No.'

'Come back in two years time.'

End of interview.

I came down the stairs feeling not so much rejected as upbraided, like a schoolboy who had been chastised for doing something he should not, but was not quite sure what it was. At the same time I felt slightly relieved, for my desire to get to Palestine was in conflict with an ambition which had long lain dormant but was now coming to the fore.

I wanted to be a writer.

I was by now in the upper school and my schooldays had become an incessant struggle to keep awake, partly because I now had my own room and could read till the early hours of the morning (and occasionally right through the night), so that I staggered around during the daylight hours in a semi-daze, and partly because the determination which had carried me cheerfully through my first three years at school was now spent. My parents knew nothing of this, or indeed anything of what I did or thought. To my mother, who watched me adoringly as I munched my Rice Krispies (over which she poured the top of the milk) and read my *Manchester Guardian* at breakfast, I was still the prospective doctor. I longed for the weekends and the two days of freedom which they gave me, and when the weekend came it was darkened by the thought of the school week ahead. There were, however, two teachers whose lessons in some way made up for the boredom I otherwise suffered. One was our History master, Monty Banks, the other was our English mistress, Alison Kidd.

Banks was a short, powerfully built man with hair puffed up to make him look taller, broad shoulders, robust chest, large horn-rimmed glasses, and a deep voice which seemed to issue from the floor below him. He was strict, as were most teachers, and could silence a class by raising an eyebrow. What, we asked ourselves, was an able fellow like that doing teaching at school and, as if by way of answer, he left to become an educational administrator.

I enjoyed History but always thought of it as a matter of kings and queens and battles and dates, all laced together with an occasional good story. Monty Banks introduced us to ideas. He began with the Renaissance and took us through the Age of Enlightenment to the French Revolution, and for the first time I became aware of the glory that was Greece, even though we were only studying its distant reverberations. I was by now teaching in Hebrew class in my free time, earning a pound a week, and was able to buy the Penguin and Everyman editions of Homer, Aeschylus, Sophocles and Aristophanes; so Athens began to vie in my imagination with Jerusalem.

There was something symbolic in this conflict, for Athens had ruled Jerusalem in the second and third centuries before Christ and Hellenism came to represent everything materialistic in this world, as distinct from Judaism which represented the forces of the spirit. It was a matter of the good life versus the higher life and I was coming to prefer the good life. Significantly, the Hebrew for a heretic is *Apikoros* – epicurean.

All this does not mean that Banks equipped me with an understanding of Greek philosophy, but he did enable me to grasp the spirit of open-mindedness and free inquiry which went with Greek thought, as distinct from the transmission of accepted wisdom which goes with an Orthodox upbringing.

Our studies of the Enlightenment, of the works of Voltaire and the Encyclopedists, though offered in mere outline (we would have lacked the capacity to take it in more solid form), both through the sharpness of the language and iconoclasm of the thought, also had their liberating effect, but I did not at first appreciate that the attacks on ancient doctrines could also be applied to the beliefs which I still cherished.

Alison Kidd was a handsome woman, rather large, but well proportioned, with sleepy grey eyes and, for a school mistress, an uncommonly varied and elegant wardrobe and, war-time or not, she did not wear the same outfit two days running, whereas the other school mistresses were frumpish old dears who looked as if they were clad in their mothers' cast-offs. Her hair was always smartly set, she wore high-heeled shoes and floated about in a cloud of perfume, which heralded her approach, and left fragrant resonances after she left. She was in her late thirties or early forties at the time and unmarried, and we presumed that so attractive a woman must have had a lover and made up limericks ascribing the role to almost every member of the staff.

She would sit on a high stool, with legs crossed, exhibiting an attractive expanse of thigh and must, I suppose, have derived some pleasure from the ogling eyes and longing sighs of the fifteen-year-olds about her. If I had come to her class in an earlier year her ability – if not her attractions – would have been lost on me, for in the first three years English lessons were given over to the mechanics of language, syntax, spelling, punctuation, all of which I found impossible to grasp. (I still do, and had problems as a writer till I was sufficiently successful to afford a secretary who could correct my spelling and syntax.) By the time we reached the upper school it was presumed that our knowledge of such details was complete, and we were concerned with the flesh and blood of the language, with writing and literature and the meaning and impact of words. Miss Kidd brought Jane Austen alive for us so that when we discussed Emma or Darcy they began to figure in our imagination as three-dimensional, palpable beings. She made words exciting, demonstrated their plasticity and many-sidedness, and to an extent imbued me with a pleasure in *vortschpilerei*, which, when I am off guard, still plagues almost everything I write.

I read a lot, perhaps excessively, and everything I wrote tended to be almost a parody of the last author I read, and it was Miss Kidd who impressed me with the fact that the secret of good writing is to find your own voice, which again I tried, perhaps excessively, to establish, and one afternoon she called me aside. The class was out of the room and I was not quite sure what to expect. 'It's about your writing, have you any ambitions in that direction?' I admitted, with some hesitation – as if I were confessing to a very private vice – that I had, and told her of the Ernespie nights when I kept my dorm enthralled with ghost stories. I had a fairly good line in polemics, she said, and if only I could keep to the subject and learn to spell and if only I would stop trying to be funny or clever, I could have the makings of a writer. There was, she said, a 'distinctive tone' to my work. I forgot the 'ifs' and remembered only the 'distinctive'. A writer I would be.

When I graduated from the fourth to my fifth year (which is the equivalent of an English sixth) school became intolerable. Monty Banks had left, and Alison Kidd was no longer our teacher and we were taken instead by a wordy old pedant. He was tired of teaching and tired of us, had obviously given up all hope of getting anywhere, and he would ramble on endlessly about the one thought which entered into his head – 'the pretty pass', as he called it, to which the world had come. There gradually came a point, especially on sunny mornings, when I could no longer force myself to go to school.

I would have my breakfast as usual, set off down the road as usual, but instead of crossing to the island site occupied by the school, I would jump on a bus to town. I was often accompanied on these excursions by a friend nicknamed Pies, who though a class below me, felt with every justification that school had nothing to teach him, and we spent our day in the Mitchell Library which is the most pleasant and, with the possible exception of the London Library, the most helpful library I have ever used.

My absences from school did not go unnoticed. I was invariably caught and punished and more painful than the physical punishment was the humiliation. The standard penalty for truancy was six of the best. My form mistress was a gentle little woman with shining eyes. She hated to use the belt and it hurt her more than it hurt me; it certainly exhausted her more. I towered a head or two above her and she almost had to stand on a chair to administer the punishment.

It was then that I learned an important lesson in life : if you are out to do something you should not do, then do it on a large scale. Instead of taking a morning off here and an afternoon off there and getting caught and punished in the process, when school resumed after Christmas I did not register at all and for three glorious months I was free to continue my education in the Mitchell Library with complete impunity. I read, I wrote, and I met with Pies and other fellow truants in the nearby Skinner's tea rooms for a coffee and a smoke (as the Talmud hath it : 'sin begets sin').

Then one afternoon as I was hurrying home I was knocked down by a bus. It didn't go right over me, but knocked me sideways into the path of a motorbike which did go over me. When I put my hands to my head I felt as if my skull was coming apart like the two sides of a walnut, which was substantially what had happened (though the brain itself was more or less intact); I was bleeding and bruised, and most painful of all, a small bit of flesh had been torn out of my side. All this happened within sight of the Victoria Infirmary. I put my one hand to my side and the other to my head, and hobbled over to the casualty department, where they washed me down, painted my wounds with purple dyes, patched me up and sent me home. I had returned in such a state before after a game of rugby. Mother took one look at me and assumed the same had happened again. Before I could stop her she strode over to the school, confronted the headmaster and demanded to know how he could allow his pupils to be mutilated and maimed on the playing fields, whereupon the school woke up to the fact that I had not been there for the better part of a term. As a punishment I was suspended from school for the rest of the year, which is rather like incarcerating an habitual drunkard in a distillery. The painful part of it all, however, was that my secret life was now revealed to my parents.

Pies and I spent endless days contemplating our future. One point we had settled. We had no intention of going to University, becoming doctors, marrying nice Jewish girls from prosperous

Jewish homes and settling down to a life in the suburbs. Pies for his part was veering towards the idea of settling on a kibbutz as an agricultural labourer, but his way ahead was comparatively clear. He was not an only son, but one of four, two of whom were already doing their bit for the family's *naches* by studying medicine. Moreover, he was untroubled by literary ambitions. Then one day as I attempted to formulate my own plans, I experienced something like a vision. I saw myself as a shepherd in the hills of Galilee, with a typewriter on my knees, and a dainty shepherdess by my side, and thought I heard the sound of pipes.

It was not the sort of vision I could communicate to my parents. They had received passing intimations, from the Principal of the *Yeshiva* apart from anyone else, that I was no longer quite the golden boy I had been in earlier years, and they were possibly reconciling themselves to the thought that I might not after all become a doctor. But as Mother said to a neighbour, a dentist also makes a living, so does a solicitor. We now had a piano in the house and its empty dust-laden top was crying out for graduation photos.

Nothing, however, prepared them for the actual turn of events. They received news of my suspension in a formal letter from the headmaster. Father could not quite understand the meaning of suspension and looked it up in his Yiddish dictionary, where it was given as hanging, and the message which he finally derived was that my behaviour was so bad that I deserved to be lynched.

It is, I suppose, impossible for Jewish parents to take a balanced view of their children as budding mortals with human qualities and defects. If I had hitherto been the source of hope, I immediately became a source of despair. The picture of the doctor disintegrated. I would not even be a schoolmaster, would never get into university and dust would gather forever on the photographless piano top. I tried to explain as best I could that I had no plans to go to university in any case, for I wanted to be a writer and live on a kibbutz. They looked at me, and at each other, wondering if I had not become unhinged as a result of my accident. The words I was uttering did not make sense. They knew what a writer was and what a kibbutznick was. The thought of my being either was ridiculous, but both together was incomprehensible.

We were a close and affectionate family and I could discuss almost anything with my parents except my plans. This was true also of my friends. If their parents wanted to know what they were doing they would ask me, and if my father wanted to know what I was doing he would ask them – not that anyone divulged anything. This was not due to any secretiveness, but a simple desire to avoid unpleasantness and recriminations. We did not expect our parents to see our case, and we did not understand theirs, and the best course for all concerned was to say as little as possible – which, however, made confrontations when they did come all the more painful.

'Vu a schreiber, vos a schreiber?' demanded Father contemptuously. Where a writer, what a writer? I was a foreigner. I did not even speak the language properly (I still don't). I did not know other writers. I knew no one in printing and publishing. I had no contacts whatsoever. How could I start? Where would I start? And even if I did start, how would I make a living? Father had actually met Sholom Aleichem, the greatest name in Yiddish letters, but even he could never make a living, borrowed from everyone he knew, lived a pauper and died a pauper. But as I explained again, I intended to live on a kibbutz.

'A kibbutz?' he said bitterly, what did I think I could do on a kibbutz? I had no qualification, no skill. I would be a *pastech*, a shepherd, because that was all I was good for.

There was no point in explaining that that was all I wanted to be. I let the storm rage over my head till it subsided, packed my bags quietly, and told them I was leaving to join a kibbutz training centre in England.

There was only a token opposition to my going. My path had been eased a little by the fact that Pies had already had his confrontation with his parents and had left for the farm some months before, but I was helped mainly by my fall from grace. Had I been their son the doctor, they would have moved heaven and earth to stop me going, but as I was their son the nobody I was free to leave. And given the sort of creature I had turned out to be, they felt that a few months on the farm could do me no harm and might even do me good.

I hate to be seen off at a port or station by anyone I care for, especially my parents. They accompanied me in the silent taxi

through the dark night to Central Station, and then to the platform where Father fumbled for small change to buy a platform
ticket, and then to my carriage.

'Why don't you take a sleeper?' said Father.

'I can't afford it.'

'I'll pay for it.'

'But I don't want a sleeper,' and we nearly quarrelled again.

It was dry outside but the platform was moist with condensed
steam. A son was being seen off in another carriage by a large,
cheerful family. They sounded as if they had all been drinking
and they began to dance on the platform, singing: 'We're no
awa' to bide awa'.'

'*Goyim*,' said father, half with disdain, half with envy.

PART TWO

I

Country Life

The roads to Thaxted have improved in recent years. One can now get there from London in a little over an hour, as too many Londoners have discovered, and one can hardly move for tourists and traffic and parked cars. There are old antique shoppes everywhere, and expensive-looking restaurants with fancy grillwork, offering scampi and chips and Spanish wines.

Early in 1948, however, roads were bad, cars were few, and one went to Thaxted by train, first from Liverpool Street to Elsenham, and thence on a local train to Thaxted.

I had travelled from Glasgow overnight, deposited my luggage in Liverpool Street, rushed about London catching a glimpse of Westminster here, Buckingham Palace there, got back on a train and reached Elsenham about six in the evening. A number of people alighted at the same time but dispersed rapidly in all directions and I was left with the station to myself. It was March, but the air was soft for the time of the year, with the glowing, lingering dusk one normally expects in summer. A man was busy in a small greenhouse by the station. One could hear the hoot of a distant train, the humming of telegraph wires, the hoarse clatter of a tractor in a nearby field.

I found the Thaxted train in a siding at the back of the station. It had a small, long-funnelled engine like something out of an Emmett cartoon. The two carriages at the back were gas-lit and a uniformed figure with a walrus moustache and bicycle clips took our fares and issued tickets with a pinging machine, like a bus conductor. The train began with a splutter and jolt and chugged its way through the gathering darkness into the misty night. When I got out at Thaxted I felt as if I had reached some never-never land, and in a way I had.

In the 1930s the various Zionist youth movements devoted to agricultural settlements began to establish training farms in Germany and Poland to equip their members with the basic farming skills and to prepare them for the personal revolution necessary for the son of an urban bourgeois Jewish family to adapt himself not merely to a rural, but to kibbutz life.

The kibbutz movement, which is not yet seventy years old, came into being almost by accident. The first kibbutz, Deganiah in the Jordan Valley, was formed after a number of Jewish employees of a land company felt dissatisfied with their role of labourers and decided to farm a tract of their own. They were on inhospitable soil, far from any Jewish settlement and surrounded by hostile Bedouin and if they hoped to survive at all they found they could do so only on a communal basis. Deganiah flourished and its example was followed by others. The ideology came later.

Many of the kibbutzim derived their inspiration from A. D. Gordon, a Russian-Jewish writer and thinker, who emigrated to Palestine in 1904 at the age of forty-eight, to work as a labourer in the orange groves of Petach Tikvah and Rishon Le Zion. He suffered every hardship and nearly died of malaria, but nothing in his experience dissuaded him from his belief that there was something inherently noble in manual work and he preached a 'religion of labour' which found many adherents.

It was a necessary corrective, for Jews in their quest for intellectual excellence tended to disdain manual effort. The *pastech*, who was held out to Jewish children as a warning, was to Gordon the ideal, not only because of the inherent nobility of the work involved, but because there could be no hope of a Jewish commonwealth without a broad base of working men. All the Zionist youth movements including the Bnei Akivah were in part, at least, based on his ideas. To this there was grafted the theories of Ber Borochov, a Russian writer, who tried to synthesise Marxist socialism with Jewish nationalism. Nearly all the Zionist youth movements were affected to a lesser or greater degree by Borochov's thinking, but the Marxism was much attenuated by the time it reached the Bnei Akivah, the religious Zionist movement. Its slogan was *Torah V'avodah* – Torah and Labour, which we translated as the Torah and socialism, and the latter was perhaps more important to us than the former which, given our upbringing, was something we took for granted. We embraced the schoolboy's usual hazy socialism, for the idea of propertyless society, in which everyone works according to his ability and receives according to his needs, is particularly attractive when one is young and propertyless.

There were a number of kibbutz training farms run under the aegis of the Zionist Organisation in Britain, and the Bachad farm in Thaxted, manned by the Bnei Akivah, was one of them. The farm consisted of about 380 acres of good arable land, devoted mainly to cereals, and shortly after I arrived they acquired a further 60 acres belonging to the farmer next door, an old widower called Coney, living by himself in a small cottage by the main Thaxted–Braintree road. He received about £12,000 for his holding and went on a prolonged drinking spree, in the course of which, or at the end of which, he fell, or jumped, into a river and, as if to complete the Englishness of the setting, it was said that he came back to haunt his cottage. I was the first person to sleep in his place after he died.

There was no electricity in the cottage and I walked down the road, bent against the wind, with a hurricane lamp rattling in my hand. Immediately I entered I had a feeling I was not alone. 'Is anyone in?' I shouted; there was no reply, but whatever it was was coming nearer. I could feel it hovering over me, I could smell it, the moist, nauseous smell of something washed up on the shore. I grabbed my lamp and fled down the road to the Bricklayer's Arms for a drink. As a result of this experience, I made up a 'true' ghost story, claiming, with a great many attendant details, that I had actually seen the risen Coney. Some years later I met a middle-aged woman who had put up for the night in the cottage with her husband, and who, turning in her sleep saw an elderly figure in a cloth cap and an army jerkin standing over her. She dived screaming under the blankets, and when her husband woke up, there was no one. 'But I saw him,' she insisted, 'an old man – his breath smelt of stale fish.' I later met several other people who claimed to have seen a vague and mysterious figure in a cloth cap and old army uniform, hovering about the cottage. Then about ten years ago there was a series of 'true' ghost stories on the B.B.C., one of which was about a woman who had bought a small cottage in Essex and who, on winter nights, was sometimes disturbed by the presence of an old man, who seemed to come out of nowhere, never said anything, and vanished as mysteriously as he came, and I am no longer certain whether Coney's ghost was a figment of my imagination or whether he in fact existed.

There were about fifty people on the farm, about twenty of whom were adults in their early twenties, who formed the staff and managed the farm, and about thirty youngsters aged sixteen and upwards, who had come to serve a year's apprenticeship as prospective kibbutznicks. We studied half the day and worked half the day, except during the hay, corn and potato harvests, during which we spent the entire day in the fields. Our studies consisted of Hebrew, Jewish history (including kibbutz ideology) and agriculture, and I picked up a smattering of everything, all of which I promptly forgot. The real education was in the company. Most of the people on the farm, including both staff and pupils, had come to England as German refugees. Jews adapt themselves readily to their surrounding culture and there was nothing to which British Jews adapted themselves as readily as British philistinism. There were enclaves of culture in London, but the provinces, certainly as represented by Glasgow, were largely a wilderness. We were a comparatively cultivated household. Father was a scholar and the house was full of books, dark in cover and dark in content, wholly devoted to holy writ. Father had never in all his life read a novel or attended a play or opera, nor ever expressed a desire to go. He had been to the pictures once, and that to see a film about Dachau. Once, when switching on too early for the news, he heard a snatch of Beethoven's Egmont overture and remarked: *Dos is doch fun himmel* – but this is from heaven! He liked the violin. A sister once took him to a recital given by Yehudi Menuhin and he spoke of the experience for the rest of his life, but he never went again, possibly because he could not afford it. Given his upbringing, his narrowness was understandable, perhaps even inevitable, and given mine, I might have been the same, but for the influence of

Monty Banks and Alison Kidd, and the B.B.C., which gave me my taste for good music.

This, happily, was in the days before good music was segregated from bad. I noticed in the *Radio Times* that an orchestra was to perform and switched on, hoping to listen to someone like Geraldo or Billy Cotton, and found myself listening instead to a symphony orchestra, but without regrets. One could get vouchers from school, enabling one to attend concerts given by the Scottish Orchestra in St Andrews Hall, for a shilling, and Pies and I went nearly every week, and also between us, built up a small collection of pop classics – the Fingal's Cave overture; the serenade from the Fair Maid of Perth, sung by Heddle Nash; Liszt's Hungarian Rhapsody; Brahms' Hungarian dances; Tchaikovsky's Marche Slave, the B Flat Minor Piano Concerto and the 1812 Overture, and several overtures by Rossini. We would also go down to Paterson's music shop in Buchanan Street, play records for an entire morning from which we might – or might not – select one. We were rather self-consciously highbrow and were disdainful of those who were not, and yet, at the same time, were a little pained by our isolation.

All this ended in Thaxted. It may seem Victorian to speak in terms of good or bad company, but if I felt myself corrupted by the Jewish Lads' Brigade, I felt a sense of betterment in Thaxted. Each boy had his own small library of Penguin books, neatly arranged in an orange box by his bed. Some had large art books, and covered their walls with reproductions by Van Gogh, Degas, Renoir, and Matisse. I had hitherto been to a gallery once in my life, and that was to see the Sword of Stalingrad in the Glasgow Art Gallery, during the war, a privilege for which I had to queue for over three hours. Now, by poring over their art books and looking at the reproductions, I was discovering a whole world that had been closed to me. The other boys extended my taste for music, from what Sir Thomas Beecham called 'lollipops' to Beethoven, Bach and Handel. They were also excited by ideas and helped me to think more clearly. To be brought up in an Orthodox family is to accept received wisdom without question, and I thought I was lonely with my doubts and my queries. Here, however, were young Orthodox Jews, who were prepared to question everything. Their upbringing, of course, predisposed them to find predictable answers, but it was something that they asked questions at all.

But with their high intelligence and high-mindedness came a heavy earnestness, and an excessive tendency to preach. I became aware of this fault even in the Bnei Akivah. Our *madrichim*, especially the German ones, could hardly open their mouths without offering a didactic aside . . . 'from ziss we know . . . ziss teaches us . . .' Western society, we were told, was basically decadent and unjust, and to embark on mere careerism was to succumb to the decadence. But in any case, they argued, the option of careerism was not even open to the Jew, and anyone who thought otherwise was repeating the tragic mistake made by German Jewry. History repeated itself and what had happened in Germany could happen in Britain. They did not suggest that concentration camps would be set up on Salisbury Plain, but the state would be playing an increasing role in the life of the nation, there would be a national health service and Jewish doctors and dentists would be unable to get jobs and Jewish businesses would be forced out of business as they had been in Germany and Poland. When we pointed to the number of Jews who were at the top of their professions, they answered that there was always room for genius, and even that was a thing of the past. And finally they argued that given the present trend in inter-marriage, Jewish life in the Diaspora would die out and anyone anxious for the Jewish future of his children had to live in a Jewish state.

I had no doubt that they were perfectly sincere, for they could not have continued with such persistence, such conviction and at such length unless they believed in what they were saying, and one of them, Benno, a tall, good-looking young man, with a great, bristly chin like Desperate Dan, went to Palestine in 1945 as an illegal immigrant, joined the Jewish underground, fought in the 1948 war of independence, was part of the column which captured Elath early in 1949 and thus opened Israel to the Red Sea, and is now a leading member of kibbutz Tirath Zvi.

The other *madrich*, whom we shall call the preacher, or rather *the* preacher, went out to Palestine about the same time. Before he left we made a small farewell party for him and presented him with a leather writing set, and as at every such occasion, there were speeches, including, of course, a speech from the preacher himself which, coming from him, proved to be remarkably brief. We should not, he said, look upon him as a hero, and to be sure with his squat shape, brilliantined hair, smart double-breasted suit with high shoulders, silk tie and stiff white collar, he did not look particularly heroic. We should not look upon him as a hero, he repeated. He was only doing his duty, and if as a result we might feel constrained to do ours, he would have achieved all he wanted. And he shook hands with each of us in turn. He was back in Glasgow a month later, looking a little shame-faced and forlorn. The weather, he said, had been uncommonly hot and it had disagreed with him. I had helped to buy him that leather writing set and wondered whether I should have asked him for my share of the money back. In the circumstances it was perhaps as well that I did not, for I was myself to be guilty of a similar act of betrayal a few years later, though, to do myself justice, I rarely preached and never denounced careerism or argued that Western society was decadent and unjust and that Diaspora Jewry was doomed. On the contrary, it seemed to me that Western society was becoming less unjust, that it held out every prospect of a good life, but that the Jewish state held out the prospect of a better one, at least as far as the Jew was concerned. I certainly entertained no worries about the Jewish future of my children.

There were too many preachers in Thaxted with too much to preach about, and two recurring topics were the *kupah* and *chevratiyuth*.

The *kupah* is the common fund which stands right at the heart of the whole principle of kibbutz life. One receives no money on kibbutz, and the *kupah* provides all, or almost all, one's needs. We had a toy *kupah* on the farm, into which we all paid a few shillings, and from which we drew cigarettes, sweets, pocket money. The light smoker took less, the heavy smoker (within reason) more. What one could not do was to supplement the *kupah* dole with private means. It just so happened, however, that as a result of pieces written long before I came to Thaxted, I had just earned my first three cheques as a writer (from the *Scottish Sunday Express*, *Galaxy*, and *Dublin Opinion* – all of

them now defunct) and I wanted to toast my success, to taste it
on the tongue, to buy some drinks.

I had occasionally been to a pub in Glasgow, but Glasgow
pubs are, or were, drab, cheerless places, dedicated to the serious
business of getting drunk. My discovery of the English pub had
nothing to do with the discovery of drink, for I had no taste for
beer then, but drank cider, or shandy or even (when no one was
looking) lemonade. I cherished the pub with its untroubled
silences as a retreat from the wordiness and introspection of the
farm. We sometimes went down to the pub in a solid group, but
the group spoiled it for me, especially as some of its members
brought their grave earnestness with them, which settled on the
pub like thick mist. I preferred to go either by myself or with
Pies, and in doing so I was committing two sins in one go. I
sinned against the *kupah* by resorting to private means, and I
sinned against *chevratiyuth* – the group spirit – by keeping myself to myself, for, as I was given to understand, the essence of
kibbutz life is to do everything as a team, work together, play
together, eat together. To which I answered that I was not un-
social, that on the contrary, I took immense pleasure in being
part of a group, and would be immensely pained to be kept out
of it. On the other hand I reserved the right to opt out of it
when the mood took me. But if each opted to go his own way
from time to time, what, I was asked, would be left of the group?
To which I replied that not everyone was inclined to go his own
way, and that the group for its own good should disperse more
than it did. But as it was inclined to stick together, I did my own
dispersing, with increasing frequency, for I had not only discovered the pub, I had discovered Essex.

This was my first long stay in the country since I had left
Barovke. I had only been a few months in Annan, and in Castle
Douglas I was incarcerated in a boarding school and was, in any
case, too preoccupied with the war. Now I spent an entire year
in the country. I arrived in March 1948, shortly after the snows
had melted, when the light brown soil was soft and moist and
the young, green tufts of corn were just beginning to thrust their
blades through the ground. Another few months and they would
grow to knee-height and turn yellow, but now the whole countryside, hedgerows, fields, meadows were fresh and moist and green

and shrill with life. There was a poultry farm next to ours, chickens, ducks, geese, turkeys, scratching and clucking behind high wire netting. Beyond it lay the broad crescent of the village green, with a pub – the Bricklayer's Arms, and several large houses on the periphery, and a sheltering wall of tall hedges. They played cricket here at weekends. I had played the game occasionally in Scotland, but I never played it well, nor had the patience to watch it for long, but the players in their white seemed so integral to the setting that I came to watch on Saturday afternoons, less for the game than the scene. It was a slow, slow game. The bowler moved towards the wicket, the batsman towards the ball, the fielders after the ball like a frozen tableau thawing into slow motion. The blue skies, the green pitch, the unhurried figures in white, the backdrop of hedges and tavern, the crescent of deck-chaired spectators, the restrained voices, the gentle clapping : to watch them on a sunny afternoon was to experience a Sabbath of the soul. The marvellous thing about England is that so many of its clichés are benign, and nearly all of them are true.

Near the green there stood, and still stands, a large, two-storey timber house, stained black, with green window frames and a garden exuberant with sweet-peas, hollyhocks and lupins, and beside it, behind a large, sagging gate, a farmhouse, its yard full of querulous poultry, which sold cream teas – toast, home-made scones, home-made cakes, with rich home-made jams and clotted cream. And beyond, one went down the hill past white farm-workers' cottages and small villas to the cross-roads, with Dunmow and Bishop's Stortford in one direction and Thaxted and Saffron Walden in another.

Thaxted is dominated by its great cathedral of a church whose dimensions bear no proportion to the town itself. It is an edifice stranded by time from the days when Thaxted was a centre of the East Anglian wool trade. Another relic of those times is the Tudor Guild Hall. Thaxted and its surroundings had declined with the general decline in British farming, which began in the last decades of the nineteenth century and continued to the outbreak of World War II. The corn trade had been particularly affected, and large parts of rural Essex were impoverished. People moved out to find jobs in London and elsewhere and the drift out from the country was not compensated by any drift in from the city. Electrification, which had reduced counties to the south, south-east and south-west of London into dormitories, had not intruded far beyond Epping Forest and left large areas of Essex untouched. The London and North Eastern Railway was happily the least aggressive and thrusting of the companies and those branch lines which served the little towns and villages around the Essex–Cambridge border, did not so much link them to London as keep them distant. One could grow marrows in some of the sidings. Essex remained the least spoilt of the Home Counties, and Thaxted the least spoilt of the towns.

There was, in 1948, still a forge in Thaxted, with anvil and bellows, and a blacksmith who might have been planted there by the tourist office, for a mighty man was he, with massive chest, and billowing moustache, and neatly brushed hair with a curl on his forehead, like a Victorian waiter. Shopping was something of a social occasion, and there was a chair by the counter even in the Co-op. No two buildings were alike, and the nearer one came to the cobbled approach to the church, the greater their antiquity, from late Victorian at the bottom, to early Tudor at the top. I was in the church almost every week and found something new to explore with every visit, but more often than not, I was content just to sit there in the broad shaft of light pouring in through the great transept windows, and felt as if God was smiling down on me. I had been to numerous places of worship in Scotland, but I found that the kirk was much like the synagogue – perhaps purposely so. It was a building to which people came with their religion and took it away with them leaving few traces of it lingering about the place; whereas I have the feeling that in England people arrive in church with empty, vacant souls and derive their religion from their places of worship. I have been to every major cathedral in England, including (in order of preference) Salisbury, York, Canterbury, Durham, Lichfield, Norwich, Ely, Wells. In York Minster the pleasure I drew from my surroundings left me with a crisis of conscience. In 1190, in the aftermath of the religious fanaticism engendered by the Crusades, the Jews of York were attacked by their Christian neighbours and took refuge in Clifford's Tower, within sight of the cathedral, and there, rather than surrender to the mob, most of them took their own lives. Those who survived were slaughtered as they emerged. Fragments from an ancient prayer inspired by the massacre passed through my mind :

'Sword, wherefore turnest thou all ways, consuming all about thee?
Thou causest the best among us to perish and decline.
Thou wendest thy way even unto the Isles of the Sea.
O Sword of the Lord, wilt thou never be sheathed?'

When I visited Norwich Cathedral some years later, I could not help recalling that the city was the scene in 1144 of the first blood libel in Jewish history, when a boy, later to become known as St William of Norwich, was found dead in the woods and Jews were accused of killing him for ritual purposes. Similar accusations were made in later years against the Jews of Gloucester, Bury St Edmunds, Winchester and Lincoln. The Jewish traveller should not perhaps be too conscious of Jewish history, for otherwise he will see blood-stains everywhere.

The very size of the English cathedrals tend to evoke echoes of their sombre past. The churches are more cheerful and evoke thoughts of Sir Roger de Coverley rather than inquisitorial bishops. The incumbent in Thaxted church in my time was known as the Red Vicar, though when encountered in full canonicals he looked as much a part of the English past as the stones of the church itself.

The nearest large town, which is to say, a town large enough to have its own cinema, was Saffron Walden. It too was dominated by its church, which was not unlike Thaxted church, except that its size bore some relation to that of the surrounding town, and it had an immense variety of architecture, Tudor, Jacobean, Queen Anne, English baroque, Georgian and Regency, sometimes all rubbing shoulders in one street. The Georgian buildings were particularly splendid, though many of them seem to have been taken over by banks, building societies, and insurance offices (all of which seem fortunately to have a penchant for the best domestic architecture in the English county towns).

One summer afternoon Pies and I had tea in Saffron Walden. The tea room was in the front parlour of a large Regency house,

with uneven floors, and with several tables of irregular size, some
oval and some square, and chairs which represented half a dozen
different periods. It was a hot afternoon and wasps buzzed round
the jam dish. We were too contented to have much to say, and
sat gazing out on a row of red-brick houses opposite, with large
polished brass-plates, carrying the names of solicitors, public
notaries, auctioneers.

'No tea shoppes in Israel,' I said.

'No,' said Pies, 'and no pubs.'

'No litany of names.'

'Steeple Bumstead and Bishop's Stortford.'

'Felsted and Stansted.'

'Thaxted and Halstead.'

'Castle Camps and Shudy Camps.'

'Great Yeldham and Little Yeldham.'

'Little Bardfield and Great Bardfield.'

'Bocking and Braintree.'

'To say nothing of Butcher's Pasture.'

'And no Gothic churches.'

'And no hedgerows.'

'And no nip in the air on brisk autumn mornings.'

'And no soft mellowness on summer afternoons.'

We walked home the five or six miles to Thaxted through the
gathering dusk, stopping at every pub on the way, from the Gate
in Saffron Walden to the Fox and Hounds on the outskirts of
Thaxted. The air was heavy with the smell of cut grass and
echoed with distant laughter. The fields glowed in the setting
sun and birds squawked and bustled in the hedgerows. By the
time we reached the Fox and Hounds it was night, and we
lingered there for a long time, smoking one Player's Weights after
another. The small front bar was deserted, save for an old man
with a bushy moustache, who sat gazing into his beer without
uttering a word, as if he was drinking it with his eyes. I was
almost equally silent. I had come to Thaxted to prepare myself
for a life in Israel and was left with a yearning to live in England.

Pies must have read my thoughts.

'Too late, too late,' he said with a flourish of his hand, which
startled the old man. 'Our course is set. We must go.'

And we went.

II

Homecoming

I arrived in Israel with a confused blur of expectations, some derived from illustrations to the King James Bible, some from my reading of Jewish classics, some from old Hollywood films, Zionist films, posters, magazines, newsreels and newspapers, and letters from friends, including Pies – who was already in the land. But nothing I imagined prepared me for what I found, the commotion, the colour, the noise, the shrill, whirring, whooping excitement of the place.

Nowadays most people fly to Israel. In the early 1950s nearly everyone went by ship, and the first sight of Haifa, the blue skies, the blue sea, the white buildings climbing the green slopes of Carmel, in itself induced an immediate sense of exhilaration.

Those were the years of mass immigration. Most of the newcomers were from North Africa, but there were still families arriving from displaced persons camps in Europe, Poles, Rumanians, Hungarians, and wherever a ship docked there were people holding up photos of wives, husbands, children, parents, in the hope that some new arrival might recognise them and have news of their whereabouts. With every boat there was a tearful reunion. As I was descending the gang-plank I heard a shriek, 'Sheika', and a tall lean man a little ahead of me, with sunken eyes and an unhappy mouth, looked around him with confusion and dismay. If it had been possible he might have bounded back up the gang-plank. But too late, a plump, bespectacled woman was upon him, and grasped him in a tearful embrace. Was this a drama within a drama, a man who had thought he'd lost his wife and would rather that she had stayed lost?

After about a week in Israel, I set out to tour the land. I was virtually penniless and hitched my way round the country – and so, it would appear, did half the population. There were strategic points outside every town where one queued for a lift. There was not much traffic around in those days and I was grateful for a lift even from a mule-drawn cart. I travelled only during the day and as darkness fell, which it does with the suddenness of curtains being drawn, I made for the nearest kibbutz.

Kibbutzim in those days offered the sort of ready hospitality to wayfarers one used to find in medieval monasteries, and one always got a meal and a bed for the night. Little was said, however, and no questions were asked, not even as much as a *quo vadis*.

I suppose if one had arrived with a bowler hat, umbrella and striped trousers, one might have got a second glance, but I was in army-surplus khaki, which seemed to be the standard uniform for the greater part of the population, and I blended in with the scene. The only place I did get a second and not entirely welcoming look was at Afikim, a wealthy kibbutz in the Jordan valley, which owned an extremely profitable plywood factory. Its dining room was large and ornate, a building of marble and cedar, with small tables neatly arranged like in a high-class cafeteria, and when I entered with my hob-nailed boots clattering on the gleaming tiled floor, five dozen heads turned round to see who I was, and for a moment I faltered in my step, and had I been less hungry or more moneyed I might have fled, but I braved their stares, sat down among them with a proprietorial air, as if I was a founder-member, and I was fed and watered.

I had friends in several of the kibbutzim, but otherwise my company was provided by other wayfarers and part of the joy of being in Israel at the time was that it was the scene of a floating youth international, but without any pretensions to being part of an alternative culture or harbingers of a new life style. Give a group, no matter how disparate its make-up, a name, and they will begin to think they have a philosophy. This was before hippies or yippies were ever heard of. We were not particularly well-kempt, but the only other thing we otherwise had in common was that we were all short of money. There were no drugs, and hardly any sex. One might find oneself sharing a hut or a tent with a girl or two, but if one has been bumped around on the back of a lorry over the hills of Galilee for the previous three or four hours, the only thing one will want to do when one gets to bed – certainly the only thing I wanted to do – is sleep. We were nearer in character to a Boy Scout jamboree than hippiedom.

The blue skies, the warm sun, the open road, the exquisite scenery, all had their obvious appeal, but being in Israel at this moment, one felt that one was seeing history in the making, one was helping to add a volume to the canon of the Bible : others could sing of a new Jerusalem, here it was being built. Yet when I actually came to live on a kibbutz, there was a sense of anti-climax, largely, I suppose, because one was finally and literally brought down to earth. There used to be a popular Yiddish song which was sung when I was a boy in Barovke :

> *Ven ven zingt a chalutz,*
> *Ven ven ven er iz in kibbutz.*
> *Und ven in kibbutz*
> *i nit to vos tzu essen,*
> *zing er a lied zein hunger tzu fargessen.*
> When when when sings a chalutz?
> When when when when he is in kibbutz,
> and when in kibbutz there is nothing to eat
> then sings he a song his hunger to forget.

But there was little hunger in the kibbutz by the time I got there, nor, for that matter, was there much singing. Israel itself was loud with song. When one passed a bus-load of youngsters, a straggle of school children (one found nothing as regular as a crocodile in Israel) or a company of soldiers, one would more often than not hear them singing on their way. In Thaxted where we played at kibbutz, we would often have a sing-song, going through the whole repertoire of melodies with which we had grown up in the Zionist movement – till the late hours of the night, and not infrequently we danced a *hora*, gathering speed with each round till we dropped with exhaustion. There was little of this in the actual kibbutz. Nowadays no one would expect it, but in the early years of the state, one arrived hugging romantic visions and one of the first facts of life to which I had to reconcile myself was that the kibbutz was no band of rustic merrymakers. I am not even sure if it is in the nature of rustics to be merry, and I asked myself how merry Merrie England could have been – except, of course, that Merrie England had the supreme virtue of being safe set in the past, whereas Merrie Israel was part of the immediate present.

The kibbutz was an earnest place seriously concerned with the serious business of earning its daily bread. The same is possibly true of farming communities everywhere. I have never seen a cheerful farmer outside a tavern and Israeli farmers are in many ways like farmers everywhere, except that they don't drink. There is a certain dourness which goes with agricultural work. It is, even on kibbutz, a lonely occupation. Nearly all gang work in the kibbutz has either been mechanised, or where it does not lend itself to mechanisation, it is generally undertaken by seasonal outside labour. The kibbutznick is largely on his own for much of his working day, driving a tractor, ploughing, sowing, reaping, watering the crops, tending the chickens, and his isolation induces a certain taciturnity. Which did not mean that he lost his Jewish capacity for argument or self-expression. On the contrary, given an ideological debate – and they were painfully frequent in those days, indeed, I began to feel the ideology was the bane of kibbutz life – they found no difficulty in finding words and, indeed, not infrequently got lost in them. What they seemed to lack was any capacity for small talk, the casual exchanges which ease social life. They were disinclined to make any effort to establish new relationships, to talk to people to whom they had nothing to say, and thus anyone who did not arrive in kibbutz with a group of friends and contemporaries, or at least with a wife, found himself in cheerless isolation.

I arrived in Israel on my twenty-first birthday, feeling rather heavy in years and I have not since been able to shake off my obsession with ageing. I had not shown any particular aptitude as an agricultural worker in Thaxted. Tractors and combines seized up at the sight of me. I had worked in the cow-shed for about a month, but was dismissed after I had allowed the bull to impregnate one of his daughters (I thought I had done sufficiently well to know the bull from the cows, let alone one cow from another, or the bull's relatives from his friends). When it came to the crops I was known as 'black-finger' – everything I touched wilted. But I showed some aptitude as an administrator and public speaker. Until 1948 the Bnei Akivah had a sufficient pool of people who had grown up with the movement in Germany, and who served as general secretaries and regional organisers, but once the Jewish state was created they emigrated almost en masse, and thereafter several of us were approached to give at least a year to the movement before going out to Israel ourselves. Thus, after I had spent a year in Thaxted, I spent a year organising the Bnei Akivah in Scotland, which I did with reasonable success, but nearly two years passed before they found a successor and I did not reach Israel until 1951.

I arrived – still harbouring Arcadian visions of myself as a shepherd in the hills of Galilee with a dainty shepherdess by my side, and one of the first things I discovered was that the local shepherdesses did not come all that dainty. These were the austerity years. One subsisted mainly on a diet of bread and potatoes, and most of the kibbutz girls tended to have the shape of an English cottage loaf. There was still in those days a belief in kibbutz that women should not look too womanly, and any girl who was still vaguely attractive tended to hide her attractions under a bushel, by cramming her head into a grubby *cova tembel*, and much of the rest of her into a hideous pair of bloomers. I still remember the sight of a group of well-built girls, bent over some planting job, all in bloomers, their great buttocks raised against the sky, like a row of giant toads squatting in the sun. When I returned to the same kibbutz some twenty years later when diet had improved and ideology had become sane, the same girls, by then on the verge of middle-age, looked like the attractive daughters of their younger selves.

The other fact, which dawned upon me rather more slowly, was that there was no place for the writer or artist in the kibbutz, at least not with the level of artistry that I was able to display, but before I reached that conclusion there were external events which made me reassess my whole attitude to the kibbutz.

The kibbutz movement consists of four different groups, of which the smallest is Kibbutz Hadati, the religious kibbutz movement, to which, as a member of the Bnei Akivah, I belonged. There were about ten kibbutzim in the group including Sheluchot, in the Beth Shan valley, founded in 1948. Sheluchot had suffered from minor religious conflicts among its members and in 1951 a number of families were expelled for alleged desecration of the Sabbath. The laws of Shabbat, of course, are so intricate that if one accepts the most rigorous interpretations one can hardly draw breath or pass water without infringing them. The particular infringement in this case was the playing of the radio, not loudly, to the annoyance of their neighbours, but privately, even secretly (though not secretly enough), in their own homes. When several hundred individuals decide to live together as family, some degree of conformity is called for, and where the individuals are Orthodox, the degree of conformity is even greater, but it never occurred to me that it could be so great that individuals could not be left to decide for themselves whether they could or could not switch on the radio on Shabbat. There is nothing in Jewish law which indicates beyond all doubt that one may not switch on electricity on Shabbat, but most Rabbis – and there is something about the very training of the Rabbi which induces him to play safe – feel that one should not. A great many people, however, do. They would not go to the stake for their right to do so, nor would they even insist that what they do is right, but if it is a sin they feel that it is the sort of sin they can live with. Much of my thinking was by then unorthodox, but all of my habits were Orthodox. I could not live in a kibbutz which was without a synagogue, where they did not eat kosher and where the Jewish festivals were not celebrated in the traditional manner. On the other hand, I could not live in a society where conformity was so strict that one could not even play the radio on Shabbat in the privacy of one's own home. The Sheluchot incident summed up for me that basic defect of any God-fearing society. Everyone tends to keep an eye on everyone else, and everyone is aware of everyone else's eye on him, so that if one begins by fearing one's God, one ends by fearing one's neighbour. In an open society, the non-conformist may incur nothing more than displeasure, but in a closed one, the conforming majority can gang up on the dissenting minority and their sanctions can be harsh and immediate.

And finally there were my own aspirations. I tried to write in my occasional free hours, but fell asleep over my typewriter, or worse, became so stimulated that I could not sleep all night, and apart from two or three newspaper articles, I did not write at all during my year in Israel. I could, I suppose, have asked for an occasional week off to write, and if I had been a Nobel prize winner for literature, I imagine I would have been given it, but as it was I did not have a single volume in print to support my claim. I had nothing in fact, save a handful of crumpled, faded press-cuttings, and as I am one of those writers who thinks he has completed a masterpiece the minute he has written it, but is too pained to read it the moment it is in print, I was rather wary of waving them about. But in any case I already had my answer from an incident at Hasolelim, a kibbutz manned mainly by Americans in Galilee, which was the home of a gifted young painter. I saw his work and admired it immensely, as did many others. It sold well and fetched a reasonably high price and he was given time off and a studio to do his work, but after a while his fellow kibbutznicks, which is to say his patrons, felt that the privileges he was given were unequal to the result. *They* did not think much of his work, and felt that it did not sufficiently reflect socialist realism, and he left.

But if I was not a kibbutznick and a writer, who was I? What was I? The unavoidable answer seemed to be, nothing. I was without a profession, without a craft, without a livelihood. I found myself increasingly alienated from Bnei Akivah ideology. The socialist part of its philosophy was becoming attenuated, the religious part more pronounced and assertive. I should have liked to continue in Israel, but what would I do? I wrote to the editor of the English-language *Jerusalem Post* asking for a job. I don't know if he got my letter, I certainly got no reply and did not feel encouraged to try again. I was without connections and without private means, and I was twenty-two. I still wanted to be a writer, but had no wish to starve in a garret in the attempt. I would have to equip myself with a profession. There was nothing for it but to follow, a little belatedly, the careerist track I had earlier disdained. I would have to go back home and go to university after all.

Before leaving, I took part in an unusual little ceremony. In Latvia I had been called a Polack, in Poland a Lett, in Scotland a foreigner. And now in Israel I came to be known variously as Scottie, Mack or Jock and, as if to live up to my name, I consciously or sub-consciously answered questions with 'och aye' and rolled my r's like Harry Lauder. I also organised what was probably the first Burns Club in the history of the Jewish state, and celebrated what was almost certainly the first Burns supper. The fare, I'm afraid, did scant justice to the immortal memory. The haggis, which was of my making, consisted of *kishke*, which is a traditional Jewish dish, with an infusion of matzo-meal (haggis proper is padded with oatmeal). We could not find pipes or a piper and the dish was therefore piped in with a recorder, but the whisky was genuine Scotch, which can give a festive touch to the most dismal occasion. And the occasion *was* dismal. It was held in what Pies called his flat, but which was in fact a hole on the ground floor of a block of flats originally intended as a garage. There were four of us round the table, three from Glasgow, one a stranger, two Scottish by birth, and all of us more than a little homesick.

Before organising the supper we toyed with the idea of rounding up any other Scotsmen to be found in Israel – there could not have been many – and even thought of approaching the incumbents of the St Andrew's Presbyterian Church to join us. The church stands hard by the British consulate, which in turn overlooks the Jerusalem railway station. There is something very British about railways and railway stations, and the British consulate, with its peculiar flying buttress, looks like the last remnant of a priory which Henry VIII might have knocked about a bit. The church, with its rounded cupolas, has an external character in keeping with its setting, but the interior is sombrely Presbyterian and one could feel the dark spirit of John Knox hovering over the place. Church, consulate and station between them formed an enclave which evoked something of the old country (if only the railway station had had slot machines selling Nestlés milk chocolate!) and I wandered from one to the other on the not infrequent occasions I was in Jerusalem. We decided, finally, not to invite the churchmen because I was uncertain how they would react to my kosher haggis. Moreover, all we had heard about Presbyterian clergymen suggested that they were but abstemious Rabbis, and might not have added much to the gaiety of the occasion.

Jerusalem can be arctic in January, but that particular night was peculiarly warm, and we were in shirt-sleeves as I rose to address the haggis:

> Fair fa' your honest sonsie face,
> Great chieftain o' the puddin race!
> Aboon them a' ye tak your place,
> Painch, tripe or thairm
> Weel are ye wordy o' a grace
> As lang's my arm.

All this uttered from a room where the open door provided the only ventilation. A small crowd gathered to watch the performance, as small crowds will in Israel (they'll gather to watch a man blow his nose).

The celebration was intended partly for amusement, partly as a token attempt to introduce our own particular element of colour in the many exotic strands which make up Israel.

Although I had by now spent the greater part of my life in Glasgow I was strangely unaware of Scotland as a distinct entity. Scotsmen had played a major role in the creation of Peter the Great's new Russia. Scottish soldiers helped to build up his army, Scottish engineers his industries, Scottish doctors his medical services, a Scottish architect his capital, yet in Eastern Europe if Scotland was mentioned at all people tended to think of it as part of England, and when we moved to Glasgow the letters we received from relatives in Latvia and Poland were all addressed in the same way:

> Rabbi A. Bermant,
> 14 Battlefield Gardens,
> Glasgow, S.2,
> Scotland,
> England.

Nor did my Glasgow schooling help me to think of Scotland as essentially different from England. This may have been partly due to the fact that I went to school during the war years when my education was in any case disrupted and when local issues may have been lost in larger ones. Scottish history was not overlooked in the curriculum. One began with the Picts and Scots, with Hibernia and Strathclyde and worked gradually through the centuries till by the time one was of an age to take history seriously, Scotland had ceased to exist. Even when I came to read and admire Burns, I thought of him as rather quaint and *haimish* and that the sort of language he used stood to English as Yiddish stands to German. The comics which provided an important part of my elementary English education, though produced in Scotland, were, as I have mentioned, angled towards England. My first taste of anything distinctly Scottish was provided by the *Sunday Post*, issued from the same stable as the comics, with its own comic section, whose main characters are 'The Broons' and 'Oor Wullie'. Both the Broons and Wullie were solidly working-class. The Broons consisted of three generations of a Scottish family, from grandfather to the bairn. Both grandfather and father wore cloth caps and although the older sons were bare-headed, no one had risen to the dignity of a trilby or bowler, and all spoke in the accents one heard in the trams. Oor Wullie was a crop-haired little chap in dungarees (which should in no way be confused with the jeans worn by middle-class children of a later generation) who, no matter how good his intentions, nearly always got into mischief, and the last box of the strip generally found him nursing a painful backside (Scottish parents evidently didn't spare the rod or the slipper).

And then, of course, there were the comedians – or the 'coamics' as they were known in Glasgow – Harry Lauder, Will Fyffe and many others less good and less memorable. When I first came to Glasgow I found it difficult to understand them, though their very sound was comical and as others laughed, I laughed too. One presumed that the true sound of English was that spoken on the B.B.C. so that any other sound struck one as vaguely funny. Regional accents, Irish, Scottish, North Country, were part of the comedian's stock in trade – he only had to open his mouth and his joke was half told. (The same is true of other languages. Yiddish is largely derived from the German and the Queen's Yiddish, so to speak, was the dialect common among Lithuanian Jews, so that Galician or Polish Yiddish always sounded humorous – at least to Lithuanian ears.) I found that the more one moved among the better educated and the better off, the more they sounded like the B.B.C. It is impossible to exaggerate the influence of the radio, and particularly the B.B.C., on an immigrant family. Those lucid, assured, measured tones, issuing from on high, had a Delphic quality about them, and the fact that they were disembodied added to their authority – I doubt if a television announcer, visible in all his nakedness, could have the same effect. It was from the B.B.C. that I received my introduction to classical music, opera, English literature, serious drama, economics and politics, and which provided us with many of our norms in life. There was a Scottish regional programme, but its announcers too had their Scottishness subdued and spoke in a quasi-B.B.C. English. The effect of all this was to leave one with the impression that if the Irish were a lower form of Scots, then the Scots were a lower form of Englishmen.

The Scottish characteristics which commended themselves most readily to the immigrant Jew were the importance attached to education, the eagerness to get on, the readiness of one generation to sacrifice itself in order to advance the next.

The Jewish immigrant tends to acquire an instinctive awareness of the dominant strain in any society, and take his cue from it, so that as one was assimilated, one tended to become English rather than Scottish and much of Glasgow Jewry tended to bypass its Scottish environment.

I only became aware of Scottish nationalism when I was an undergraduate at Glasgow University (and felt tempted to join the Scottish National Party because it had so many attractive women, including Winifred Woodburn, a contemporary from Queens Park School, who, as Mrs Winifred Ewing, became the first woman Scottish Nationalist M.P.). As a Zionist it was of course easy for me to sympathise with Scottish Nationalism, and I could see many arguments for a greater degree of Scottish autonomy, but the one argument which I could not accept was the one which was most frequently and vehemently advanced, the economic one. Scotland, it was argued, was pillaged and plundered by the English and never allowed to develop its full potential, but it was in fact the English connection which enabled it to develop what little potential it had. Scotland, though a small, poor and barren country, had, by the end of the sixteenth century, four large universities which were among the foremost seats of learning in Europe. Scotland itself could never have employed the talents it nurtured, and if it had not been for the openings provided by England and her colonies, much of that talent would have been soured and frustrated. I have often had the feeling that the Act of Union put England in the grasp of Scotland rather than the other way about. I do not think that the mere list of Scottish Prime Ministers from Bute to Sir Alec Douglas-Home is particularly significant, for most of them, like Bute, Rosebery, and Sir Alec himself, were Englishmen, who happened to have Scottish titles and Scottish estates. What is far more significant is the number of Scotsmen one finds in leading positions in industry, commerce and the civil service.

When I was at Glasgow University, Arts graduates were virtually unemployable in Scotland unless they went on to take teaching diplomas and became schoolmasters or divinity degrees and became divines. I had no ambition to be either, and in my final years at university filled in countless applications for jobs, all of them in the south, for apart from anything else, it was a way of seeing England at someone else's expense. I found, as did several of my friends, that the preliminary interviews were generally conducted by some glossy underling, usually an Englishman with a public school accent, but if one was short-listed and brought before a senior figure, one generally came face to face with some rough-hewn Scot. There is, in fact, a Scottish freemasonry as there is a Jewish one and no doubt one reason why we were short-listed was the fact that it was often a Scot who did the listing, but when this happened with Shell Oil and Shell Chemicals, British Petroleum, Proctor and Gamble, and Mars (Bars) it seemed to be too much of a coincidence. It happened even with Marks and Spencer where I thought I had a special entry and when I was invited back for a second interview, I fully expected to be received by Lord Marks himself, for were not his parents and mine immigrants from Russia? But I was not seen even by Spencer. I was received instead by a tall, lean, white-haired man called McPherson or McLean (and I didn't get the job).

If Scottish nationalism is now becoming a potent force, it is, I believe, because the pickings in the south have become thin and the prospects in the north, with the discovery of North Sea oil, are becoming fat. It seems to me that Scottish nationalists are acting like brash nephews, who have lived off a rich and indulgent uncle for many years and, on coming into their own inheritance, are preparing to renounce the relationship.

On the other hand I regret the blurring of the Scottish identity which has arisen out of the association with England and I have always had a slight twinge of regret that one does not pass any striped barriers or have one's passport stamped as one passes from England into Scotland. One of the great disappointments of travel in America is that one can traverse vast areas without being quite certain as to where one is or where one has been, without any sense of coming upon anything new. This is beginning to happen in Europe, and the same could happen to the British Isles.

I am also afraid of bigness, big crowds, big buildings, big cities, huge entities. Big to me means worse, that nations can get to a size as many have done where they are ungovernable, and there is much to be said for staying small – provided, of course, one can get away with it. The main drawback to being small is that one is so often swallowed by the big. Latvia, Lithuania and Estonia were all small, but given their neighbour they would have had slight prospects of survival even had they been big. In Western Europe, however, it has been possible to be small, and stay small with the minimum of molestation, but as the political need for union has declined, the economic need has increased. There are, of course, obvious economies of scale and the larger the market, the greater the scope for economic growth, but I doubt if, given the present standard of living, the benefits accruing from a larger market are equal to the social loss involved in the fading of national identity.

If one argues, as I would, that Britain should have stayed out of Europe, one can equally argue that Scotland should get out of Britain, and, indeed, there are many who have put forward this argument, but if there are virtues in smallness, it does not mean that the smaller one is, the greater one's virtues.

Scotland and Israel are both about the same size (or were before 1967) with about the same population. Although there is much to be said for being small, both have seen in their smallness something like a proof of excellence and, as if it is not sufficient proof, both point to the Diaspora beyond them to show that they are less small than is generally believed. 'Wha's like us?' the Scots will ask. In Israel they don't even ask; they already have the answer. What is often maddening to outsiders is that the good conceit which both have of themselves is not entirely unjustified.

Scots conceit, however, is at least mundane.

The Scots believe there is no one like them on earth, the Israelis that they are unmatched in either earth or heaven. About fifteen per cent of Israel's population are believers to the extent of voting for the religious parties, about forty per cent to the extent of sending their children to religious schools; perhaps half of the population attends synagogue more than once or twice a year. The other half is either non-religious or anti-religious, but nearly all have a lingering belief that they are, in the words of Isaiah, 'a light unto the nations'. It is a comforting belief and is not in fact peculiar to Jews. 'All my life I have thought of France in a certain way', wrote de Gaulle in his *War Memoirs*, 'as dedicated to an exalted and exceptional destiny. Instinctively I have the feeling that Providence has created her either for complete success or for exemplary misfortunes.' Jewish misfortunes have been exemplary and not even the non-believer likes to feel that they have been gratuitous.

And there is, of course, more than misfortune to sustain the belief. Israel's population is extremely heterogeneous but nearly all have this much in common, a close knowledge of the Old Testament. The knowledge may not always convince one – it certainly has not convinced me – that Jews have a right to Palestine by divine promise, but it is difficult to read, say, the Psalms, in Hebrew, or indeed in English (except perhaps in the New English Bible), and not feel that they are divinely inspired, and the Bible is accepted even by many so-called non-believers as an expression of the Jewish mission.

There are Israelis – *kleine Israelites* one might call them – who would like to rest from this burden and be a nation as other nations. This feeling became fairly widespread in the mid-1960s, when Israel had been at peace for almost a decade, and there came into being a group called the Canaanites who wanted to shrug off their Jewish past and Jewish connections and so to speak, turn native, very much as many individual Jews in the

Diaspora have yearned to shrug off their Jewishness and blend into their background. But to an extent Israel is sustained in her Jewishness, very much as individual Diaspora Jews were sustained in theirs, by external hostility. The so-called Canaanites were among the first casualties of the 1967 war and they have hardly been heard of since, and the very isolation of Israel, the extent that she is kept distant by man, has tended to enhance the belief that she is cherished by God.

III

England, Mine England

I returned to Glasgow with the intention of going to university, but without any qualifications to do so, and almost as soon as I unpacked, I sat down to prepare myself for the entrance examinations. It was the beginning of February 1952, the examinations were at the end of March, and I had, in the course of seven weeks, to go over the ground normally covered in school in two or three years. I surrounded myself with the necessary books and papers, and for the next seven weeks buried myself in them, surfacing only for meals, and sleep (and not much of that either). I saw no one, spoke to no one, did not listen to the radio or read a paper, and the only recreation I allowed myself was a two-mile walk round the periphery of the park last thing at night. When Father or Mother put an anxious head round the door to ask if I wasn't over-doing it, or if I wanted a cup of tea, I snarled at them.

A day or two after the examinations I had to attend a Jewish wedding, and, as was the custom in those days, they played the National Anthem after the loyal toast. We all stood up and a stout woman next to me even sung the words, her under-chin quivering with patriotic fervour : 'God save our gracious Queen, long live . . .'

'Our gracious *queen*,' I said when she had finished. 'What's wrong with our king?'

'Didn't you know?' she said in amazement. 'He's dead.' He had died the previous month. I felt like Rip Van Winkle.

To the surprise and delight of my parents (and not a little to my own surprise) I passed the examination and my father asked a little diffidently if I would perhaps like to study medicine. No, I said firmly, I would study economics. He was not quite sure what that involved (neither for that matter was I), but he was grateful enough for the fact that I was going to university at all and did not want to expect too much of fortune : I was a son reclaimed. My mother dusted the piano top.

I hoped to become a journalist and contemplated reading English Language and Literature, but the literature course, I discovered, was largely devoted to Beowulf and Chaucer, so I turned to economics and politics instead, but at the end of the first year my ambitions took a different course. The old Jewish love of study for its own sake was asserting itself. Glasgow University, though founded in the sixteenth century, was moved to its present site in the nineteenth century. Its architect, Gilbert Scott, one of the great figures of the Gothic revival, was also the architect of St Pancras Station, and it indeed bears a close resemblance to St Pancras, though its stones are of a more sombre hue. I loved the place, for all its mock antiquity, the tiered lecture halls, the company of learned men and learned books, and wondered if I could not perhaps settle among them for good.

I did reasonably well in my first year. When I did even better in the second year I allowed myself to believe that I was possibly in line for a 'first'. There were no new universities cropping up all over Britain in the early 1950s and one did not even consider applying for an academic job with anything less than a 'first'. At the same time I was troubled about the three years I had spent in the Bnei Akivah and the kibbutz. I later came to appreciate that those were possibly the most productive years of my life and allowed me to acquire the maturity necessary to benefit from university, but at that time I regarded those years as lost, and was obsessed with the need to catch up on myself. I decided to attempt a four years' honours course in three years. My tutor thought it could be done, but it was not a prudent thing to do. And indeed it was not, for I was at the same time headmaster of the religious classes in the Pollokshields synagogue, which took up most of my evenings and Sunday morning, I was an active member of the University Union and secretary of the University Labour Club. I was also founder of the Adam Smith Society, which I believe is still flourishing, and, most time-consuming of all, I kept falling in and out of love, usually with the same girl, but I nevertheless telescoped my last two years into one, sat my finals in May 1955, and in June went off to a post-graduate seminar in American Studies in Salzburg. My tutor had kindly undertaken to cable the result and I found it waiting for me when I arrived – SECOND. It blackened my summer. I don't know how, given the circumstances, I could have thought that I was even within sight of a 'first', but I had decided finally and firmly that I would be a writer/academic and would not even allow myself to contemplate the possibility of a 'second'. More-over, I had an eye on a post-graduate award tenable at a Cam-bridge college, which would have required a 'first'.

I have in recent years been to about twenty or thirty different universities in Europe and America, but I know of none with the tranquil beauty of Cambridge. In 1955 it still basked in the glory of Keynes, and apart from its physical and social attractions, it had a natural attraction for anyone who hoped to become an academic economist; but what particularly drew me to Cam-bridge was the memory of my Thaxted days. Cambridge was about twenty miles from Thaxted and I had been there on a number of occasions to visit the colleges or to go to the Arts Theatre. One autumn evening I was walking along King's Parade, with undergraduates on bicycles hurrying in all directions, their gowns flapping in the wind, and heard the sound of a choir coming through the mists and felt a sharp pang of regret that I was about to leave England and was not going to university. Now that I was back I wanted to savour thoses scenes and those sounds.

The picture of Cambridge vanished from my mind as I crumpled the telegram. I had no idea what to do next. The Salzburg seminar was housed in a magnificent eighteenth-century rococo palace, once the home of the Bishops of Salzburg, with formal gardens like a minor Versailles. But I was almost unaware of my surroundings and spent much of my time in the library sending out letters in all directions applying for every grant, award and scholarship I had heard of, and quite a few I hadn't heard of, and finally I found a small bursary which enabled me to enrol for a post-graduate degree at the London School of Economics. Harold Laski, who was to the L.S.E. what Keynes had been to Cambridge, had died in 1950, but something of his spirit still haunted the place, and it was then perhaps at the height of its reputation. It also, of course, meant that I would be able to live and work in London, which I thought would also have its compensations. I was mistaken.

If the year in Breslev had been one of the darkest in my life, I was now entering upon another. I suppose if one proceeds through one's university years gently and leisurely, one can approach the period beyond with equanimity. I had gone through mine at a gallop, rushing from lecture to tutorial, to library, to committee room, to debate, to Hebrew class, always trying to make up for lost time, and going about my work as if the end of the world were nigh. And then, as if they had crept up from behind, the finals were upon me, and day after endless day, bent over examination papers, one eye on the clock, one eye on the paper, wondering how to cram in all one has to say in the little time in which one has to say it, the hand almost paralysed by the need to rush. And then the Great Day. Mother, in an outfit she normally wears at weddings, among the great crowd in the Bute Hall, and me, in tuxedo and gown, among the graduates in the front row. There is a loud bustle, a cheerful expectant chatter. The platform before us is empty but for the chairs and desk. Somebody begins to hum 'Why are we waiting?' and we all take up the song loudly, boisterously, so that when we come to 'Why, Why, Why?' we almost raise the great, vaulted roof. A janitor comes on to straighten the chairs, and gets a loud cheer, and a minute later the platform party enters, preceded by a mace bearer, and behind him, in his richly embroidered gown, the Chancellor, Lord Boyd-Orr, looking like an overblown carica-ture of a Scotsman, with a face like hewn granite, and a lordly nose which is not merely one feature among others, but presides over his face, and a pair of shaggy eyebrows that almost brush the lapels of anyone who comes near him. There is a brief speech, but not brief enough for some of us, who are beginning to get a little restless, and then to the business of the day. First the D.Scs., then the D.Litts., then the Ph.Ds. As their names are called, they rise, advance, shake the hand of the Chancellor, and are handed their diploma, all in alphabetical order. I am the first of the M.A.s to be called. I rise, advance, stretch out my hand to be shaken, and it is left in the air – only post-graduates receive a handshake. I am given my diploma in a narrow roll like a truncheon, and I emerge into the lobby where the photographers are waiting, Chaim Icyk Bermant, M.A. A few days later there is a graduation photo on the gleaming piano top. (It was later to be joined by others, as I acquired further degrees, mainly I suppose, to compensate my parents for the long wait they had for the first one.) And then the anti-climax. I had redeemed myself in my parents' eyes, and Uncle Louis and Aunt Leibe Sheine also looked on me as a man reborn, but the world otherwise seemed strangely unimpressed that there was a full-blown Master of Arts abroad among them. One felt a chilly sense of anti-climax.

But worse was to come. I had, during those last, sad days of summer, cheered myself with thoughts of London. Londoners can probably not appreciate the extent to which London dwells in the imagination of the provincial. I used to study the theatre and concert reviews in the *Manchester Guardian* and the *Observer,* the advertisements for political meetings and rallies in the *New Statesman* and *Tribune,* the social meetings and dances advertised in the *Jewish Chronicle,* and took a vicarious pleasure in merely reading them. Here were the great galleries, the National, the Tate, the Courtauld Institute, the Victoria and Albert, here was the Albert Hall and the Festival Hall : here were the Proms. And the place was steeped in literary associations, Dickens, Galsworthy, Thackeray. I would visit the house where Dr Johnson lived and worked, and the taverns where he held court, visit the Fitzroy and the other Soho taverns, the Louis Macneice country, where men of letters assembled to talk and drink. The more I thought of London the more I felt almost compensated for the fact that I had failed to get a 'first'.

The first shock of London was the expense of just being there. I had been living at home nearly all my life and although I used to pay a pound or two towards the housekeeping I had no inkling of the financial realities of independence. I descended on London with the vague thought of finding myself a small flat not too far from the London School of Economics. I tried first in Bloomsbury and was quoted a rental for which one could have bought a flat outright in Glasgow. I lowered my sights and tried for a room; found I could not afford even that, retreated further and further back up the Piccadilly line from Holborn, settled finally in a chilly ruin beyond Finsbury Park, and found that after I paid for my rent and fares, I hardly had anything left for my meals. For the first time in my life I was poor. We had been penniless in Barovke, but there we were paupers among paupers and had never, in fact, thought of ourselves as poor. In Glasgow I had been among the golden boys. While everyone about me subsisted on tiny bursaries, I was earning nine pounds a week as headmaster of the Pollokshields synagogue classes, and the occasional thirty shillings from one of the local papers. I bought books, papers, gramophone records, carpeted and furnished my room, travelled. Semi-strangers would approach me in the Union bar, staring hopefully into my beer and ask my opinion on the events of the day. While others drank draught bitter, I had Carlsberg Special. Now suddenly I found myself a pauper. I remember standing outside Lyons' tea-shop by Holborn station one bleak November evening, counting my pennies to see if I could afford a cup of tea and still have enough money to get to my lodgings.

There is a scroungers' international nowadays, who seem to live out of each other's pockets, but if it existed then I felt too old to be part of it. I went to the theatre once or twice, and only sat in the gallery of course.

Galleries are built in the belief that the poor are also short, whereas I am (or was, for I have shrunk in middle-age) well over six foot and I sat in great discomfort. I had found the 'gods' uncomfortable even as a schoolboy, but survived the discomforts cheerfully; now I found it not only discomforting, but humiliating. I felt that at my age and with my qualifications I should have had a place in the stalls. Moreover, the main pleasure (and, given the quality of some of the plays, the only pleasure) in theatre-going was to go with a pretty girl, and with provincial sense of chivalry I felt that one could not take a pretty girl, or indeed a plain one, to the 'gods'. But what I felt was academic, for not a girl I knew would have gone to the 'gods'.

Although I was by now more or less a confirmed heretic, I was still an incorrigible synagogue-goer. I would set out on Shabbat morning with the intention of going for a walk, but would find myself straying almost without thinking into synagogue. There one would get talking to strangers, be invited home for a glass of whisky and lunch and more often than not, there would be a daughter or daughters in the house. I came to London with mild hopes of debauchery, but found myself a prisoner of my own respectability, going out with nice Jewish girls from nice Jewish homes, and nice Jewish girls expected to be taken out and paid for, and given what was called a 'good time', which is to say, an expensive time. My own idea of a good time would have been wholly inexpensive, but they were not the sort of ideas which one could, in those days, put to a nice Jewish girl of good, or, indeed, bad family, and I remained celibate and alone.

Apart from visits to the synagogue, the nearest thing I found to company was in the crowds at the Promenade concerts in the Albert Hall, but there too, hemmed in among schoolboys and teenagers, I felt very conscious of my age. Gradually, after some weeks in London, I became aware of others in the crowd who experienced the same difficulty of blending in with it, or being swept along by it, people of about my age or a little older, the genteel poor of London, who were beyond the age to find poverty a joke – schoolmasters, clerks in insurance offices and travel agencies, counter-hands in the Knightsbridge stores, junior, and perhaps not so junior, editors in the large publishing houses, minor civil servants, people with some taste and discernment brought up to enjoy things they could not afford. They were not, I should imagine, people in reduced circumstances, but like me, people from humble circumstances, who had entertained the hope that they might rise to something better. I would see them at the bleak little meetings in the cheerless little venues advertised in the back pages of the *New Statesman*. I had the advantage over them in that I had no need to keep up appearances. The only person I saw with any frequency was my supervisor, an elderly bachelor, who looked and sounded as if he had just got out of bed and was about to get back into it, and I rarely had to change out of my corduroys, whereas the others were, in comparison, immaculately dressed and spent much time scratching stains out of their Burton suits. Though well-kempt, they had the slightly harried look of people in lodgings, men without mothers, wives, girlfriends, who slept alone, and more often than not, ate alone and who could not even cheer themselves with a hot bath without giving due notice to their landlady. It was, I discovered, one thing to have rooms in London, and quite another to have a room. In the former, one is a man about town, in the latter, a prisoner. We were lower-middle-class people, with upper-middle-class aspirations and working-class incomes. This urge to be away from home was largely a middle-class phenomenon. Working-class people, I found, were content to stay at home till they married or even after, so that they were left with surplus funds to buy a drink, go to a dance hall, buy motor bikes and even cars, and to enjoy life while still of an age to find it enjoyable. Besides which, even in the 1950s, a factory hand in Dagenham or a dock worker in West Ham was often earning more than a school teacher, and infinitely more than a research student.

I was particularly unfortunate in my lodgings. There is, between the expensive terraces of inner London and the leafy suburbs of outer London, a vast crescent of decaying boroughs, which once formed the homes of the Victorian middle-class, Holloway, Hornsey and Harringay, Stoke Newington and Hackney, Leyton and Leytonstone, composed of large, crumbling, three-storey dwellings, sliced up into flats. I lived in a house which had not yet been converted into self-contained apartments, but every dank corner of which was let out to different families and individuals. The proprietor and his wife lived in the basement. He was a small, sickly looking man with thick glasses. She was a tiny bag of skin and bone, with high, flushed cheek-bones, and eager, malicious eyes behind large slant-eyed glasses, which made her look almost demoniac. She was a splendid cook and house-keeper, but as seems often the case with good cooks, she was a vicious little woman, with a pointed, restless little tongue which seemed to glisten with poison. The world had done her some terrible little wrong; I wasn't sure what it was, but she had no conversation beyond complaint and denigration. If she was poisonous, he was cantankerous, and ill-will radiated from the iron grill about their windows.

A large television set with a tiny screen dominated their small living room and they would settle down before the set when even-ing transmissions began and not stir until the news, when they would rise for a cup of tea and a biscuit, and then settle down again till God Save the Queen.

The phone was in their living room. One night it rang and they didn't answer. It continued to ring and they still didn't answer. I had a feeling that the call was for me, and it was important. I rushed downstairs and barged into the living room. It was for me, a long distance call, but it was not a particularly good line and I could hardly hear the caller above the noise of the television. 'Would you mind turning the set down?' I said. 'It's long distance.' They ignored me.

'Would you mind turning the set down?' I shouted. They still ignored me, and I strode over and switched off the set. They looked at me, and looked at each other, open-mouthed, aghast, as if I had strangled someone before their eyes, and it took them some time to find their voices. I finished my call, put down the receiver, and went back upstairs, without saying a word.

A few minutes later there was a knock at my door and I found them both outside.

'You'll have to go,' he said.

'I'm going,' I said.

And I went.

I missed Glasgow and in particular I missed Glasgow University, and couldn't help comparing it with the London School of Economics, which had neither the look nor feel of a university. It was tucked away behind the huge office blocks in Holborn, looked like an office block itself and might have been erected to accommodate the London branch of a provincial insurance company. It was not built round any sort of courtyard, as, say, the Prudential is. There were no quads, no trees, not a blade of grass in sight, but asphalt, concrete and Portland stone. It was not a particularly spacious place at the best of times and between lectures there was such a milling of crowds that it was impossible to move. Porters and other non-academic staff in Glasgow had been genial, friendly and helpful; here they were gruff and insolent, as if the revolution had come and the workers were already in control. The food in the canteen was at best inedible and at worst poisonous, and students came out on strike against it – which is about the only time in the history of the L.S.E. when its students struck with just cause. The library was overcrowded and uncomfortable and one could not use it without being searched for stolen books (in Glasgow one came and went at will, and even undergraduates had access to the shelves). I attended some undergraduate debates, but found them disappointing. This may have been due in part to the contempt which new graduates have for undergraduates, but it seemed to me that in Glasgow students were more inclined to think things out for themselves, and even where their arguments were facile, they were generally good-humoured and sometimes witty, whereas here the reasoning seemed to be pre-packed and clogged with clichés and slogans and utterly humourless. They had the presumptuous gravity of people who think they can put the world in order.

Nor did I have a particularly high opinion of my fellow research students, most of whom seemed to be from Africa and Latin America, though there was also a considerable sprinkling of tall, lean, earnest young graduates from North America. We had our own common room and most of the discussions seemed to be about the enormities of British and American colonialism. British colonialism I could understand, but American colonialism? My research work was concerned with a comparative study of parliamentary institutions which involved me in much reading of modern history, and it seemed to me that no great power in history had ever acted with such lack of arrogance and such a deep sense of responsibility. The Korean war was behind us, the Vietnam war yet ahead, and it seemed to me that if Britain and France had acted with the alacrity in the thirties which America showed in the fifties, we would have been saved the horrors of World War II. One sensed an idealism in American policy, which, even if wrong-headed, was distinct from the grubby opportunism one found elsewhere, and what surprised me in particular was the extent to which the American students joined in heaping calumnies upon American policies, institutions and office holders. Eisenhower was President, a cheerful nonentity, who spent most of his time on the golf course, and I could not see how anyone could view him, as they did, in a sinister light. I had the feeling that exile makes patriots of us all, and that if I was exiled from hell I would find a good word to say for the devil. I wondered if there was anything in the upbringing of those young, privileged Americans which made them regard their homeland with contempt.

As it was I found myself defending even Britain's imperial

record and argued that in any case what Britain had done in India after 1857 and in South Africa after 1900 was a great deal less important than what she was doing now. To which a very tall, very lean young man from Karachi retorted that Britain may be pulling her people out, but that her money was still there, strangling the economies of her former colonies; and he added in the same breath that the rich countries such as America and Britain were doing nothing to help the economies of the poor. 'These people should be taken seriously,' a young, curly-haired Israeli urged me, 'tomorrow half of them are going to be Prime Ministers.' And, alas, almost half of them are.

The saving grace of the L.S.E. – indeed the only grace it had – was its teachers, but they did not, so to speak, live above the shop as they do in Oxford and Cambridge, or near the shop as in Glasgow, nor did they linger about the place for a moment longer than they had to, and as soon as their lecture or tutorial was finished, they would rush out to keep an appointment with a television company, or in the City, or in one of their half a dozen or so extra-mural activities, which seemed to occupy them more than their intra-mural ones. The only time my own supervisor, a brilliant scholar and likeable man, showed any alacrity at all, was when the time apportioned for our meeting was up, and even as the clock approached the hour, his hand would, quite instinctively, reach out for his brief case, and if I ever tried to engage him on a topic outside my subject, he would say: 'Interesting point, young man. Let's talk about it when we next meet – what?'

I applied for a supplementary grant at the L.S.E. but failed to get one and seeing no other escape from poverty, got myself a job as a supply teacher. This, strictly speaking, was against the rules, but again strictly speaking, I had to eat and I had no compunction on the matter. My economic problems were doubly solved. I now had money, and no time in which to spend it, and I would rush straight from school to the L.S.E., or rather the library in Senate House, Bloomsbury, where I now did most of my work. I was back in double harness as I was in Glasgow University, working long hours at great speed, but I felt that I was at least beginning to catch up on myself, and sheer weariness was a far more wholesome sensation than the constant feeling of constriction which comes with penury.

I spent some three years at the L.S.E., had many changes of address, and lived for a time near Tunbridge Wells (which had an excellent train service to Charing Cross, which in turn was about ten minutes walk to the L.S.E.). During my excursions through the surrounding countryside on Sunday afternoons I made a number of friends, including one elderly lady who was an earnest student of the next world, because, as she put it, 'I think this world has had it, don't you?' She would invite me to tea on Sunday afternoons and introduce me to friends : 'You must meet Mr Bermant, he's a Jew,' which made it sound like a profession (which it can be), and I began to feel a sort of Jew in residence. I was not the only Jew in Tunbridge Wells, but I was probably the only one who could quote scripture. I was also going through one of my several bearded phases and looked as if I might be vaguely related to one of the minor Prophets, and became something of a social lion. The inland watering-towns are the last resort of Godliness in the British Isles, for a large part of their population is of an age where the hereafter is of more than mere academic interest. They also harbour a large number of maiden ladies, often elderly sisters living together, with private means and ample time to speculate on this world and the next, and the church and church affairs formed their principal occupation. Churches would be the scene of traffic jams every Sunday morning as chauffeurs pulled up in large cars and unfolded wheelchairs. Even the back streets rang with religion at such a time and were free of the boisterous paganism one found in the working-class areas of other English towns, for here, eking out their small pensions, lived women who had been in service, and who had received their religion as a hand-me-down from their employers.

I became particularly friendly with two old ladies, white-haired, blue-eyed, red-cheeked, who looked alike – possibly from their long years together – though they were not in fact sisters. They must have been dazzling in their youth and looked almost radiant in old age. Had I met them nowadays, I suppose I might have suspected they were lesbians, but I don't think I was even aware of the expression then. They were so devout, so unobtrusively kind, so incapable of uttering an uncharitable sentiment, that I thought of them as nuns in mufti. One of them would break off her conversation from time to time to have a lump of sugar soaked in brandy, and would apologise : 'You will excuse me, my dear, but my heart will keep stopping.' Their talk, presumably for my benefit, was almost all of the Bible, and Job and Amos and Nehemiah and John the Baptist would enter into their conversation as if they were people they had known at some earlier stage in their career.

They had numerous friends who lived in large houses gloomy with religion, with stained glass windows on the staircase landings and grandfather clocks and large oak chests in the hall, and large drawing-rooms full of brass and copper ornaments and boxes inlaid with ivory, Hindu idols, hookahs, Persian miniatures and Chinese vases, all of them suggesting a lengthy sojourn in the east, and here and there the haughty portrait of some sashed proconsul. Both homes and owners looked as if they had seen better times.

There was an International Spiritual Congress during my year in Tunbridge Wells. The Imam of Woking was present, as was the Archimandrite of some Greek Orthodox sect, a Jesuit father in monkish garb, a plump, androgynous representative of a Hindu sect with sleek, black hair and eyes like door-knobs, and a lean, crop-haired figure in saffron, whose teeth chattered for much of the cold afternoon, and who spoke with a broad Yorkshire accent. I, hardly less incongruously, represented the Jews. The star of the occasion was the late Air Chief Marshal Lord Dowding, a tall, lean man, with a quiet voice and neat little moustache and eyes that looked as if they beheld scenes invisible to others, and when he spoke, it was clear that they had – objects from outer space. There was also a handsome young curate with black hair and pink cheeks, who looked like an over-grown choir boy, who presumably represented the Church of England.

Each of us had to read a small extract from some writing illustrating our philosophy and I came equipped with a story of Rabbi Akivah, who was a sort of pre-Panglossian Pangloss, to the effect that all is for the best, in this the best of all possible worlds. However, the chap in saffron, with the north country accent, got in first with a quotation from Krishna which said much the same thing, and therefore when it was my turn I quoted a famous saying by Rabbi Hillel : 'Love thy neighbour as thyself.' It was the shortest contribution to the conference, and caused a buzz all round the hall which, I later discovered, was due to the fact that no one had understood a word I said. The *pièce de résistance*, perhaps, came from the young curate, who read a lengthy extract from Ella Wheeler Wilcox, the gist of which was that if you look after your dog, mankind will look after itself. I have heard similar utterances from other Anglican clergy and was sometimes left with the impression that the Church of England was the R.S.P.C.A. at prayer.

I became friendly with the vicar of a parish no great distance from Tunbridge Wells, and I envied him his ancient church, his spacious vicarage, his large library, his beautiful garden, his china tea-service, his whole way of life, and sitting in front of his drawing-room fire with a cup of tea in my hand one bleak afternoon, I confessed that if I were to choose my reincarnation I would opt to be an English country parson.

'But why wait till then?' he asked. 'What's to stop you being one now?'

'Several things.'

'Such as?'

'I can't accept the divinity of Christ.'

'But my dear boy, who does?'

In addition to my several friends, who lived mainly on the periphery of the town, I found Tunbridge Wells itself very attractive, and remained there, teaching at a local college after I had taken my degree at L.S.E. One thinks of it as the redoubt of blimpish colonels nursing their prejudices and gout in chandeliered pump rooms. There was a pump room, but it was used as a venue for chamber music concerts, which went superbly with the Regency setting. The colonnaded 'Pantiles' with it bay-windowed restaurants and tea-shops formed the most exquisite promenade in the British Isles, but with the original well, which is the source of Tunbridge Wells's prosperity, it became of course a tourist show-piece, and tends to belong to the visitor rather than the inhabitants. But it was the town beyond the Pantiles, its nineteenth-century buildings still intact, that I found particularly attractive, and the stately villas on the edge of the town, the exuberant gardens, the lawns that looked as if someone had been over them with an electric shaver. Many of the villas have been broken up into flats or converted into hotels, guest houses and private schools, but their stately, external character remains.

I was a teacher in one of those private schools, which was basically a very expensive, well-equipped crammer for the sons of Arab oil sheiks, but it also housed a number of tall, lean Persians, tiny, dusky Yemenites, a few bombastic Greeks and the occasional dumb, hulking Swede. Most of the boys were in their late teens, and at weekends the place was besieged by teenage girls from town. They were not allowed on to the grounds of the estate itself, but they clustered round every entrance and exit and the police sometimes had to be called to clear them away.

I saw one of my students, a young Arab of about twenty, going into town with a fresh faced youngster of about twelve, and I later asked him who his friend was.

'Friend, sir? He no my friend. He come invite me fuck his sister. You fuck her too, sir, I pay.'

Events had turned full circle and Tunbridge Wells was coming to assume the role of Port Said.

I might have settled in Tunbridge Wells. The job was undemanding, I liked my students, the pay was adequate, my quarters comfortable, the setting beautiful and on free afternoons I went exploring Kent as far as the Weald and the Medway towns on one side, and Sussex as far as the Downs on the other. I also found time to write, contributed occasional articles to newspapers and magazines and was gathering energies to begin my first novel.

London had been too vast to be encompassed even mentally. One had to settle oneself in one particular quarter and seek one's milieu there, and had I been content to think of myself as a citizen of Stoke Newington or Ilford, or even Golders Green, I might have been less unhappy, and in fact I came to enjoy London only after I moved to Tunbridge Wells, which being fifty minutes from Charing Cross (it used to take me almost as long to get in from Stoke Newington), is hardly more than an outer suburb. It offered all the facilities I needed in a town, a good shopping area, three or four cinemas, a good library, excellent bookshops, including one of the best second-hand bookshops in the country.

It was compact enough to be crossed on foot, and on every side lay the orchards and woods and fields of Kent. What more could I want? Very little as a matter of fact, but I was aware of distant expectations and anxieties.

I was twenty-eight, almost thirty. I had already provided not one graduation photo for the piano, but two, but my parents would have gladly forfeited the second photo – perhaps even the first – for a wedding group.

I used to return to Glasgow every spring and autumn for Passover and the High Holidays, as did most of my contemporaries who, like most Scottish graduates, had felt compelled to seek a living in the south. It was a biannual roll-call and if any-one failed to appear in synagogue for both the spring and the autumn festivals, knowing heads would nod sadly and presume that the worst had happened. The worst usually *had* happened, and whenever I came home, Mother would reel off the list of further acquaintances who had married shikses, and she made it sound as if they were victims of an epidemic. 'The nicest boys, from the most Orthodox families.' Doctor this and doctor that (physicians seemed to be particularly prone to the disease), and this dentist, and that solicitor, 'a solicitor', repeated Mother, as if lawyers should have been above that sort of thing. The obvious inference from this litany of misfortune was that I too might fall victim to it. Indeed how could it be otherwise, surrounded as I was by all those goyim? 'In what do you call it, Coatbridge Wells?' A place without even a synagogue. There was no use pointing out that I spent many of my weekends in London and the festivals in Glasgow. She heard that I'd been out with a blonde shikse. That's how she imagined them, tall and blonde, and abandoned and scheming. Of course I had been out with shikses, but never with a blonde, because I'd never found blondes attractive.

I was coming out of the Aldwych theatre one evening with a young, dark-haired, very attractive girl and was walking towards Charing Cross, when I bumped into a Glasgow Jewish business-man who was staying at the Waldorf and he asked us in for coffee. I was on fairly friendly terms with him, was always glad to see someone from Glasgow, and couldn't refuse. The girl's name was Collins and the first thing he asked her was if she had relatives in Glasgow, which she had. Collins is, of course, a common Scottish name. It is also the name of a fairly prosperous Jewish clan, whose name had probably at one time been Cohen.

'Yes,' she said, 'in fact I'll be spending Christmas with them.'

He then asked her where she lived.

'Hampstead.'

'A nice area. Do you go to the Dennington Park Synagogue?' and she, at once sensing the role in which she had been cast, said 'Yes, regularly.'

A week later I got a letter from my mother which had an oddly cheerful tone to it. The actual words she used in her letters rarely expressed her fears and anxieties, but one could feel them ooze forth as one opened the envelope, but here was the letter of a reassured woman. She was obviously standing by for good news, but after a month, when none materialised, and when I had not uttered as much as a word about the company I kept, she asked why I was so secretive. She had heard that I had been out with a very pretty, very religious girl, who was related to the Collins family. Why was I ashamed to say so? I was to be sure and introduce her when she was in Glasgow for Christmas.

Although I had by now almost drifted from my faith, there was never any prospect that I could have married out of it, for my happiness was too tied up with that of my parents and I could not for my own peace of mind have done anything which would have caused them lasting grief. But there was no point in explaining that either to my father or my mother, for the sort of conversations we had never approached that level of intimacy. I knew that they were troubled by the fact that I was away from any major centre of Jewish life, and the fact that they were troubled, troubled me.

Then, as if in answer to my mother's prayer, a letter came out of the blue. John Grierson was setting up a production unit with Scottish Television in Glasgow, would I care to join him? I had, of course, heard of Grierson as the father of British documentary, and had seen and admired several of his films, but his name was so much part of the past that I was surprised to hear he was alive. I soon discovered that he was very much alive, and kicking. He was looking for a young man who could write, had great

stamina, a decent academic degree and wide curiosity, and I
had been recommended to him by the University Appointments
Board.

I phoned my parents to say I was coming home.

'Are you bringing anyone with you?' asked Mother.

IV

The Return of the Native

He asked me to meet him somewhere in Paddington. I expected
to find him in the grand suite of a large hotel, surrounded by
secretaries and assistants. I found him instead in a seedy little
place, smelling of urine and mildew, nursing an aching head and
drinking black coffee. He was a small man, grey haired, with a
red face and bristling moustache, and grey, piercing eyes behind
thick glasses. He looked up from his coffee and did not seem too
reassured by what he saw.

'So you want to work in television?' he began.

I said that I wasn't sure that I did, but wanted to know what
the work involved.

'Not sure? Of course you want to work in television, they all
do. Well let me tell you for a start, it's the lowest form of existence, but – '

And I waited.

' – the money's good – Christ, it has to be. But in this case it
also means going back to Glasgow. Can you face that?'

'Readily,' I said.

'I'm surprised. It's one thing being in Glasgow and staying
there, but to leave it and come back, Christ, who can face that?'

Grierson could not for one. He lived in Wiltshire and flew up
to Glasgow for a few days every fortnight.

He was planning a programme to be called 'The Face of
Scotland' which would take a close look at the shipbuilding industry, the Grangemouth petro-chemical industry, Dundee jute,
electronics, the Caithness nuclear reactor, and it was my job to
prepare a series of reports on each of these, which Grierson would
then use as a basis for his programme.

I spent some six months on the project before it became obvious that it would never get off the ground. It would have been feasible only if the networks had been prepared to take it, and the networks were not interested in 'the face of Scotland' or, as Grierson put it, 'its arse'. Grierson himself was amply employed on another programme, and his film editor and director joined other units, but it was not at all certain what could be done with me. I was enjoying a substantial salary and discovered to my surprise that there were some excellent restaurants in and around Glasgow. I took a brief holiday in Florence and Madrid, I went to see *The Magic Flute* in Salzburg, and I occasionally surfaced in Glasgow to show that I was still around and to see that the monthly cheques were still being paid into my account.

It was during one of those visits to Glasgow that I bumped into Grierson. He was having a large gin and he ordered me a whisky : 'a good malt – none of your proprietary piss', and we sat down to drink.

'Well, Chaim' – he pronounced it Chime – 'what are you doing with yourself?'

'Nothing much,' I said.

'That's what you usually do, but who are you doing it for?'

'You,' I said. And his eyes grew large.

'You're still on Roy Thomson's pay-roll?' I nodded.

'Christ, we'll have to do something about that', and he got on to a former protégé, Denis Foreman of Granada Television, and a month later I was back in London. I now took *rooms*, in Highgate. I had arrived. I was a 'writer', or at least was classed as such in the internal directory. I had a spacious office, an elegant secretary. The only drawback to my situation was that after an initial frenzied spasm of activity I had no work. I came south, bent for action and found myself a pensioner. These were the early days of commercial television and Sidney Bernstein, the head of Granada, kept buying up 'bright young men' as he called them, without knowing what to do with them. Indeed as I found my way about the place, I also kept stumbling upon numerous highly paid, middle-aged men, who were not quite sure what they were doing there, but seemed perfectly content not to be doing it.

I was attached to a documentary production unit and my function was to write the outline script as a rough guide for the film crew. Then, when the rushes were available, I re-wrote to fit the pictures. I tried to – tried to? I couldn't help myself. I introduced little twirls into the script and what I fancied as small felicities. The late Kenneth Allsop, anchor man of the programme, also added his little twirls, by which time there were more twirls than script, and finally Tim Hewat, the Ritchie Hook of television, lately of the *Express*, who was in charge of the programme, took me aside and in the friendliest possible way put it to me that if I could not cut the twirls he would have to cut my throat. I got the message, took a more self-effacing view of my role, and gradually self-effaced myself out of the programme. I had arrived as the creative element in the unit – or so I thought – and remained as a caption writer, and when the programme was over, even that was over, but whether out of charity or forgetfulness, I still remained on the payroll. I still came in every day, for I had a comfortable office – which was more than could be said of my rooms – and wrote articles for newspapers and magazines, but I got little *naches* out of them, even though an increasing proportion of them were accepted. There is something rather pathetic about a tangled heap of faded newspaper cuttings no matter how well they may have read when they first appeared; they were more ephemeral even than television scripts. I felt the world was ready for my first novel. I cleared my desk. I brought in my secretary's electric typewriter. I loosened my tie and rolled up my sleeves. I turned the central heating off and opened the window. I inserted a clean sheet of quarto in the typewriter, lit a *Passing Cloud*, and began. Within a week I had drummed out twenty thousand words and blown a fuse in my typewriter.

In the next-door office there was a girl from South Africa, called Pat Williams, the author of a successful musical *King Kong*, which was to come to the West End the following year. She too was on the Granada payroll, she too had nothing much to do with herself, she too was writing a book, and one afternoon in a spare moment, sat down to read what I had written and was sufficiently impressed with it to take it round to Tom Maschler, then fiction editor of Penguins. He asked me to come round to see him the following day. 'Marvellous stuff . . . unique flavour

. . . an English Sholem Aleichem.' Could I, would I, let him see it when it was finished?

With these words ringing in my ears I returned to Granada and sent a memo to the programme controller, to say that I felt too young to be a pensioner and that I was leaving to write a book. A few minutes later his secretary asked me to come and see him. I did not wait for the lift, but rushed up the stairs two at a time. I presumed that my note of resignation had startled him into recognising what hidden talent the company possessed – a prospective author, no less – and I thought he might offer me a function worthy of my ability. But he did not offer me another job; he did not try to persuade me to stay; I suppose he was curious to see who I was.

I now returned to my beloved Essex, though not to Thaxted. All my friends were in London and I was writing a weekly column for the *Jewish Chronicle* and I wanted to be within easy reach of a good train service, and I found a place near the village of Ingatestone, from which I could get to London in an hour. Ingatestone had an attractive main street and a beautiful church in rich red brick, with a splendid fifteenth-century tower, but it and the surrounding villages were, I discovered, dormitories, not for London, but Chelmsford, which was twelve miles away, and which, for all its antiquity, was, with its engineering, electronic and food processing industries, becoming a large and charmless place, like Luton and Dunstable, a sort of jumped-up Birmingham with signs of prosperity everywhere and taste nowhere, small houses crammed with gadgets, picture-windows with venetian blinds, formica kitchens with split-level cookers, tiny gardens with tiny lawns and hedges, and sparkling little Minis everywhere.

This was not rural Essex, the Essex I had known, the Essex of the rolling corn-fields and the distant vistas, but perhaps above all I was missing the kibbutz training farm in Thaxted, the Jews who were Jewish when I was a Jew, the Friday evening service at sundown, the hymns at the Sabbath table, the animated discussions. What I wanted was rural England with a synagogue. Not that Ingatestone was wholly devoid of Jews. There was a landed family, several young scientists working at Marconi's in Chelmsford, a number of commuters with jobs in London, I sniffed them out one by one, for I can sense Jew as dog can sense dog, but I

F

wanted synagogue Jews, whereas the sort of Jew who made his home in the countryside was often the sort who wanted to escape his Jewishness.

Some five or six years later I did discover a synagogue in rural England, and a splendid one at that – perhaps the most attractive synagogue building in the British Isles – at Carmel College, the Jewish public school, near Wallingford in Berkshire (now Oxfordshire). The school owned a building site in the nearby village of Crowmarsh, which they were prepared to lease at a nominal price for the development of a Jewish housing estate. Here one would have everything, a synagogue, an excellent Jewish school, fellow Jews, possibly even a kosher delicatessen. We would have a small Jerusalem on the banks of the Thames and I wrote about the idea in glowing terms in the *Jewish Chronicle* and invited interested readers to contact me. I received one reply. The synagogue Jew, I discovered, is a congenital urbanite. There is something about his upbringing which blinds him to the beauty of the world about him. His rituals call for fellowship. Without other Jews about him he is not quite a Jew himself. He is gregarious by instinct and upbringing and towns alone, usually large towns, assure the numbers he requires, so that even where he forms his own village settlements, as some Hassidic sects in America have done, he turns his back upon the countryside.

I was six months in Ingatestone when I was overtaken by a calamity. I had finished my novel, and delivered it in person to Tom Maschler, by now transferred to Cape, and I thought that his face fell a little when I unloaded the five or six hundred foolscap pages on his desk. I did not expect him to read it on the spot, but when a month passed – the longest month in my life – and I still had not heard, I descended on Bedford Square in person and demanded to know what was happening. When I saw Maschler's face I could see what had happened. I don't know if he read it – he may only have weighed it – but in any case he didn't like it. It was too big. Books of this size weren't published any more, he said. If Tolstoy had come in bearing *War and Peace* he would have told him the same. My effort, he thought, wasn't wasted, but why didn't I go home and extract a novel from what I had written?

I stood in Bedford Square, hugging my great bulky manuscript, wondering what to do next. I had saved up a few hundred pounds during my years in television, but I spent as much when I was out of work as when in work. Within a few months my savings were gone, and my sole income was now ten pounds a week from the *Jewish Chronicle* and, as before during times of need, I turned to teaching and became a master in the village school.

The school was a modern secondary one and served a catchment area with few grammar schools, so that it had a considerable proportion of intelligent, hard-working youngsters, who would have given a good account of themselves in any grammar school that I had known either as a pupil or teacher, but they did not remain in the school long enough to form any substantial grammar stream. I got the impression that local authority schools in the home counties were used by the working class; and of the rest, those who couldn't get a place in the grammar schools were sent to private schools which had neither the facilities, nor the staff, nor the interest to offer the level of education available in the modern secondary schools, but which exploited middle-class snobbery. Later when I became a father and listened to the endless debates which middle-class families – and Jewish families of all classes – have over the education of their young, I came to wonder what it was all about. A whole race of soothsayers have come into being, educational counsellors, education correspondents, educational advisory centres, child psychologists, all of them offering mutually contradictory advice, battening on the worries of parents anxious to do the best for their children and who sometimes, through their very anxieties will, even when taking the very best – or at least the most expensive – advice, tend to do the worst. There are so many imponderables involved, so much depends on the headmaster, the teachers, the fellow pupils, all of whom are constantly changing, that what may be true of a particular school in one year, may not be true – usually is not – in the next. I was once a teacher in a so-called grammar school which I had no doubt was the worst school in England, yet many of its pupils have done well, found places in good universities and two or three even won open scholarships to Oxford and Cambridge, and it seems to me that where a boy is sufficiently intelligent no sort of schooling will do him much harm.

Ingatestone was a good school, which is to say, it had more than the usual quota of good teachers, people not only with the necessary paper qualification, but the necessary sense of vocation, who could control a class without raising their voice or their hand (which I could never do), but even they could make little headway with some of their pupils. I had a number of fourteen- and fifteen-year-olds in my class, mostly the children of small farmers (the children of large farmers went to fee-paying schools) and farm labourers, and they came eager and open-faced, carrying the fresh smells of the countryside, speaking with an attractive rural burr (most of the other children had the incoherent quasi-cockney of the Greater London area). They had benefited from their earlier classes and could read, write after a fashion and add. They were not dull, but whenever I tried to explain why Hamlet did not get on with his mother a slightly dazed look came into their eyes. They were bored, and I was frustrated. It is possible that a better teacher might have had happier results, but I doubt it, and in any case the better teachers took the better pupils. In England, as elsewhere, talent in education is applied to where it is least needed and withheld from where it is most needed.

Teaching did not solve my financial problems, for a teacher's salary did not go with the tastes or the company I had acquired in television, and the editor of the *Jewish Chronicle*, taking a look at the frayed cuffs of my Jermyn Street shirt, offered me a full-time post which carried a reasonable salary and left me with sufficient time to continue with my own writing, and a year later my first novel appeared.

But before that something rather more momentous happened. I got married. I was thirty-two by then and coming to an age when one begins to think one is ageless, so that the older one gets, the younger the female company one keeps. I was at lunch one Shabbat afternoon and found myself next to a pert, pretty little girl with large, lively eyes and an animated manner of speaking. Our paths had not previously crossed, but they had followed a strangely similar course. She had been a pupil at the nameless London grammar school where I had been a teacher, but left the term before I came. Then, after a period in art school, she joined the kibbutz training farm in Thaxted and from there moved on to Israel, where she worked as a commercial artist with a Tel-Aviv advertising agency. She happened to be on holiday in London when we met and I tried to persuade her to delay her departure. It was no slight undertaking, for her commitment to Israel was less trammelled than mine. Any ambition she had did not conflict with her desire to be there, and she was infinitely more religious than I was. She took her religion religiously while I took mine pleasurably. She believed not only that the written law as enshrined in the Pentateuch was divine, but that the oral law as culled by the Rabbis also contained its divine element, whereas I was not even sure whether I believed in God. But I did, and do, believe in ghosts, not of the headless nun variety (though if I had lingered amid the Essex mists sufficiently I might have come to believe even in them), but in the non-material, so that certain parts of the liturgy have meaning for me, not because I believe anyone on high might be listening, but because the ancient prayers with their ancient tunes link one in communion with earlier generations.

There was a year in the late 1950s when I could not get up to Glasgow for the Day of Atonement. I was living in New Cavendish Street at the time and was hurrying across Regent's Park to get to St John's Wood Synagogue, when I stopped in my stride and asked myself what was the hurry. Did I believe in God? I was not sure. Did I believe that by fasting and prayer He would forgive the sins I had committed in the past year? No. If not, did I think I would become a better man through the very act of fasting and prayer? If my experience of the past thirty years was anything to go by the answer was again no. So what was the hurry?

It was a clear morning in early October. The sky was blue and framed with the autumnal tints of the surrounding trees. The park was beginning to fill with nannies and small children and I sat back to enjoy the nannies and the day, but I did not. I was tugged, as a falling object is tugged by the force of gravity, by a consciousness of Jews at prayer, of my father in synagogue, my mother, my sisters, my friends, pious and impious, believers and sceptics, by the whole congregation of Israel, living and dead. I had no feeling that I was missing something, or that I was guilty of a dereliction of duty. The sensation was rather one of isolation so cheerless and profound as to amount almost to an ache.

I was more aware of the synagogue by staying out of it than by being in it. All this could no doubt be dismissed as withdrawal symptoms, and that if I had stayed away from synagogue long enough I would, over the years, have become inured to the feeling. My lack of belief, however, was not so pronounced that I felt that need to martyr myself for it. I shook the grass from my trousers, picked up my hat, my prayer-book and my prayer shawl, and continued to synagogue.

One does not, in short, have to be a believer to enjoy religion, or to be pained by the lack of it, and I conform to observances which I cannot in logic defend – because they defend observances which I cherish. I take pleasure in the ceremonies and ritual of Judaism as impalpable antiques, Mings of the mind. To my wife, however, it is all far more positive and emphatic, and among the reasons why she was anxious to get back to Israel was that it gave her a feeling of religious fulfilment. Even had she disliked it, she would probably have been compelled there by a sense of duty. When I first decided to go to Israel I was moved by a mixture of feelings the strongest of which was, perhaps, the insecurity induced by the holocaust. The Germans may have launched the holocaust but it could not have assumed its massive scale without the ready co-operation of Poles, Russians, Rumanians, Hungarians, Frenchmen, and I sometimes asked myself if the English would have acted any differently had the Germans crossed the Channel. These thoughts troubled me less and less as time passed and after my year in Thaxted they almost ceased to trouble me at all.

The second motivation was religious. I was increasingly beset by scepticism and doubt as I moved from my early to my late teens, but Zion and Jerusalem had figured so much in my imagination and prayer that I experienced a constant yearning to see them.

The third was a naïve romanticism. Being in Israel in the early years of statehood, with all the hardship that it involved, was part of being young and Jewish. I had dozens of friends in Glasgow and there was hardly one among them who did not experience this feeling and did not respond to it.

Three things happened during my stay in Israel. I lost my obsession with the holocaust, and it seemed to me that anyone who felt insecure in Europe would not feel particularly safe in Israel. I did not lose my religion, but my doubts outweighed my beliefs. And finally, I grew up. I still wanted to go back to Israel, but for one reason only, because I liked it. This may have been no more than a simple liking for sunshine and it is possible that had I spent a year in Italy, Spain or Greece, I might have had the same yearning to go back. It may also be that I was by now English enough to have acquired the Englishman's passion for Mediterranean lands. But I doubt it, for apart from anything else I am not all that fond of the fierce heat and the loud colours of the Mediterranean (except for short visits) and much prefer the temperate climate and pastel shades of the north. I did miss Jerusalem, I doubt if anyone can live there for any length of time without being gripped by it and, as I was later to discover, my religious feelings, even if not founded on actual belief, were perhaps stronger than I imagined, but the main reason that I wanted to go back was that I liked being among Jews and that I was at ease among them in a way that I could not be among anyone else.

But if I should have liked to return to Israel, I was not prepared to go back at any price. I still hoped to be a writer, and had nothing to show for the hope save determination. I was earning a reasonable salary on the *Jewish Chronicle*. Some of the things I have written in the *Chronicle* are as good as almost anything I have between hard covers, but I was still scratching in the merest foothills of literature. I had a mound of mouldering press-cuttings, and a stack of television scripts, but not a single book in print. And, as I said, I was thirty-two, yet I was still naïve enough to believe that once my name appeared on hard covers, I would be made (I suspect I shared this illusion with every unpublished author in the land) and that I would be able to pick up my typewriter and set up home wherever I wished. It was on this shaky hope that Judy finally agreed to marry me.

I phoned the news home and the first question Mother asked was :

'Is she Jewish ?'

'I think so,' I said.

'You think so ?'

'She's Jewish.'

I had achieved all that a Jewish mother may reasonably expect of a Jewish son. The rest – such as children – was in the hands of Providence. From that moment I felt free of the burden of parental anxiety. Hereafter it would be my turn to be anxious about my parents, who were getting on in years and shaky in health.

My wife's family was second generation English on her father's side, fourth generation on her mother's. Both stemmed from Frankfurt and both carried about them traces of pre-Bismarckian Germany, or rather Hesse-Cassel, when Germany was regarded as a quaint place and Germans regarded as a quaint people, with oompah bands and merry beer-drinkers, and yodelling yokels in *lederhosen*, and rustic wood-carvers. Their house was a large, double-fronted, three-storeyed Victorian edifice, standing a little apart from a street of large, terraced houses. The others had more bells to their portals than there are tits to a sow, whole banks of milk bottles, and had obviously been converted into flats, but this one, with its muslin curtains billowing in the breeze, its uncluttered approach, suggested gentility and a determination that, whatever was happening elsewhere in the street, it would remain the same. The interior was in keeping with the exterior, large armchairs and a large sofa, all with antimacassars, grouped around the three sides of an ornate fireplace, with an open fire actually burning in the grate, and dogs and cats and maids. There were six children in the family, of whom my wife was the oldest, and when they were young they had their meals in the nursery with nanny, while Papa and Mama ate theirs at opposite ends of the long dining-room table – except on Shabbat, when parents and children ate together.

When I first spent a Shabbat with my wife's family, I wondered if they were perhaps converts to Judaism, for their whole establishment was so goyish. There was first of all the livestock, the cats, the dogs, the white mice, the budgerigar. In *der heim* every home had its mice (not white mice, though), which is why most homes had their cat, but whoever heard of a Jewish household – and an Orthodox household at that – with a dog – or, for that matter, a budgerigar? (The budgie, I later discovered, belonged to Grandma's companion and was a weekend guest.)

Then there was the fare. In a traditional Jewish home, one

can savour the Sabbath on the tongue, chopped liver, kishke, cholent, kugel, lokschen pudding. Here I was given roast beef and Yorkshire pud. But perhaps more astounding than the fare was the ritual surrounding it. The joint – bound and trussed – was brought in by the maid on a small bed of nails, and placed before my prospective father-in-law, a red-faced, jovial figure, with a large white napkin tucked under his ample jaw, who carefully primed knife on hone, and then proceeded to carve the meat up with the ceremonial flourish of a high priest performing a sacrifice. We sang the usual table hymns to unusual German tunes, and in the evening, when the Sabbath was over, I was entertained to Gilbert and Sullivan on old 78 r.p.m. records. This was something of a diversion for the parents (although they know all Gilbert's lyrics by heart), for on most Saturday nights, they would sit themselves on either side of their walnut-veneered radiogram, which was about the size of a small wardrobe, he smoking a cigar, she knitting, while they both listened to Saturday Night Theatre on the radio. There was no television in the house till all the children were grown up and away from home. In the summer they took houses in Bognor or Frinton or Rye, and rain, hail or sunshine, were out on the beach every day playing compulsory beach cricket. In winter they went to *Peter Pan* and *Toad of Toad Hall* and on Sunday afternoons made excursions to the museums, the Victoria and Albert, the Natural History Museum, the Science Museum.

I had stumbled, as I discovered after I married, upon the final remnants of a particular segment of Anglo-Jewry which, in preserving its type of Jewishness had preserved something of Victorian middle-class England. For the attitudes which are now spoken of as Victorian were not indigenous to this country, but brought from Germany by the Prince Consort and transplanted in England where they flourished with rather greater vigour and at rather greater length than on their own native soil. A German making his home in England before the First World War – as a great many did – could thus feel very much at home, and the German Jew doubly so, for Victorianism propagated and preserved many of the attitudes, the puritanism, the soul searching, the consciousness of a personal God, which the Jew had tended to regard as peculiarly his own.

But England was changing and Anglo-Jewry was changing and the German Jews who had made their homes here felt that it was changing too fast, and that in particular, Chief Rabbi Adler was leading English Jewry downhill towards outright assimilation. In the early years of this century they broke away from the main body of the community, to form a more Orthodox body of exclusive brethren, which they called the *Adath*, under the presidency of my wife's great-grandfather. And yet, for all their exclusiveness, they managed to integrate themselves fully into English life, acquiring all that was best in their new environment, without discarding anything worthwhile in the old. Nevertheless, anyone who tries to live in two worlds is involved in a constant struggle to maintain his balance between them, and it cannot always be done. Some of the *Adath* families have thus drifted out of Judaism, while others have drifted out of this world. They may trade with it, or even study in it, but otherwise keep their distance from it, and my wife's family was perhaps the last living remnant of the old *Adath*.

Having decided that we could not, for the time being at least, hope to live in Jerusalem, my wife and I did the next best thing and bought a flat in Hampstead. Four years later we moved to Hampstead Garden Suburb. By then our second child was born and my fifth book was in print and I felt sufficiently confident to leave regular employment and live on my wits. Moving to Israel was always in the forefront of our minds but, as our family grew in size and expense, the prospect receded further and further into the distance.

We were living from hand to mouth. It was a large hand but an even larger mouth, and it left us without any surplus for foreign adventures. Any self-employed writer who manages to feed his family and himself and keep his house in a reasonable state of repair is extremely lucky. We did not want a higher living standard than we had, though it would have been nice to have had the money to pay for it. There were moments when we were threatened and a little worried by the prospect of riches. When my third novel, *Berl Make Tea*, appeared, someone bought an option on the film rights and at once thoughts of Hollywood sprung to mind, private swimming-pools, fast cars, winters in Jamaica, a house in Israel. It did not occur to me that anyone in his right

mind would pay £500 – which is more than I got from the publisher – for an option which he would not bother to exercise. Since
then, I've sold options of four or five of my books and have
pocketed the money without giving it a further thought, but in
one case the matter went well beyond the option. The director
himself materialised, and asked whether he could induce me to
work on the film script. He hoped to have John Gielgud for this
part and Ralph Richardson for the other and Avis Bunnage for
the third and he couldn't see how the film could fail to gross a
fortune. My Ford Cortina had conked out and for a day or so I
toyed with the idea of replacing it with a Rover. A week later I
received a cable of apology : his backer had backed out and he
was not in a position to take up the option after all. Such disappointments are so common to writing that I now take nothing
for granted till I have both the contract and cheque in hand and
even then I wait till the cheque is cashed and spent before I am
sure it is mine.

In 1973 my tenth book, *The Cousinhood*, broke through to
something like best-sellerdom in America and for the first time
since I married I found myself not only without debts, but with a
small surplus. I was, by the standards with which I was familiar,
rich, though well within the dreams of avarice, and the embar-
rassing thing about riches is that they encumber one with options.
Our plans were no longer settled by our circumstances. We could
afford to make a break for Israel without sinking into irretrievable
debt. Moreover, our eldest daughter, Alisa, would be going into
her final year in prep school and we would not want to disrupt
her education once she was in high school. It was now or
never.

There was finally one other factor. I had for most of my life
been out in the cold, on the periphery of things, and had almost
grown to like it. Now, certainly by the level of aspirations with
which I had set out, I was something of a success. I remembered
having long walks on blustery autumn afternoons across the
Queens Park playing fields, day-dreaming that I was a writer,
sitting in my own study, surrounded by books, bent over the
typewriter, and even now, after ten years as a full-time professional writer, I sometimes pinch myself to make sure that I am still
not in one of my Glasgow reveries. I am one of the very few people

who have had the extreme good fortune to have set out with an ambition and to have fulfilled it. At sixteen I had decided that I wanted to be a writer and at thirty-two a writer I was.

I got fairly generous – my publishers would say extravagant – advances on my books. They did not sell by the hundred thousand, but given the state of the book trade, it was something that they sold at all. I had wide contacts in Fleet Street, so that as a break between books, I could travel abroad on newspaper assignments, or could travel the length and breadth of America on a lecture tour and come away with money in hand. There was hardly a month in which I was not taken out to lunch by one publisher or another and although the ideas they offered were seldom up my street, it was good to feel wanted and delightful to eat well and drink superbly well at someone else's expense. My wife and I were often at the theatre or opera, entertained frequently and were frequently entertained. We also had a comfortable five-bed-roomed, suburban house, semi-detached, privet-hedged, bay-windowed, with neat garden back and front, a large, gleaming kitchen with a dining area and walls of knotted pine-wood, Danish furniture, and acres of bookshelves lined with acres of books and I sometimes looked into the advertising pages of the Sunday colour supplements and saw people uncomfortably like ourselves. Most important of all, I had lately acquired the one thing I had always dreamed of, my own private study, sacred to me, sound-proofed and insulated from the rest of the house, lined with book-shelves, with a sitting desk and a standing desk, and a swivel chair and armchair, and foot rest, and filing cabinets, and a large picture window which looked out onto the back garden and which, alas, was a constant inducement to idleness.

All that and heaven too. On Fridays, as the sun began to set, I would return my typewriter to its case, clear my desk, polish my shoes, have a bath, change into my 'Sunday' suit and walk slowly through the declining day to synagogue. The Sabbath does not enter at a fixed hour, but at sunset, so that in the summer evenings I would set out about eight, and in the winter about four, but always amid the dying embers of the day. A walk at such a time is almost a form of prayer in itself and I have often had to ask myself during my promenade whether I am the heretic I think I am. One does not, however, have to be a believer to enjoy the Friday evening service (which is largely drawn from the Psalms):

'O sing unto the Lord a new song: sing unto the Lord all the earth.

Sing unto the Lord, bless His name; proclaim His salvation from day to day.

Recount His glory among the nations, His wondrous work among all peoples . . .'

The Sabbath was a day out of time. I did not open mail, answer the phone, use the car.

I belong to two synagogues, a large one, which is part of the United Synagogue group, and a gilded little bethel with about two dozen members we called a *shtieble*. The United Synagogue is the Church of England of Anglo-Jewry, and is in many ways modelled on it, and like the C. of E. everyone berates it but no one would wish to be without it. It is rather formal and staid, whereas the *shtieble* is none of these things, and I went to the one to offset the effects of the other.

Synagogue services are much longer than church services (on the Day of Atonement they last all day) so that one cannot expect – certainly one rarely finds – the level of decorum usual in church. There are, indeed, Jews who would find something vaguely church-like about a well-behaved congregation, and thus if the decorum in the large synagogue was imperfect, it verged on the riotous in the small and my wife tended to regard it as a place of low resort. Children played with their toys or ran hither and thither among the congregation, men gossiped, told jokes and there was the frequent sound of ribald laughter. They also found time for prayer and after prayers there would be a *kiddush*, with herring, cakes, wine, whisky. The word *kiddush* means sanctification. Before anything was eaten, the Rabbi would make a blessing over the wine, and after the tables were cleared, different members of the congregation would offer a *vertel*, a brief word, a didactic thought, all of which raised a mere *nosh* or booze-up to the level of a religious experience, and it left one with a feeling of elevation which was not due entirely to the whisky.

When the Sabbath was over, I felt a man refreshed, braced to cope with the rigours of another week, and its most rigorous day, Sunday, when I had to mow the lawn and help cope with the children.

I had, in short, found myself a particularly snug corner of the universe, in snug circumstances and felt comfortable to the point of discomfort. One can, I suppose, learn to live with success as much as with failure. I was not so successful that I had to make a great effort, but successful enough to feel a slight sense of suffocation. We had to go to Israel.

When we were packing, one of my sisters said to me : 'Are you sure you want to go? There's trouble on the border.'

'There's always trouble on the border,' I said.

V

The Man in the Grey Trilby

There was a man who sat a few rows in front of me in the Yeshurun Synagogue, Jerusalem, who is implanted in my memory as clearly as my own late father, yet we never exchanged more than a nod. He is small and dapper, with a dark complexion, a bushy moustache and wears a grey trilby. He must be in his fifties and often has his grandchildren sitting by him. I do not even know his name, but every time I see him, I hear the sound of sirens.

At about 5.30 a.m. on *Yom Kippur*, we were awakened by the roar of jets flying low overhead. The windows rattled and the house shook as they passed, and we took it as an ominous sound, for it seemed unlikely that the air force would go in for joy-rides on the Day of Atonement. About eight, on a clear, fresh morning, I set out for synagogue and on the way bumped into Dr Yosef Burg, Minister of the Interior. Dr Burg is a large, red-faced, ebullient man, whose glasses smile out on the world even when his eyes do not. He is the Brother Cherryble of Israeli politics, but that morning, in spite of the bright sunshine, and the tingling freshness of the air, he seemed strangely sombre. I greeted him cheerfully and he nodded without a word, like a man preoccupied with some private grief.

In the synagogue everything seemed normal, but as the morning proceeded, I sensed a build up of tensions and looking through the narrow windows, I noticed a growing volume of transport, army jeeps, lorries, even buses, in streets which were usually deserted on *Yom Kippur*. More ominous, young men came into the synagogue on tip-toe, tapped other young men on the shoulders, who immediately folded their prayer-shawls and slipped out.

The Israel mobilisation plan is, or at least was, based on a simple – though by no means fool-proof – chain letter system. Reservist A had a list of fellow reservists B, C, D, etc. in his region, and at a given signal, he alerted them. B, C, and D, in turn had similar lists, until within a day or two, the entire reserve corp was mobilised. As the morning wore on, the congregation was gradually denuded of young men, then of the older ones. By one o'clock the synagogue, which had been packed in the morning, was half empty. Then someone entered and tapped the man in the grey trilby on his shoulder. He quickly pulled off his prayer-shawl, rammed it into its bag. 'If they're already calling me,' he said to a neighbour, 'they must be in a bad way.' At which point the sirens went.

The sound took me right back to wartime Glasgow and my immediate reaction was one of nostalgia rather than apprehension. My wife had gone home some time earlier to give the children lunch. I hurried back to the flat and found the children jumping up and down with cheerful anticipation. My wife had told them that we were probably at war, which was something they had read about in books, or watched on television, now they would be seeing it with their own eyes. There was a hurried scramble for pandas and teddies, and reading matter for all ages, Ant and Bee, Topsy and Tim, Bedknobs and Broomsticks, and we hurried down to the shelter. By then the other families in the block had also come down and looking around I discovered that I was the only adult male in the company. All the others were in the army or out of town. I immediately took charge and put on my best A.R.P. manner. 'Women and children first,' I said, pushing ahead of the rest, 'no panic,' but when we got to the shelter there was a slight panic. Every family was provided with a key to the shelter but none had remembered to bring it down. Someone rushed upstairs for his key, while the old wartime repertoire of shelter-songs went through my mind, *Roll out the Barrel, Knees Up Mother Brown, It's a long Way to Tipperary, Wish me Luck as You Wave me Goodbye* (sung in the one air-raid which I had sat through, to a Charlie Kunz record). The boy couldn't find his key and I rushed up to look for mine. By the time I got down the all clear had sounded. The children were inconsolable.

There was one other air-raid alarm during the war. We were

at lunch at the time in an hotel with about a hundred other guests. They all looked up when the sirens went, but it was a good meal and no one went to the shelter. Jewish phlegm!

In May 1967, when Nasser closed the Straits of Tiran and another Israel–Arab war seemed certain, a number of Jewish writers were hurriedly called to a meeting in the Maida Vale home of the novelist Gerda Charles. There were about twenty of us in the room, some of whom I had not known were Jewish – some of whom, indeed, may themselves have not thought of themselves as Jews, until this moment of crisis. I had been to Israel on one newspaper assignment or another at least once a year since 1961, and in 1966 I had spent some time there writing a book on the country, and though deeply concerned about the impending loss of life, I had no doubt that Israel would emerge victorious, but the others sensed Armageddon and we all wondered what we could to do help. The result of our deliberations, which continued far into the night, was a letter which appeared a few days later in the *Sunday Times*:

'Sir – Israel is a country the size of Wales. Today it is mobilised to prevent itself becoming another Auschwitz. The Arab states which surround it have declared their intention of exterminating it. There are two and a half million people in Israel whose right to live is threatened, behind the political game, this is what the present crisis is about.'

It was signed by more than thirty authors, including Dannie Abse, A. Alvarez, Alexander Baron, Myrna Blumberg, Caryl Brahms, Gerda Charles, David Daiches, Lionel Davidson, Marty Feldman, T. R. Fyvel, Larry Gelbart, Lewis Greifer, John Gross, Ronald Harwood, Ronald Cass, Sid Colin, Diana and Meir Gillon, Martyn Goff, Dan Jacobson, Bernard Kops, Philip Levene, Emmanuel Litvinoff, Wolf Mankowitz, Luis Marks, Robert Muller, Denis Norden, Harold Pinter, Frederick Raphael, Mordecai Richler, Jeremy Robson, Reuben Ship, Jacob Sonntag, George Steiner and myself.

Denis Norden became our Chief of Staff, and his office, off Regent Street, our centre of operations. We organised petitions, demonstrations, protest meetings, fund-raising drives. The war began on Monday 5 June. On Wednesday, when it was effectively over, we drafted a letter to the Prime Minister, and Wolf Mankowitz, Bernard Kops and I were delegated to deliver it. Wolf is over six feet tall, broad-shouldered, with a massive chest and I am not much smaller, so that Kops came between us at a rapid trot looking like some minute malefactor being taken into custody by two burly plain-clothes men. That, at least, must have been the impression we gave to cameramen, and cameras clicked on every side.

At Number Ten, Mr Wilson did not come to the door. Neither, for that matter, did Mrs Wilson, but a helmeted policeman appeared and behind him a bent, white-haired figure in black, who took our letter, thanked us, and closed the door.

We felt that the masses were not sufficiently appraised of Israel's case and took full page advertisements in the *Mirror* and the *Express*. I don't know how much all this helped Israel, but it helped the *Mirror* and the *Express*. The incessant activity made us feel that we were somehow involved in Israel's battle, so that it also helped us, but not sufficiently, for beyond the anxieties about the outcome of the war, the excitement during the fighting, and the exultation at the result, was a nagging frustration that one could not be there. So that when, in 1973, I realised that Israel was engaged in yet another war my first reaction was a determination that I would somehow, in one way or another, be in on it.

As soon as *Yom Kippur* was over, and I had had my usual breakfast snack of herrings and beer, I rushed down to the government press office to contact Eric Silver, the Jerusalem correspondent of the *Guardian* and *Observer*, but he had already left for Tel-Aviv. I therefore phoned Bill Millinship, Foreign Editor of the *Observer*, and asked if I could be one of their war correspondents. 'Gladly,' he said. 'Copy by 4 p.m. Friday, please.'

As I made my way home, through the darkness, I passed the narrow lanes of *Nachlat Sheva*, one of the older and more attractive quarters of the city, inhabited mainly by Orthodox artisans and craftsmen, and heard the sound of a hammer on wood echoing through the streets. It is customary among Orthodox Jews to start building booths for the joyous Feast of Tabernacles immediately on the close of the sombre Day of Atonement, and war or no war, someone was abiding by tradition.

In the press office the next morning, everyone was self-assured, ebullient, jolly, the foreign correspondents rather more than the local ones. 'Second day of war, and no end in sight,' said someone, only half humorously. Old hands familiar with the ways of the army press office were troubled by the fact that there was no access to the front either in the North or the South and that all the information was second-hand, but there was no rumour of setback or retreat on either front. We were all waiting for good news, and on Monday, the third day of war, we received the first hint that it was coming. It was announced that the Chief of Staff would be addressing a press conference in Beth Sokolov, the government press office in Tel-Aviv.

The conference was scheduled for six. The large hall began to fill up at five, by five-thirty there was not a free seat in the place. Whole ranks of cine and television cameras were drawn up, down the side of the hall, and correspondents squatted among the tripods. There must have been about five hundred press and cameramen present, plus a leavening of local celebrities. The pianist and conductor, Daniel Barenboim, was there. He had attended the press conference at which the triumphs of the Six Day War were first announced and he was anticipating the same again. 'This is becoming routine for me,' he said. In the row behind him sat the film-star Chaim Topol, in uniform. He was acting as an army press liaison officer, and cameras swivelled to catch him in their lenses. The place buzzed with expectancy.

At six precisely, a tall, moustached, British-style R.S.M. entered the hall, followed by the Chief of Staff, a powerfully built man, with broad shoulders, massive chin, wavy black hair and craggy good looks. He had an erect soldierly bearing, but without a swagger and everything about him suggested strength and confidence. One felt that if a bus went into him, it would get the worst of the encounter. His statement was brief :

'This morning we embarked on a counter-attack simultaneously on both fronts. I am happy to tell you it is succeeding. We are advancing on all fronts. We shall destroy them wherever it is possible. We shall strike them, we shall beat them, we shall break their bones.'

It was not quite the recital of victories we had been expecting and some of the local correspondents went away with glum faces.

One can always tell there is a war on by a glance at the cocktail bar in the Dan Hotel, Tel-Aviv. The Dan is the oldest of the large luxury hotels, and one of the most expensive, and on a normal evening one may find a young pair perched on its high leather stools, drinking a Schweppes or Coca Cola – Jews are God's gift to the soft-drink trade – but when the foreign press descends the gin begins to flow, and the gin was flowing in a torrent that night. 'None of your local piss, old chap,' said a lean, moustached figure, 'make it a Gordon's.' It was like a regimental reunion with much talk of campaigns gone by and wars long ago, Suez, Cyprus, Vietnam, Biafra, Ulster.

As wars went the Middle-East 'punch-ups' (as one man put it) were everything a journalist could want, for they tended to be swift, sharp, dramatic and bloody and, moreover, the best side won. Most of the foreign correspondents were overwhelmingly pro-Israeli, though it is not unusual for pressmen to adopt the sides they have to cover.

I joined the conversation, laughed at the jokes, stood my round of drinks, but otherwise felt like a spectre at a feast. This was my first campaign and I could not compare it with any previous 'show', or view it with the same feeling of detachment as those around me. I could only think of the young boys in the white shirts at prayer in the Yeshurun synagogue two days before, called suddenly to arms. I had seen them pile on to lorries and buses, being driven off to unnamed destinations. How many would return? I was troubled by the manner and tone of General Elazar's statement. It had the hollow sound of a morale booster, and morale does not need boosting when things are going well. I was troubled by the fact that there was still no access to the front.

The following day, however, we were allowed up to the Golan, and went in a whole convoy, buses, jeeps, private cars, taxis, and my spirits brightened, especially on the approach to Tiberias when we heard the distant rumble of shell-fire, a low, drawn-out 'crump,' like the sound of the earth being torn apart. I wondered at my reaction, for I thought I would be nervous and frightened. I suppose both fearlessness and fear are contagious. I was in a bus-load of people who had spent most of their mature years at scenes of carnage. They had seen it all and had been through it all, and were eager to see it again. The nearer we came to the front, and the louder the sound of battle, the more their faces brightened. They reminded me of a charabanc outing of schoolboys impatient for their first glimpse of the sea. We alighted near Kuneitra, the biggest Syrian town to have fallen into Jewish hands, and then, as if for our benefit, the ground around us began to erupt with rockets and shells and shrapnel flew over our heads. I stood a little bewildered, for rather too much was happening to be taken in. There were people diving in all directions, some for shelter, but most, it seemed to me, for the best camera angle, though I would have thought that the sight of one exploding shell was very much like another.

The shell-fire apart, the trip was something of an anti-climax. I wasn't quite sure what to expect. My knowledge of battle was largely derived from films and books, mostly Tolstoy, and although I did not expect to see one army formed up in solid ranks against another, with officers at their head leading the charge, I did anticipate a certain regularity or pattern, with line massed against line, but there was nothing of the sort. One saw a cluster of tanks here, the occasional artillery battery there, some infantry units on half tracks, each of which seemed to be in business on their own. Jets screamed and whined and turned on what I later discovered were victory rolls – overhead – like swift, sharp-winged fowls, out to enjoy the sunshine, and helicopters, like giant dragon-flies, kept ascending and descending, throwing up great clouds of sand every time they approached or left the ground. Movement was limited by the traffic jams, which stretched across the plateau round Kuneitra, downhill to the Jordan, over the Jordan, and all the way back to Tiberias, with swearing and cursing red-caps trying to restore order. It reminded me of the Exeter by-pass on a bank holiday in the 1950s. Most of the paralysis was caused by broken-down civilian vehicles, pressed too hurriedly into service, which steamed, fumed and clogged the narrow roads of Galilee and the Golan, tank-trailers, container-lorries, pick-up trucks, private cars – including one gleaming Jag – Egged buses, jeeps, taxis – ice-cream vans.

The next morning I had a coffee in Dizengoff. It was early in October, which is often the best time of the year to be in Israel, for the worst heat of the summer has passed and there is a sort of cheerful, sunny, smiling warmth that one gets on a perfect summer's day in England. Dizengoff is the Champs Elysées of Tel-Aviv. It is lined with cafés and restaurants, with tables arrayed under bright awnings on the broad boulevards. I had first one coffee, and then another (for I had had little sleep the previous night) and then a large brandy, and sipping my drink slowly, I wrote my first dispatch.

Everything I had to say could have been written from the bar of the Dan hotel, or this café, and indeed, Eric Marsden, the resident *Times* correspondent, who remained at his typewriter in the Government press office in Jerusalem, rarely went anywhere, or saw anyone, but filed some of the most informed dispatches to come out of Israel.

But after a day or so in Tel-Aviv I was anxious to get out to the front again, not because, as a colleague suggested, I had a death wish – I know of few people more eager to stay alive – or because of a reporter's instinct for action – but because the war front was infinitely less depressing than the home front.

Israel had been the victim of a surprise attack by two armies both larger than hers and both armed with the latest and best equipment Russia could offer, including Sam 2, Sam 3 and Sam 6 rockets, which limited the air-cover the Israeli airforce could give the troops, and the deadly Saggar missile which cut through Israeli armour like a knife through butter; and yet after the initial retreat Israel recovered sufficiently to hold the Egyptians on one front, throw back the Syrians on the other and to advance within thirty-five miles of Damascus. Elsewhere this would have been treated as a miracle of deliverance, there would have been dancing in the streets. In Israel all was gloom.

Before the fighting broke out my family and I had arranged to spend *Succoth* in a small hotel in the seaside resort of Nathania some thirty miles north of Tel-Aviv and I saw no need to change our plans, especially as I had made the Dan hotel my base of operations and it was easier to get from Tel-Aviv to Nathania than to Jerusalem.

The hotel was a drab little place and would have been depressing even on a gala night, but in the war, in the blackout, with half its rooms empty and most of its staff mobilised, it was cheerful as the grave.

There was a small hall adjacent to the hotel, with tables in festive array – red table-cloths, wine glasses, red napkins, gleaming cutlery and crockery. It was laid for a wedding to have been held the previous day. On the morning of the wedding the bridegroom was called up to the army, and went, and the father of the bride ordered the tables to be left as they were, with cutlery, crockery and glasses in place, till he came back, like Miss Havisham's wedding breakfast.

A holiday resort out of season can be a desolate enough place, but it is even more so when it is in season but without guests. The hotels large and small crowding the sea-front stood empty or half-empty, with the footfall of an occasional visitor echoing through their tiled halls, and every hour on the hour the pip, pip, pip of the news bulletins, when all life stopped, as if for a two-minute silence, as people crowded round the nearest radio for the headlines. There were shorter news bulletins at half-hour intervals, and at various times round the clock there were news broadcasts in French, English, Russian, Polish, Rumanian, Arabic, Yiddish, Ladino. Radios never stopped their crackling and people went about with transistors to their ears. It was a bit like England during the final days of a Test Match, and by the look on the faces it didn't seem as if the home side was doing too well. The actual news bulletins were, or should have been, reassuring, and the news commentators were certainly so, but there was hardly a family without a father or son at the front and the fact that the war continued was bad news in itself. Everyone still went about his work at the usual hurried pace, and argued as loudly in the cafés and restaurants, but as darkness approached and the blackout descended, all life faded out, as people huddled round their television sets in darkened rooms to watch the rushes from the front.

A week passed before the first casualty figures were announced. The numbers were not high, but they were felt as a personal bereavement. One might have thought that a people whose recent history has been one of almost ceaseless torment would have had their feeling cauterised sufficiently to be inured to further suffering. Every generation in Israel had had its baptism of fire. One Israeli in five is a survivor of the holocaust. The Jewish state had to be hacked out of an unyielding womb and more than five thousand lives were lost in the War of Independence in 1948 out of a Jewish population of less than a million. Nor did the end of war bring peace. There were Fedayeen incursions from the Gaza strip and Jordan, so that hardly a week passed without further loss of life. The lightning strike against Egypt in the 1956 Sinai campaign brought what was perhaps the most trouble-free decade in Israel's history, but then came the Six Day War.

In 1948, although the casualties had been much larger and the population much smaller than in any of the later wars, the losses were accepted with comparative stoicism, but in 1948 it was touch and go whether the state would survive at all. In 1967 Israel lost 777 men, and although no Israeli will ever speak of casualties as being low or light – the loss of even a single soldier being deeply felt – they were light compared to the magnitude of the victory. The war, moreover, had not come out of a sunny sky. The public had been bracing itself for weeks and the build up of tension was so acute that the actual outbreak of fighting came as a relief. After 1967, with a triumph so complete, and with more distant frontiers, the Israelis allowed themselves to relax and to live a little. The country, partly with the help of German reparations, but largely through its own efforts, was experiencing something of an economic miracle. People were better dressed, better fed, better housed. There was wider choice and sounder quality in the shops. More people took holidays abroad, in spite of a severe travel tax, which was virtually a fine for leaving the country. There were more – indeed, far too many – cars on the road, and Tel-Aviv was racing towards its assumed destiny of a poor man's Los Angeles. Thus, when the Yom Kippur war suddenly came, not only was the army unprepared, but emotions were unprepared, and the mood of euphoria gave way immediately to one of grief. The army recovered its balance, the public mood did not.

The main anxiety of troops at the front seemed to be the worry they were causing at home, and every correspondent who moved among them was piled high with telephone numbers. Could I phone a wife, a mother, a girlfriend and tell them everything was all right? It proved to be a more difficult undertaking than I imagined, for apart from anything else it is a good deal easier to phone London from Tel-Aviv than to phone Jerusalem, or even another part of Tel-Aviv; then, when one finally did get through it was not all that easy to keep the conversation brief. One sometimes got the impression that the entire population was sitting by the phone hoping for, and yet dreading, a call. The receiver was snatched as soon as the phone rang, and there came an anxious, troubled voice: 'Yes, yes, who's that? What is it?' And the grateful relief when one finally delivered the greeting. There was one exchange in particular which I noted down, for it summed up for me the Jewish capacity to shore up real fears with imaginary ones:

'Hullo,' I began.

'Hullo? Who's that? What's that? Who are you?'

'My name is Bermant, I'm a journalist and I've just met your son.'

'My son? How is he? Where is he? Is he all right? Nothing's the matter?'

'Not a thing. He's in fine spirits, fine shape.'

'And?'

'And he asked me to give you his regards, and to tell you not to worry.'

'Not to worry? If you had a son at the front, wouldn't you worry?'

'Of course I would, and he knew you would, that's why he asked me to tell you he's fine.'

'He asked you to tell me?'

'Yes.'

'You mean he's not fine, but he wants me to think he is?'

'No, he is fine, I saw him myself.'

'Fine?'

'Perfectly.'

'Then why didn't he phone himself?'

'Because he's in the middle of the desert.'

'My neighbour's son is in the middle of the desert, and he phoned.'

'Maybe he was near a telephone.'

'If my neighbour's son could get to a telephone, why couldn't he? I've been going crazy with worry.'

'Look, I saw him with my own eyes, and I can tell you've nothing but nothing to worry about.'

'You sure?'

'I'm sure.'

'You're not just saying it to cheer me up?'

'I'm not just saying it to cheer you up.'

'Because if there's something wrong I want to know it. People treat us like children, we're not children, you know.'

'He's in perfect shape.'

'Perfect?'

'Perfect.'

'When did you see him?'

'Yesterday.'

'And he was all right?'

'Fine.'

'You speak Hebrew with an odd accent, who are you?'

'I'm a foreign correspondent.'

'If you're a foreign correspondent, how come you speak Hebrew?'

'Because I was interested in knowing Hebrew.'

'You don't speak it very good.'

'I'm a bad learner.'

'What did you say your name was?'

'Chaim Bermant.'

'Chaim?'

'Bermant.'

'Any relation to the Bermans of Pardess Hannah?'

'Not that I know of.'

'Like it here?'

'Very much.'

'It's even nicer in peace-time.'

'I'm sure it is.'

'Why don't you come and settle?'

The turning point of the war came on 13 October. The Egyptians made a desperate attempt to break out of the perimeter in which they had been held after their initial advance, and were thrown back with the loss of over two hundred tanks. They had formed two bridgeheads, one to the north of the Great Bitter Lake, with the Second Army, and one to the south, with the Third Army, but the two armies did not quite meet and on 16 October a brigade led by General Ariel Sharon, Israel's own Marlborough, moved through this gap, crossed the canal and established a bridgehead in Egypt proper on the west bank. In the next few days, after pausing for reinforcements, he advanced to a point sixty miles east of Cairo, and then, thrusting south-ward, penetrated the town of Suez and cut off the Egyptian Third Army.

At the end of the fighting an Israeli intelligence officer summed up Israel's achievements. The army had occupied one thousand two hundred square kilometres on the west bank of the Canal. The thrust into Syria gained a further six hundred square kilo-metres. The Egyptians had lost two hundred and forty planes and a thousand tanks; the Syrians two hundred and twelve planes and a thousand tanks. 'It is a very big victory,' he said, 'which could have been bigger.'

It did not feel like it in Tel-Aviv.

The ceasefire came into effect on 25 October and the same night the lights came on, flickering, uncertain. The blackout was over, but the black mood remained, indeed it was intensified. During the fighting the pace of events kept people too active to ponder unduly on what was happening and what had happened, but now, with the immediate tensions over they could sit back and count the cost, and Israel was a nation in mourning. For the next few weeks half the population seemed to be engaged in comforting the other half, and even I, a comparative stranger, found myself going from *shiva* to *shiva*.

A *shiva*, I should perhaps explain, is the seven-day period of mourning observed on the death of a close relative. One does not work during that period, or go out, but remains at home, to be visited and comforted by relatives and friends. The custom is not very widely observed by Jews in the Diaspora, but in Israel I noticed that even people who would disregard the Sabbath and ritual laws, observed the *shiva* meticulously. When children come together to mourn for the death of an aged parent the atmosphere is not too depressing and can at times be cheerful, but when one comes upon a middle-aged couple mourning for the death of a young son, their anguish stabs everyone who comes into their presence. I do not think I have cried more than three or four times in my adult life, and one family must have been startled by the unexpected appearance of a tall bearded stranger with suede boots, who came into their tiny overcrowded living-room, tried to mumble something, broke down and fled.

I had last seen their son in a field hospital near Kuneitra. He was so small, slight and young that looked a mere schoolboy, and he lay back, his face white, his eyes large and incredulous, as if unable to take in what had happened to him. An arm and part of his shoulder had been blown away. The surgeon had told me that he had a reasonable chance of recovery, but when I phoned the hospital a week or so later, I was told he was dead.

Israel's main quality is compassion, but it is also its main weakness. Every casualty was felt as a personal loss by every member of the public, and the country was buckling with grief. This, I believe, was the main reason why Israel accepted a ceasefire when every military advantage was on her side, and when every military consideration should have induced her to continue. She could not allow the bloodletting to go on for another minute.

There is no one more courageous than the Israeli soldier, no one more vulnerable than the Israeli civilian; and the pain is intensified, I believe, by the degree with which grief is celebrated in Jewish life.

A death in the family is followed not merely by the *shiva*, which might be called the primary period of mourning, but a secondary period, or *shloshim*, which lasts a month, and a tertiary period which lasts a year. During the *shiva* one is incarcerated, a prisoner in one's own home. One may not work or study, and one's reading should be confined to sad stories of misfortune and travail, like the book of Job. If for some reason one must go out, one has to put gravel or peas in one's shoes as a constant reminder of one's grief. One may follow one's normal occupation during *shloshim*, but one should not have a hair cut or shave, or wear new clothes, and during the tertiary period one must not attend any wedding, festive occasion or place of entertainment.

And even that is not the end of it, for on every anniversary of the death – the *yohr-tzeit* – one lights a candle in memory of the deceased and says the *kaddish* for the repose of the soul. And four times a year special remembrance prayers, known as *yizkor*, are read in synagogue!

'My God, remember the soul of my honoured father, who has gone to his eternal home. O may his soul be bound up in the bond of life, and may he rest in honour, with fulness of joy in Thy presence, with pleasure at Thy right hand side for evermore. Amen.'

The darkest curse known to the Hebrew language is *yemach shemo vezichro* – may his name and remembrance be blotted out. The purpose of the *yizkor* – the word means memorial – and the *yohr-tzeit* candles answers to a certain Jewish yearning for immortality and as long as someone is recalled among his beloved ones, he is not entirely dead, but the *yizkor* can also be a periodic opening of wounds, and it is not uncommon for congregants to break down in the course of the prayer, sometimes with hysteria.

Israel's war-dead are first laid to rest in what are called temporary military cemeteries in the north and south of the country and are later reburied in a cemetery of the family's choosing, which means that many families suffer the ordeal of two funerals and the scenes of grief at the second are perhaps even more heart-rending than the first, with mothers tearing their hair, fathers jumping into graves and clinging to the coffins of their sons. One young widow with a small son who had lost her husband in the Yom Kippur war told me she was dreading the reburial. It had taken her something like six months to pick up the shreds of her shattered life and build up a new existence, and to accommodate her child to his new fatherless situation, and now she would have to start over again.

One day, my two daughters, Alisa and Eve, returned tear-stained from school. The day had been set aside as a memorial to the holocaust, and classes assembled in the darkened hall, a candle was lit and the children sang the sad songs of the ghetto.

The following week they were again in tears. This time it was a memorial day to the fallen in the War of Independence.

In June I attended a third memorial meeting. It was not a national occasion, but many meetings like it are held up and down the country every summer. Every group in Israel has its own *lantsmaschaft*, Polish, Bulgarian, Rumanian, Hungarian, Persian, Iraqi, even so-called Anglo-Saxons, and within every local group there is a sub-group consisting of immigrants from a particular neighbourhood.

I attended the annual meeting of the Jews of Breslev. There were about six thousand Jews in the towns and the surrounding area when the Germans invaded in 1941. Many of the young and able-bodied fled to Russia, among them my mother's youngest brother, Rachmiel, who had been a Communist, joined the Red Army and, in the words of one of the survivors, suffered a *gutten teit* – died a good death – he was killed in action. My other uncles died a *shlechten teit*, a bad death. They were married and kept immobile by the number and age of their children, and for a time they remained in hiding in the cellar of my grandmother's house, with several dozen other families. They had laid in a large store of food which was soon exhausted, and the menfolk took it in turn to venture out at night, to bring fresh milk and water. One night it was the turn of an uncle, Chaim Kasre, to go out. He was spotted by a German guard, shot and wounded, but no attempt was made to arrest him. He was left writhing in his own blood all that night and much of the next morning, his cries audible to his wife and children in the nearby cellar. To have gone to his help would have meant certain death, not only for his helper but the whole group, and they remained in the darkness listening to his agonies till his voice died away. A survivor told me later : 'I can still hear him every time I shut my eyes.'

In a cellar in another part of Breslev, there was another group in hiding, among them a young mother with a newly born child. When the Germans with guard dogs began to search the house, the baby started crying, and the mother, fearing for the safety of the group, stifled her child with her own hands. It was of no avail. They were all discovered and rounded up and taken with the other Jews of Breslev to the nearby woods, made to dig their own graves, and shot down in two days of slaughter.

I learned all this from a cousin of my mother's and her husband who had fled shortly after the Germans marched in and had joined the Polish partisans.

There were only a handful of survivors from the entire neighbourhood. Most of them live in Israel now and they come together with their wives and children every year to talk of those times, to light candles, utter a memorial prayer, shed a tear.

One might have thought that there was sufficient in the present and recent past to satisfy the lachrymose instincts of even the most morbid individuals, but Judaism also delves into the remote past to add a further area of darkness to existence. There is a fast to commemorate the assassination of the Babylonian governor of Judea (sixth century B.C.), and a fast to commemorate the slaughter of the firstborn before the exodus from Egypt (2000 B.C.), a fast to mark the fast undertaken on behalf of Persian Jewry by Queen Esther (fourth century B.C.), and three different fast days connected with the destruction of Jerusalem by the Babylonians (sixth century B.C.), the first to mark the beginning of the siege, the second, the breach in the city wall, and the third the fall of the Temple. The three weeks between the second and third fast are treated as a period of semi-mourning when no weddings can take place. The seven-week period between the feast of Passover and Pentecost is likewise treated as one of mourning connected with various calamities in Jewish history, some going back to Roman times, some as recent as the Crusades. The ten days between the Jewish New Year and the Day of Atonement is a further solemn period, rather like Lent, and altogether twelve weeks out of the fifty-two are for one reason or another designated as periods of mourning during which one should not cut one's hair, buy new clothes, attend a place of entertainment or celebrate a wedding. It is only the very Orthodox who will in fact observe these weeks with the solemnity that tradition demands, but in Israel, a large part of the population still observes *Tisha B'Av* with fasting and a succession of sombre rituals. Men assemble in the synagogues, all ornaments like the cover over the ark, are removed, and they sit on low stools to read from Jeremiah's *Lamentations*:

'How doth the city sit solitary that was full of people! How is she become as a widow! She that was great among the nations and a princess among the provinces, how is she become tributary.

'She weepeth sore in the night, and her tears are on her cheeks : among all her lovers she hath none to comfort her; all her friends have dealt treacherously with her, they are become her enemies ...'

There is a certain sweetness to the melancholy and to an extent the beauty of the language rises above the darkness of the subject. The *Lamentations* are too articulate to be lamentable, but they are accompanied by special prayers called *kinoth* which, once one becomes familiar with the language, are exercises in masochism. One set of *kinoth* commemorates the final agonies of a group of martyrs who died at the hands of Rome, another a massacre in Mayence, a third a massacre in Paris, a fourth the massacre of York. One also finds among them sublime elegies. But in the main they are a catalogue of torment, many of them read to a mournful refrain – *Alalai li* – O woe is me – which sounds a good deal more mournful in Hebrew than it is in English, especially if repeated time after time :

'When women could devour their young ... O woe is me.
'When compassionate women could boil their own young ... O woe is me.
'When the flesh of the fathers was prepared for their children ... O woe is me.
'When the tongue of sucklings could cleave to their tongues through thirst ... O woe is me.

And so on, one line more dreadful than the other. The effect on those who understand the language and have any imagination at all is more painful than flagellation and one emerges from a synagogue not a chastened, but a broken man.

Tradition has made the Jewish people legatees of grief but such rituals re-enacted year after year, with their shedding of tears and the beating of breasts, are a strain on national morale.

VI

At the Sign of the Brief-Case

The emblem of the Jewish state is the seven-branched candelabra. It should have been the brief-case. Everybody who is somebody has one, and in Israel nobody is nobody. Children carry their books to school in one, plumbers their tools, building labourers their sandwiches, public officials (and private) their public and private papers. It is part receptacle, part status symbol, part talisman and even where it no longer indicates status or calling, it at least indicates aspirations.

The founding fathers of Zionism sought to change the whole structure of Jewish society as it had existed in the Diaspora with its large strata of business and professional men and small working-class base, and hoped to create a co-operative commonwealth of working men. Their ideal was a class of philosopher farmer and the typical kibbutznick is not all that far from the ideal, but, partly because of the very demands kibbutznicks make of themselves, they have always remained a small class and today comprise less than three per cent of the population.

Between 1881 (when a succession of Russian pogroms induced a great westward movement of Jews) and the outbreak of war in 1914, something like 2,000,000 left Russia and the eastern provinces of the Hapsburg Empire. Of these over 1,600,000 went to America and under 80,000 to Palestine. The latter were mainly from better-off homes. What there was of the Jewish proletariat headed en masse for America. Between 1919 and 1939 there were only two periods when Palestine immigration rose above the 10,000 a year mark. The first was in the mid 1920s when the economic nationalism of the Polish government ruined or threatened to ruin many Jewish businessmen; the

G

second was after the rise of Hitler in the mid 1930s. The inflow in both cases was overwhelmingly middle-class. It did not mean that they all found themselves middle-class occupations. Many became labourers, but they regarded themselves what they were in fact, middle-class people in temporarily straitened circumstances. As soon as the situation improved they scraped together enough to go into business, or the administration. The Jewish working-class was in the main transitory; it was a state through which newcomers passed on the way up. The permanent working-class was Arab. That this might happen was becoming evident in the earliest years of Jewish settlement, and in 1908–9 a convoy of Yemenite Jews was brought up from Arabia, partly because of their renown as hardy working men who were, moreover, content to remain working men.

The situation changed dramatically in the first years of statehood when over 600,000 immigrants poured into the country within three or four years, most of them from North Africa, and almost overnight a community which had been predominantly European in origin became predominantly Sephardic or Oriental. This did not mean that the character of the country was transformed in the same way. The Ashkenazim, though by now in the land for several generations, had never turned native. In a sense the snow had never melted on their boots. Their European attitudes and outlook were still intact, and they inculcated them in every successive wave of immigrants. They controlled the schools, the universities, the press, the radio. One still heard occasional voices preaching 'the nobility of labour'. Society was certainly more egalitarian than anything to be found in Europe. Welfare benefits were substantial and an unskilled manual labourer with many children could earn more than a university lecturer with few. But the European belief that a desk job carried more authority, dignity and grace, even where it carried less money, persisted, and persists still, and with it, the European, or at least the Euro-Jewish determination to get on. Baron Hirsch, a Jewish philanthropist, and friend of Edward VII, who was possibly the richest man in the world, complained of this as the source of all Jewish misfortune. It was not something which affected the Oriental Jews to the same extent. They came with a more relaxed attitude which, however, changed under Ashkenazi tutelage, and the Yemenites in particular have become as ambitious and as go-ahead as any Galician Jew on the make.

Israel with a population of about 3,000,000 has seven universities, but they are not sufficient to accommodate everyone anxious for a place and thousands of Israelis study abroad. All this may be but a further example of the old Jewish hunger for learning as the highest good, but it is also, in part, a hunger for degrees. A first degree, possibly because so many people have one, is no longer taken as a sign of arrival and if one stops almost any Israeli under the age of fifty (and sometimes beyond) and asks him what he is doing, he will answer : *'Any ose kurse'* – I am working on a course. B.A.s are striving for M.A.s, M.A.s for Ph.D.s and Ph.D.s in one discipline are seeking qualifications in another. A neighbour of ours in Jerusalem, the mother of two children, a lawyer by training (and an excellent plumber and electrician), was working for a doctorate in biochemistry. I was in Israel once on a newspaper assignment and anxious to interview a certain Cabinet Minister. 'You've come at a bad time,' said his secretary, 'he's trying to polish off his doctorate.' A middle-aged man, the head of a major national institution, felt that his office called for something grander than his B.A. from Manchester University, and got himself a pseudo-doctorate by post from an American university. A friend, a highly skilled dentist from Glasgow, decided to call himself Doctor on settling in Israel. 'Not for the glory of it,' he assured me, 'but unless you're doctor somebody they'll not open their mouth to you here.'

Not everybody who wants to make it, of course, makes it, but nearly everybody feels that they should, and by way of compensation they are given, or more often, assume, high-sounding titles, which I once summed up as *menahel-mania. Menahel* is the Hebrew for manager, and rare is the individual who will confess to being anything less. If he is a mechanic he will, or if he will not his relatives will, speak of an engineer; if a schoolmaster, as headmaster; if he's a doctor, as specialist. I knew numerous civil servants, but not one who was less, or described himself as less, than head of his division. And if one is a writer or a poet or a painter or a composer or an instrumentalist, one is always 'the famous' or 'the well known'. *'Yedua'*, well known, is used so promiscuously, that it is almost the Hebrew for unknown. If Israel were ever to have a memorial to the Unknown Warrior, it would, I am sure, be referred to as the Tomb of the Well-Known Warrior.

I once came upon a photograph of myself in the daily *Davar*, with the caption : 'Chaim Bermant, the famous English poet'. When I pointed out that I was neither English, nor a poet, nor, indeed, famous, I suspect that my protest may have been taken as an example of subtle English conceit. Did I think I was so well known that I could be introduced without a prefix?

What I describe is not peculiar to Israel. I once had to call on a certain Rabbi in London. He had to go out and left a scribbled note pinned to his door : 'Will be back in ten minutes, please wait. Rabbi . . . B.A. (Hons).' The Classified Advertisement department of the *Jewish Chronicle* used to be plagued by advertisers – especially those announcing an engagement – who gave themselves outlandish degrees which no one had ever heard of and which, on closer examination, proved not to exist, and the paper eventually had to introduce an index of acceptable qualifications. It is also troubled from time to time by visiting foreign Rabbis who describe themselves as Chief Rabbi of this or that place when they are no such thing, or where, at best, they are the only Rabbi in the place named.

All this may, for all I know, be common to all immigrant groups. The newcomer needs external proof that he has arrived and Jewish presumption and pretension are among the by-products of Jewish wandering and exile. These characteristics, however, have not changed with his homecoming; on the contrary, they have become more pronounced. The Israeli is like other Jews, only more so.

After the Balfour Declaration promised the creation of a Jewish state in Palestine, the World Zionist Organisation established a Jewish Agency which was a sort of government in exile. When Israel became independent, Ben-Gurion and others, who were the heads of the various departments of the Jewish Agency, became the Government of Israel. The Agency itself, now that its work was complete, should have fallen away, but it continued in business and even expanded and formed a sort of second division government from which one could rise to the first, or to which one could be relegated from the first. There is also the *Histadrut* which is in some ways equivalent to the British T.U.C., but which is very much more, for with its sick fund (which is the nearest thing in Israel to a national health service), its industrial holding company, its banks and insurance companies, it is a government within a government. Hospitals may have a shortage of doctors, nurses and orderlies, but there is no shortage of clerks. The Hebrew University has twice as many clerks as teachers. The country is awash with paper and groans under the weight and number of its bureaucrats.

This is in part due to *rachmanut*, the very Jewish quality of mercy. There is a feeling that no one is so helpless, or useless or feckless that he should be deprived of his livelihood. It is difficult to demote a man and almost impossible to dismiss him, and incompetents will be moved upwards or sideways, but rarely down and never out, and if necessary someone will be brought in to do the job. Someone in the end has to pay for mercy, and in this case it is the general public. The quality of such mercy, from my experience of it, is twice cursed.

Politics and vanity also enter into it. The number of government departments (and departments of the Jewish Agency) is based not on administrative need but on the number of partners to the coalition – and the Government alone has no less than twenty-three departments. Some Ministers, moreover, measure their importance by the number on their payroll, which is also the measure of their patronage. Senior officials build big empires, junior ones small empires and everyone makes jobs for everyone else. The very number of officials makes it impossible to pay them all a living wage. Even senior men supplement their income by taking two or three jobs and they are too tired and too jaded to do any of them well. But that is only part of the trouble. Israel is largely a co-operative state, and the public official looks upon himself less as servant than proprietor.

The founding fathers of Israel, moreover, were brought up in Russia. Many Russian habits still prevail, and the Russian civil servant has always regarded – as he still regards – the general public with contempt.

All of which would matter little if one could go through life – as one does in Britain – without encountering more than two or three officials a year, but in Israel one cannot draw breath or pass water without a permit. One stumbles upon officials at every turn and there is many a jack-in-office with the authority to affect the happiness of entire households, who should not have been entrusted to issue a dog licence.

My own contacts with bureaucracy were largely confined to the government press office and the army censors, whose staff were never less than courteous, competent and helpful, but they were so unlike the staff encountered elsewhere that one presumes they were hand-picked. The overseas counter of the General Post Office was rather more typical. There were two large wenches in their early twenties behind the counter, chewing gum in unison like browsing cattle, chatting together, and usually loth to interrupt their conversation to attend to the waiting customer. At a branch post office which I sometimes used, there was a little stubby clerk, with a stubbly chin, thick glasses and thin hair, who was usually eating, sometimes tea and a bun, sometimes yoghurt, occasionally an apple, sometimes all three. He did, I admit, eat briskly, but he hated to be interrupted in mid-nosh, and there was frequently a line at his counter while he scraped the last reluctant smear of yoghurt from the corner of his yoghurt cup.

When we arrived in Israel I was anxious to take out a health insurance policy for my family and myself, and I was advised not to use the Kupat Holim, the Histradruth Sick Fund, because one could expire while waiting for a doctor, and I therefore went to another group called Kupat Holim Amami. The first time I called I found a large milling crowd and I was advised to come back in the afternoon 'when the place is almost empty'. I came back in the afternoon and the place was closed. When I returned the following afternoon the clerk looked at me and looked at the clock. 'We close in quarter of an hour,' he said. 'But you're still open,' I said. 'Yes, but if we started seeing people quarter of an hour before we closed we would be open all night.'

I returned yet another time to find that the clerk who deals with the new applications was off, and nobody else in the office was prepared to handle them, upon which I decided that no possible malady to which we could become victim would be half as hazardous as an insurance policy with that particular concern.

I went along to another company called Hashiloah where they were efficient and brisk and where the secretary was so attractive that I was hoping to have cause to return a second, third or even fourth time. She disposed of the matter in ten minutes. The fees were reasonable, till I discovered that they provided for almost every contingency short of ill health, and I finally went along to the group I was originally urged to avoid – the Histradruth Sick Fund. I enrolled in one building which took a mere hour, and was sent along to another where, after a morning's wait, they took blood and urine samples. I was then sent along to a third building for an X-ray which took the better part of an afternoon, and then spent yet another morning waiting to be seen by a doctor, to have my blood pressure measured and other tests, and in due course we were admitted as members. Some time later my wife collapsed and had to be rushed to hospital for a major operation. We presumed that the costs would be borne by the Sick Fund. It was not. We had only been members for five months, and one only qualified for benefits after six.

'Why wasn't I told when I originally enrolled?' I demanded.

'You're right,' said the official with unusual candour, 'you should have been', and he suggested that I take the matter up with head office. When I spoke to head office, I was told that as a mere visitor I should not have been allowed to join in the first place. I was given apologies in plenty, but no recompense.

When we came to Israel I had to pay £28 in customs duties on an article which I later discovered was customs free. I wrote about it to the official concerned at the customs house, who referred me to a colleague at the Jerusalem head office, who referred me to another colleague in another office, who referred me to a third, who referred me back to the first, who then suggested that I travel to the customs house and take it up with the official originally concerned. I finally called in a lawyer who cleared the matter up in a day. The lawyer was a friend who refused to take a fee, otherwise the cost would not have been far short of the sum involved. In Israel one needs lawyers not so much for the intricacies of the law, as the intricacies of the administration.

One sometimes feels that time is no object in Israel. The merest transaction can take a morning, provided always that the official one wants to see is available. One reason why he may not be available is that he could be on reserve duty in the army. Another is that he is probably himself waiting to see another official in another department, who may in turn be waiting ...

Now if all this was due to a cosy doziness, a *manana* tradition, it would to an extent be forgivable, but it comes with a sweaty eagerness to get on. Israel is a great, buzzing, restless hive, agitated, fidgety, loud with bother and pother, a nation in a hurry. One can understand why it is in a hurry and why it might never have come into being if it were more relaxed, and yet for all the frantic energy generated not all that much gets done.

There is a refrain which one hears everywhere in Israel at all times of day and most times of night – *rega, rega,* a minute, a minute, shouted loudly and frantically (there is even a gesture for it, involving the thumb and forefinger drawn closely together and waved up and down). One hears it most often on the buses, for drivers always hurry to get started before all the alighting passengers have got off and before most of the prospective passengers have got on. And everyone shouts *rega*, and they stop. But what happens if the alighting passengers are on a train? This is what happened to us.

On a bright spring morning, my wife, my brother-in-law, and my four children, aged ten, seven, five and two, set out on a picnic to Beit Shemesh. Beit Shemesh is in the plains and involves an hour's journey, through what is perhaps the most beautiful route in the world, round the wooded Judean hills, through a landscape that might have been familiar to travellers in David's time. When we reached Beit Shemesh we found that the doors on the platform side were locked, but we saw some passengers alighting on the railway side, and Eve (aged seven) and Azriel (aged five) followed them down. I then alighted, and as I reached up to bring Daniel (aged two) and his push-chair down, the train began to move. I immediately jumped back on and snatched wildly in all directions for the communication cord. There was none, and I finally found a communications lever at the end of the carriage. By then the train had picked up speed and was travelling at sixty miles an hour. I rushed along the length of the train – the picture of my two crying children on the railway track before my eyes – to find a guard, but there was none in sight. At this point the train stopped for a minute, but we were by then two or three miles from Beit Shemesh, and I did not want to risk getting off in case it should move on before I had collected my whole family. And the train indeed moved on after a minute. Then, after a clamour from other passengers, a guard materialised, and suggested that we stay on till Ramleh, which we would reach in another twenty minutes, from where I could get a bus and be reunited with my children in Beit Shemesh in an hour, maybe two, but when he noticed the murderous glint in my eyes, he quickly ran along to the engineer, and the train finally pulled up at Nahal Sorek, a deserted station. From there they radioed to Beit Shemesh, and a small clatter-buggy was sent to collect us. For the children it was a joy-ride. For my wife, who had recently come out of hospital after her operation, it was a nightmare, and she was in constant fear that her stitches might come undone, but we reached Beit Shemesh in one piece. The family was reunited and we had our picnic, and the children had something to write home about.

So did I, but first I wrote to the Minister of Transport and Communications, whom I had met at various press briefings, to give him an account of the day. Communications in Israel are not what they ought to be and by the time it reached the Minister he was out of office and over a month passed before I got a reply, from the director of railways. His letter is framed on my study wall:

Israel Railways,
Plumer Square,
Haifa.   26/6/1974

Dear Sir,
    Your letter addressed to the Minister of Transport, dated 19.5.74. was forwarded to us and after thorough verification we found the following:

    The doors of the carriage in which you travelled on the 10.52 train on Yom Ha'atzmauth, were *not* locked, but unfortunately could be opened only with great difficulty. The train guard gave the departure signal to the Station Master at Beit Shemesh when he saw all the doors shut on the platform side and it was only after the train had left Beit Shemesh station, that the station staff there saw the children on the track . . .

We most sincerely regret the incident and are doing everything to see to it that coach doors open properly, though such defects are liable to occur.

May we point out that you should not have risked alighting on the off-side of the train, with the small children, push-chair, etc; continuation to the trip to the next stop would have been preferable . . .

Now if a matter like this occurred in Britain one could take it up with one's Member of Parliament who might either raise it privately with the Ministry or table a question in the House of Commons, but the Israeli M.P. does not function in this way. There are no constituencies. At elections the public is presented with a list of candidates by each of the political parties. One does not vote for any individual but for the party as a whole, and the seats are then allotted in proportion to the votes cast for each party. There are a hundred and twenty seats, so that if a party gets, say, ten per cent of the votes it will receive twelve seats. It may submit fifty to sixty names to the electorate, and the electoral hopes of a candidate are based on his position in the list. Politicians, therefore, are rather more concerned to remain in the good grace of the party than the electorate. Individuals and groups with any serious grievances have to take to the streets to make their case heard, and one can rarely pass the *Knesset* (Israel's Parliament) or the Hakiryah (its Whitehall) without seeing some sort of demonstration in progress.

To protect oneself, to get anywhere, to be anyone, one is almost compelled to be part of a group, and the most effective groups are the political parties. The parties may at one time have represented distinct ideologies and to an extent they still do, but they also mean jobs, preferment, influence. Jews may be the most individualistic of people, but one needs more than an ordinary streak of individualism to survive on one's own in the Jewish state and one is aware of a constant thrusting for place, an elbowing for position.

My misgivings about Israel seemed very petty once the Yom Kippur war broke out and I came into contact with the men in the fighting lines, tough, lean, swarthy, intelligent, alert, high-spirited and resourceful and it seemed to me that there could be little fundamentally wrong with a society which produced such men.

And yet once the fighting was over some old doubts crept back. There had been a great deal of muddle and disarray which were at least partly due to some of the characteristics I have described and although there were few complaints about the courage of the soldiers, there were a great many about discipline. Every Israeli soldier not merely believes that he has a baton in his knapsack, but that he has a baton in his hand and if given an order he will be inclined to argue the matter and even to ignore it.

I have already described one typically Israeli gesture involving the thumb and forefinger, and meaning *rega, rega*. There is another involving the forefinger and the flat of the hand. One taps oneself on the chest with the forefinger, and puts out the palm of one's hand like a policeman halting traffic, and it means: *Tishmoach alai* – leave it to me! There has been a conscious endeavour among Israelis to shrug off the habits of exile, and in some respects they have succeeded to excess. I am not sure that the diffidence of the ghetto Jew was more wholesome than the swaggering self-assurance of the Israeli, but it was infinitely more becoming.

I also had misgivings about more serious matters. One of the reasons why we were anxious to live in Israel is that there is something vaguely unreal about being an observant Jew in the Diaspora and although I enjoyed the Sabbath and festival rituals I had an odd feeling that I was taking part in a charade, whereas Israel seemed to be the natural setting for the sort of Jew I was and the sort of Jewishness I revere.

More important, our two daughters were of school age and in England I had yanked them out of the mainstream of their English contemporaries and sent them to an expensive Jewish prep-school. It was, I felt, not wholesome to isolate one's children excessively from the wider society in which they should have to live, but we were anxious that they should have a sound Jewish education. In Israel, I felt, there would be no such conflict, and we enrolled the girls in the Evelyna de Rothschild, which, we were assured, was one of the best girls' schools in the country, and which perhaps it is, but when I opened their maths books on the first day of term I almost removed them there and then. For the Evelyna is a religious school and in religious schools they have taken care to doctor the history books so that they should not conflict with the Old Testament, which I expected. What I did not expect was that they would doctor the cross in the arithmetical tables and instead of the vertical bar over the horizontal thus, $+$, they have an inverted St Anthony's cross, thus $\perp$, and I felt that any schools which went to such lengths to guard the souls of their children against external influence could not be entrusted with their education.

And then there were the old wives' tales. One teacher actually told her class that the Yom Kippur war was a punishment from God because Jewish women went about immodestly dressed. The children were given a constant diet of superstition and bigotry. Happily the girls laughed at it, and I took no action. Moreover, it is often the case that people with the most absurd ideas have the most wholesome instincts, and this was certainly the case with the teachers at Evelyna, who were so approachable, so considerate, so helpful and went to such inordinate pains to integrate the girls into their classes, that I found it difficult to remain critical of them. But I remained, and remain, critical of the system. In England if I removed my children from daily contact with other English children, they at least moved among all kinds of Jewish children. In Israel they were confined to contact only with the Orthodox. I was also troubled by external events.

Outside Israel, even in the larger Jewish communities, the Orthodox usually form an amiable and unobtrusive minority who add warmth and colour to Jewish life, and whose example is sufficiently attractive to be followed by many people who may not share their beliefs.

In Israel, however, Orthodoxy is neither amiable nor unobtrusive, but bloody-minded and aggressive. Let me give an example.

If one drives a car on the Sabbath through any ultra-Orthodox quarter of Jerusalem, one is likely to have a brick heaved through the windscreen. I have much sympathy for such heavers. They

have a right to enjoy their Sabbath in peace and one can get
about Jerusalem without driving through their areas. To which
I would add that such is the nature of Israeli drivers and driving
that I often feel tempted to heave a brick through their windows
even on week-days. It is not, however, illegal to use a car on
Shabbat, but there is no public transport, except taxis which
charge double rates. Israel, moreover, has a six-day week, and
thus while the well-to-do can drive out to the hills or the forests
or the sea, on their one free day the poor are left to swelter in
their slums. And this situation exists through the ill-grace of the
religious parties in the Knesset who, though they have never
received more than fifteen per cent of the vote, use their political
position to impose their ways upon the entire country. I believe
this to be not only morally wrong, but corrosive to the very
traditions it is trying to preserve, and I came round to the view
that Orthodoxy is benign only where it is impotent.

I was in Israel on newspaper assignments on several occasions
after the 1967 war and interviewed leading figures in all walks
of life and nearly all took it for granted that, apart from Jerusalem
and minor border rectifications, the conquered territories were
being retained merely as a bargaining counter and would be
returned in the event of a peace settlement. By the time we came
in 1973 all this had changed and there was a formidable movement against returning even the sands of Sinai, and nothing at all
of the West Bank areas taken from Jordan. Rabbis issued edicts
that it was against the Torah to return one inch of the sacred
soil of the Holy Land to alien hands. Herut, the small extreme
right wing party headed by Menahe Begin, the former chief of
the Irgun Tzvei Leumi, led the movement and in 1973 the
National Religious Party was committed by its annual conference
to the principle that the West Bank was not negotiable. This
was politically important because the N.R.P. has been an essen-
tial element in every government coalition, and if its members
were committed to opposing the return of any part of former
Jordanian territory then, of course, it would hamper any government efforts for a peace settlement.

It was important also on a personal level. The National Religious Party, which used to be known as the Mizrachi, has branches
throughout the Diaspora, and I was for many years a member

of the youth group of the British branch, the Bnei Akivah. It seemed to me now that I had devoted some of my most formative years to a pernicious and destructive cause. Peace prospects were slight, and certainly distant, so the fact that they might be hampered was a comparatively minor matter, but supposing the N.R.P. had its way and the West Bank became a permanent part of Israel? What would happen to its 1,000,000 Arabs? No one, not even the National Religious Party, suggested that they be expelled. Yet if they were given full rights they could, together with the half million Arabs already in Israel and their very high birth-rate, eventually outgrow the Jewish population (whose birth-rate was rapidly declining). What would happen then? 'We'll face that when we come to it', an N.R.P. leader told me, but it would invariably involve a Rhodesian-type constitution with one electoral register for Jews and another for Arabs so that the former could always have the upper hand.

That, however, was a distant fear. There were nearer ones. The whole basis of the Zionist creed was that Jews should return to the land as self-employed labourers tilling their own soil. I was on a tour of Israel in the summer of 1974 and one hot and hazy afternoon, I took a wrong turning and drove into a *moshav* – a co-operative agricultural settlement – to ask the way. I found the place asleep behind shuttered windows. The only people about and working were Arab labourers.

I am not suggesting this was a typical scene, but more and more *moshavim* are coming to rely on Arab labour and one can see the emergence of a class of gentlemen farmers, like the colons of Algeria and Rhodesia. If that should happen – and if the conquered territories are retained one cannot stop it happening – then Zionism will have lost its moral basis and the whole Zionist experiment is doomed.

We lived in a part of Jerusalem much favoured by Cabinet Ministers, with the Prime Minister, Golda Meir, around one corner, and the Foreign Secretary, Abba Eban, around the other. When Dr Henry Kissinger descended for his round of negotiations early in 1974 the whole area was virtually impassable as he moved in closely guarded convoys from the one to the other. And every time he appeared there would be a crowd of demonstrators, composed largely of Bnei Akivah youngsters in their knitted skull-caps, waving placards and chanting slogans. The future of the West Bank was not on the agenda, but Sinai and the Golan were and there were people who were opposed to handing back anything at all, on the grounds that if you give back anything you would in time be compelled to surrender everything, or, as one demonstrator put it, 'Jerusalem is being defended on the Suez Canal.' 'Would it not be even better defended on the Nile?' I asked ironically. 'It would,' he said, 'but we don't happen to be on the Nile.'

I encountered these crowds on my nightly walks and was less troubled than amused by them. One evening, however, I returned home shaken. Kissinger had lately taken another wife, who was not Jewish, and as he emerged from Abba Eban's residence in Balfour Street and stood for a while on the threshold, he was faced with a crowd of youngsters shrieking in unison : 'Go back to your *shikse*, Kissinger!' I was aware of the strong Jewish feeling against marrying out of the faith, but this was brute racialism. I described the incident to my wife and wondered, if this was the situation to which a religious education could lead, whether we were right in sending our children to a religious school, more, whether we were right to give them a religious upbringing at all.

My wife, for all the depth of her convictions, understood, and to an extent shared my doubts and anxieties and agreed that some dreadful things were being said and done in Israel in the name of Judaism, but her attitude was that I should stay and fight it, which showed a touching faith in my prowess as writer and publicist. It reminded me of a monologue by the late Robb Wilton which began : 'The day war broke out my missus said to me, you've got to stop it . . .'

VII

Mrs Tittlemouse

'Once upon a time there was a good mouse, and her name was Mrs Tittlemouse. She lived in a bank under a hedge. Such a funny house! There were yards and yards of sandy passages . . .'

One of my more pleasant evening chores was to read bed-time stories to the children; when Azriel, our eldest son, was four his favourite was Beatrix Potter and, in particular, *Mrs Tittlemouse*.

My father never read me bed-time stories, but he told me some, about Rabbi Akivah, how he left his wife and children to study in Yeshiva, and how he became a great scholar with thousands of disciples, how he was tortured by the Romans for keeping the Jewish religion alive, and how he died in agony with the name of the Almighty on his lips. I listened enthralled but would, I think, have preferred Mrs Tittlemouse, and I eventually discovered her for myself when I was eight or nine years old in the Langside public library in Glasgow. The illustrations, the subject matter, the very size and format of the Beatrix Potter books suggested that they were for little people, whereas I was a growing lad, and I read them furtively behind larger books.

Parents like mine would do anything for their children, but they were impatient of childhood. One is not – unless one is part of a particularly poor family – lumbered with adult responsibilities but there are attempts to imbue one with adult attitudes and tastes. Playtime was resented. Football and other games were for *shkotzim* (young gentiles). One went from school to *cheder*, from *cheder* to homework, from homework to prayers and bed. The only permitted pleasures were those associated with the Sabbath and festivals I only ever had one toy as a child, a pistol and caps, and even they were connected with a festival, *Purim*, when a certain degree of riotous behaviour is permitted. When I came to Glasgow I discovered children's comics and children's books and children's games and *Children's Hour*, and I immersed myself in Beatrix Potter to catch up on everything I missed. It was only then that I began to be a child and I am not sure I have ceased to be one since.

I had never been taken to Christmas Pantomime as a child (I never in fact set foot in a theatre till I was fifteen), but when my eldest daughter was five we took her to *Peter Pan*. For my wife it was a return to scenes of childhood, but for me it was an introduction to one of the rituals of English middle-class life. The audience knew all the cues, much as a Jewish child might know his *shema*, when to hiss Hook, when to clap hands for Tinker Bell. The parents, I could see, enjoyed it as much as, if not more than, the children, and I think that Peter Pan represents an ideal in English life, the eternal child.

There can be few cultures in which childhood is so richly celebrated with nursery songs and nursery tales and nursery rhymes and dramatis personae of nursery folk who people the imagination of every child. And even now there is hardly a town in England where one cannot come upon the gabled roofs, the cobbled walks, the stone walls, the oak doors, the mullioned windows, where once upon a time there lived, or could have lived . . . There is something of Never-Never Land about England. And for all the changes that countryside remains much as I have known it. There are beautiful areas which have been swallowed up by the growth of towns, but I, who take so much pleasure in my many children, am hardly in a position to complain of the growth in population. Rural England tames and transforms innovations till they blend with the past. There was a time when electricity pylons were regarded as an eyesore, but a line of pylons striding across a wind-swept moor have an austere beauty of their own. One misses the horses and the cheerful clatter of mower and binder, but a fleet of great combine harvesters moving line abreast through a field of corn have something of the majesty of galleons. A car abandoned in a city street blights its surroundings, a rusting piece of farm machinery, even before it is engulfed by vegetation, assumes something of the dignity of sculpture. Certainly the countryside evoked by the stories and illustrations of Beatrix Potter, was substantially the countryside I had known in Annan and Thaxted and which greeted us on our Sunday excursions in the car.

Read in Jerusalem, *Mrs Tittlemouse* evoked not only my childhood and my Glasgow, and the glass-topped tables and the panelled walls of the Langside Library, but my England, the moist meadows of Thaxted, the bustling hedgerows, the waving corn fields, the warm, sunny, harvest days and, alas for Mrs Tittlemouse, the mice scurrying from the combine blades, moving ever inwards into denser packs, to be slaughtered in the final swath so that the straw emerged caked with their tiny corpses.

I wanted everything, a countryman's life with a townsman's sentimentality about animals, a goyish sense of liberty with a Jewish sense of tradition; I wanted my Essex with my Jewish contemporaries; I wanted my Jews to be a little less earnest and a little more bucolic, a little less in synagogue and more in the pub; I wanted Jewish warmth and English detachment. In fact, I wanted such a conflicting mass of things that I came to realise that perhaps the most English thing about me was my failure to grow up or rather, as Polonius might have put it, in England such a failure can pass unnoticed, for it is a country where even the mature pretend to be childish.

'Mrs Tittlemouse was a most terribly tidy particular little mouse, always sweeping and dusting the soft sandy floors.
Sometimes a beetle lost its way in the passage.
"Shush! Shush! little dirty feet!" said Mrs Tittlemouse, clattering her dust-pan . . .'

Reading these words one hot, windless Jerusalem night, with my parched voice crackling in my ears, I experienced a pang of longing that brought tears to my eyes, and my son looked up to see what was wrong : and I sometimes asked myself if the faults I found with Israel arose out of my longing for England, for they seemed so slight when set against the achievements and so natural when set in their circumstances. A people which has fought four wars in twenty-six years and which is constantly under threat of annihilation has a great deal to be agitated about, and all things considered it is perhaps a cause of surprise that Israelis should be as sane and as stable as they are.

But why did I need an excuse? Is it a moral crime to leave Israel? In a sense it is, certainly for any Jew who has any pretensions to being a Zionist, or who draws reassurance and pride – as I do – from the existence of Israel. I felt this even after my first stay in Israel and felt it more intensely now, for I had witnessed at first hand the anguish borne by most Israelis in their day-to-day life, and no sacrifice made by Jews outside Israel, no matter how much time and money they devote to Zionist causes, can compare to the burdens undertaken by the least-burdened Israeli. After the war, moreover, I was intensely aware of the desperate sense of isolation felt in Israel. The Arabs, the Communist bloc, the so-called 'Third World', were all against her. France, a former ally, was siding openly with the Arabs. Britain, nervous for her oil supplies, had adopted the Munich stance again. Of the European nations only Holland seemed ready to brave the Arab oil boycott, and Israel went wild about everything Dutch. There was a rush on the Dutch lager at our local supermarket, and some Dutch lorry drivers who had come under contract with their lorries to help out in the post-war transport crisis, were pulled from their cabins, hugged, garlanded and borne shoulder high by cheering crowds. There was, of course, the help flowing in from America, but Israelis were accustomed, not without cause, to look American gift horses in the teeth. There was a Sinn Fein atmosphere, the feeling that in the last resort they could rely only on their fellow Jews, so that they drew new reassurance from every new Jewish face. Israel studies her immigration figures as anxiously as a sick man studies his temperature. The first question the Jewish visitor will be asked is: 'You like it here?' and the next – whatever the answer – 'Why don't you come to settle?' or 'When are you coming to settle?' It is part inquiry, part challenge tempered usually with solicitude. Israelis may not be particularly accommodating once you are there, but they want you there, and they want you badly and I feel that they have a right to expect you there.

The Hebrew for an immigrant to Israel is *oleh* – one who

ascends; for an emigrant, it is *yored* – one who descends. Both are loaded expressions. The *yored* is regarded as a type of defector, and here I was about to defect for the second time in twenty years.

The first occasion one could easily excuse. I came young, semi-formed, with romantic illusions and no skills or qualifications, and that year in Israel was a stage in my education. But what could I say for myself now? I was on the verge of middle-age, indeed beyond it, a married man with four children, numerous qualifications and (in ordinary circumstances) an income which, by Israeli standards at least, was considerable. My family was perfectly happy and seemed to thrive on what I thought of as harassment. There was never a dull moment. My two daughters came home from school one day and the following conversation ensued :

'Mummy, there was a bomb in the school gym this morning.'
'It wasn't in the gym, it was in the refectory.'
'It was in the gym.'
'The refectory.'
'Gym.'
' 'fectory.'
'Well, the police closed off the gym, see.'
'But the bomb was in the refectory.'
'Well it didn't go off anyway.'

Israel is a paradise for children (though it is sometimes hell for everyone else) and everything is built round them and revolves round them, with organised activities in the museums and parks, and with excursions and hikes and summer-camps. There was a blizzard in January, which cut Jerusalem off for a day or two, and the municipality used the occasion to organise a snowman competition in which prizes were awarded to all participants (including my children, although they used my bow tie and dinner jacket as garb for the snowman – the only occasion that the jacket was used during my stay in Israel). But apart from the organised activity, there is the climate, the sun, the blue skies, the clear air, which – until the dog days set in in June or July – give one a constant sense of well-being. The children romp around for most of the year in light shirts, tiny shorts and sandalled, sockless feet, their limbs and features a tawny brown, living in each other's homes, cheerful, clamorous, vivacious, free.

I derived pleasure from their pleasure and if it was not quite sufficient to compensate for the clamour, it was something which I had to take into account. And there was, above all, the deep feelings which my wife had about staying in Israel and particularly Jerusalem. My children missed their cat, their Grandma, pantomime and Smarties. My wife missed nothing. We had been happy in Hampstead Garden Suburb and lived a fairly good life, but what with its cocktail receptions and dinner parties and theatre evenings and the constant convoying of children here, there and everywhere and the elaborate birthday parties and the 'Mummy-why-can't-we-go-to-Via-Reggio-Samantha-always-does?' it was not quite the sort of life she sought. As soon as she set foot in Jerusalem, she felt this was it, her homecoming, and there was nothing she wanted except to remain.

All of which suggests that I was the only fly in the ointment, but it was not as simple as that, for my feeling of unease, my yearning for England were week-day, workaday phenomena. Came the seventh day and I rested and was satisfied. Indeed, I was more than satisfied, for as the Sabbath approached one became conscious of a softening of mood, an inexplicable gladness of heart akin to serenity. The hurried working week comes to a climax on Friday morning and then subsides. Factories, banks, offices, close. There is a frantic rush for last minute purchases, usually the small luxuries brought home by the men, nuts and sweets for the children, wines for kiddush, flowers for the table, and then the shops shut. The commotion dies down, the traffic thins out, the sun begins to sink, the skies turn red and I swear there comes a moment when one almost hears the soft beating of wings, as the Sabbath peace descends.

On Friday evenings we all went to the Yeshurun synagogue. It was round the corner, and we all loved the choir, and then after supper with the children all asleep, and the poplars swaying in the evening breeze, we would sit out on the balcony, gaze out on Jerusalem, too glutted with gladness to talk.

On the Sabbath morning we rose early. The girls went to synagogue with an aunt, my wife remained at home with the baby, and my elder son and I went to the Old City, down the

Mamille Road, into the Jaffa Gate, and then through the Arab Bazaar, to the Western Wall.

There is a Yiddish expression, *reid tzu em, reid tzu di vant*, speak to him, speak to the wall, meaning that he is wholly impenetrable, but walls are not wholly inanimate objects, and stones are not impervious to experience. The charm of walking through an old English town – say Lavenham – is that its stones are stained with life, and the walls breathe their past back at you. It is the same with the Wall, though in a much exaggerated form. Prayer, as an act of holy communion, is not something which any serious worshipper will seek at the Wall, for the masses there do not form a united congregation speaking with one heart and one voice. They are fragmented, with perhaps thirty to forty *minyanim* (quorums) trying to engage in worship at the same time, with each out-shouting the other, so that God in His heavens must quake at the noise. They made an unlovely sound, and, indeed, an unlovely sight, the milling crowds, the late-comers elbowing their way forward to touch the stones, tourists with paper hats and clicking cameras in search of local colour, screaming and scrimmaging children, and individual worshippers, swaying amidst the crowds in a silent, private ecstasy of prayer. The first impression is thus one of bedlam, but the ancient stones – some of which date back to the time of Herod and beyond – radiate back the heartfelt supplication they have received in their two thousand years, and merely to be there is a religious experience. It may be a sanctimonious expression to use in our unsanctimonious times, but I came back feeling a better man, and I realised that no matter how well I re-established myself in England the Sabbath and festivals would never be the same again.

But in the six days that I laboured I hankered for London. In London I had my sound-proofed study, insulated from the rest of the house, custom-built to my needs, a controlled environment. In Jerusalem we had a four-roomed flat. It was beautifully situated in an English country-lane of a street in the heart of Jerusalem, but when the children were home from school – and in Israel they come home about noon – I had to flee. I worked in libraries, waiting rooms, restaurants, cafés, taxis, on park benches, frustrated and harassed, a refugee from my own home.

This was a problem which with time and money could be overcome but the other problems could not. I was a writer who lived on the use or abuse of English and I missed the sight and sound of English, the stimulus of England, the meetings with publishers, editors and other writers. Several friends suggested that they might get me teaching jobs in university. I doubt if such jobs were available, and in any case I had long ago forgone the chance of academic work because I still hoped to be a writer, and now that my hope was realised I had no intention of grubbing around for a job which would give me little of the satisfaction, nor even the income that I get from writing. I know some Hebrew, not enough to write in, but enough to know that I shall never be able to write in it. It is a beautiful language, but the phrasing is brittle and has none of the plasticity or flow of English and even if I could write in it I could never earn enough to support my wife and children.

I was also uncertain whether some of the frustration I suffered was due to the fact that I was an English writer in an un-English setting, or because I was an *andante* being in a *presto* setting.

One could perhaps argue that the English pace of life is a little too slow. I recently came upon a letter, which Chaim Weizmann, a future President of Israel, wrote home from Manchester:

'No one hurries in England and the wheels turn slowly. The same is true of everything – their entire way of life – and that is why they have fallen behind. I must confess that we used to have false notions about the English and England. They have much that is good, but obtuseness prevails in everything. Well, God be with them.'

It is a familiar complaint (though what is perhaps unusual about it was that it was made in 1905), but it seems to me that English lethargy is about as misleading as Jewish speed. I sometimes feel that a cross between an Englishman and an Israeli would be the ideal citizen, for they both have virtues which they carry to a fault. I do not, for example, know which is worse, Israeli intrusiveness or the English passion for privacy. I read the English papers in Jerusalem and there was hardly a week without some dreadful story of a child being maimed or murdered by his parents who in most cases would still be alive if the neighbours had been rather more intrusive. The Englishman's home is his dungeon.

If the Israeli sometimes likes to give the impression that he knows everything, the Englishman will often refute the suggestion that he knows anything at all, which, if due in some cases to genuine modesty, is due in others to a lack of purpose, a hesitancy to transmit anything because they are not really sure what they stand for. Israel is loud with didacticism. Everyone, priest and layman, the religious and secular, is conscious of some received truth which he is anxious to transmit, and even the mass circulation dailies like *Maariv* and *Yediot Achronoth*, are full of substantial matter, and there is an honest attempt to inform, to instruct, to elevate. The reader is treated, if not as an informed, intelligent being, at least as one who would like to be informed and intelligent. In England one often gets the feeling that the popular papers regard their readers with contempt, and occasionally they read like the creation of half-wits for the edification of nit-wits. People are afraid to instruct in England, to preach, and what is worse those who do are dismissed as hypocrites and humbugs. It was painful to see the treatment accorded to Lord Longford in the so-called liberal press. He looks eccentric and sometimes sounds eccentric, but he is a devout and saintly man (qualities which in England are taken as forms of eccentricity in themselves) but even where his critics dismissed his arguments one might have expected them to accept the sincerity of his feelings. It is, I suppose, difficult for people who have no faith or convictions to recognise the sincerity of those who have and Lord Longford was either lampooned as a joke (Lord Porn) or regarded as a publicity-hunting fraud.

There are various teachers at school and university whom I regard as my mentors, but my supreme mentor – and I would say this is true for most people of my class and my generation – was the B.B.C. It is to the B.B.C. mainly that I owe my love of literature, my love of music, my understanding of politics and economics. In our house we took several papers, which we regarded as entertainment, and for serious information we turned to the radio. I grew up to regard the B.B.C. as a sort of antidote to Fleet Street, but now the former has become a resting place for the clapped-out hacks of the latter, with the same shoddy attitudes, the same search for sensations, the same triviality. The legacy of Lord Reith is being quickly debauched.

There is a new expression much in use, 'elitism'. I am not quite sure what it means, which is a quandary I share with most people who use it. The expression is not to be found in any dictionary, but I presume that it refers to the endeavour of the commanding elements in society to transmit their values and beliefs. In that sense Reith was a supreme, perhaps *the* supreme elitist and he was, I suppose, trying to create a universe in which John Knox would not have felt out of place. It would not have made for a very cheerful kingdom, but it would have resulted in a much more wholesome one than we have now, for if the elite cease to have any belief in themselves, if they become apologetic about their role, if they abdicate or resign – as they seem to have done in this country – then they leave something worse than a mere vacuum, and instead of 'elitism' we have, if one may coin an equally ugly expression, 'scum-ism'.

Here too we have an area where a cross between English attitudes and Israeli would be the ideal, for in Israel one has elitism run amok. In the early years of statehood every political group had its own school system because each was determined that its values should be transmitted throughout the generations, and even today, in a country of three million Jews, there are no less than three school systems, secular, Orthodox and ultra-Orthodox. The place throbs with conviction and if the Jews did not have the Arabs to contend with they would have been at each other's throats long ago, but the alternative to the fierce convictions of the typical Israeli, need not be the aimlessness of the typical Briton.

We came to Jerusalem initially for an experimental year, and my wife and I agreed that it had not been a fair try, for though no year in Israel is usual, our year was more abnormal than most. We arrived in Jerusalem at the end of August. By the time we settled down the Yom Kippur war was upon us, and I was away from my desk for a month. There then followed a month in which I shared something of the depression of the people around me and I found it impossible to work. It was December now and by the time I settled back to my old routine the snows descended. We were left without heat for weeks on end, and sometimes without gas, light or water. The cold did not bother me. Indeed, it made me feel at home, but in the evenings, when the children were asleep, and I sat down over my typewriter for what were usually my most productive hours, the lights went out. When spring dawned and the lights went on, my wife, who has never been seriously ill in her life, collapsed with an internal haemorrhage, was on the danger list for a week and out of action for nearly two months. And so it went till the year was almost over, and we decided to give it a try for another year or two, by which time my wife hoped I would get England right out of my hair, but by then the decision was out of our hands, for I had done so little work and acquired so many debts that if I didn't return to England to recoup, we might have to run for it.

It is strange that my wife, who is fourth-generation English and whose family is integrated so fully into English life, should have missed England so little. I once discussed this matter with Lionel Davidson, of *Rose of Tibet* fame, an English writer who has made his home in Israel. His family too had lived in England for generations and he had served in the navy during the war, and although he missed the company and stimulus of other English writers, he never gave a sigh for England itself.

A friend of mine, a member of an old Scottish Jewish family (insofar as there are old Jewish families in Scotland), who was a prosperous jeweller, sold out his business and took a job as a schoolmaster in Israel. When I visited him in his Herzlia home some months later he was a new man. 'I bless the day I came here,' he told me. 'Every morning when I wake up I feel as if I'm born afresh.'

I knew the sensation for I often felt it in Jerusalem. Elsewhere in the world one has to go places, see things, do things to enjoy oneself, in Jerusalem one can have a sense of exhilaration through merely being there. I feel it every time I return. It lasts for a week, a month. It did not last for a year; it wouldn't last for a lifetime.

Jerusalem is home in many ways which London is not and can never be. I have been to Westminster Abbey several times and marvelled at its splendours, but always as a visitor and never with any feeling that it was part of my past. The *Kotel* in Jerusalem may be the ruin of a ruin, something that Titus knocked about a bit. It is not beautiful, in some ways it is rather ugly, but its ghosts are my ghosts. In England I am still conscious of restraints and constraints and still feel the need to be on my best behaviour, but not in Israel (neither does anyone else, which is one of the reasons why it is such a loud, rude and brusque place). But above all, and this I think is the truest test of home, events in Israel trouble me more – and not necessarily because they are more dramatic – than events in Britain. What might merely irk me in the latter can incense me in the former. Home is where you lose your temper, but this may be because concern is contagious. One may care less about what happens in Britain because Britons are less caring.

And yet I yearned for Britain for much of my stay in Israel. One's attitude to a place – as to a person – is not based on any careful appraisal of virtues and defects; one likes it in spite of its defects. Moreover, for all the changes that I abhorred there are many things about Britain which are changeless. It is still with all its crazes and defects the most calm, the most sane, the most relaxed place on earth. It also used to be the most prosperous. It is now being overtaken by country after country in the race for the largest gross national product and one hopes it will have the sense to stay behind. Economists speak of her economy as 'stagnant', when they mean simply that it is not growing. One could, with rather greater accuracy, describe an expanding economy as cancerous. Given a fair distribution of wealth – and we are moving towards it – a country should not want to be much better off than Britain is now, and what it lacks in prosperity it may yet gain in grace. There may come a time when Britain is awash with oil and makes her great leap forward to become the richest country in Europe, with great eight-lane highways slicing through London, fast cars whizzing in all directions and multi-storey blocks on every horizon; then it will be time for me to pack my bags, gather my wife and children about me and head once again for Jerusalem; but while anything of the Britain I know and have known remains, it will always have its peculiar hold upon me. Which is not to say that I am completely at home in England, I am not – except that a language is also a homeland of sorts. Every word of English evokes English scenes, English thoughts, English ways; and I am at home in English in a way that I never shall be in Hebrew, no matter how lovely its cadences and how ancient its echoes.